WHEN BOXING
WAS A
JEWISH SPORT

WHEN BOXING WAS A JEWISH SPORT

Allen Bodner

Foreword by Budd Schulberg

Westport, Connecticut
London

Library of Congress Cataloging-in-Publication Data

Bodner, Allen.
    When boxing was a Jewish sport / Allen Bodner ;
  foreword by Budd Schulberg.
       p.   cm.
    Includes bibliographical references (p.   ) and index.
    ISBN 0–275–95353–X (alk. paper)
    1. Jewish boxers—United States—Biography. 2. Boxing—United
States—History. 3. Jewish boxers—United States—Interviews.
I. Title.
GV1131.B63   1997
796.83′092′2—dc21   97–14469
[B]

British Library Cataloguing in Publication Data is available.

Library of Congress Catalog Card Number: 97–14469
ISBN: 0–275–95353–X

First published in 1997

Praeger Publishers, 88 Post Road West, Westport, CT 06881
An imprint of Greenwood Publishing Group, Inc.

Printed in the United States of America

The paper used in this book complies with the
Permanent Paper Standard issued by the National
Information Standards Organization (Z39.48–1984).

10 9 8 7 6 5 4 3 2 1

Copyright Acknowledgment

The author and the publisher gratefully acknowledge permission for use of the
following material:

Excerpts from *The Ray Arcel Oral History* interview. Used with permission of
The American Jewish Committee.

Every reasonable effort has been made to trace the owners of copyright
materials in this book, but in some instances this has proven impossible. The
author and publisher will be glad to receive information leading to more
complete acknowledgments in subsequent printings of the book and in the
meantime extend their apologies for any omissions.

Dedicated with love and admiration to my father, Leo Bodner, who, when reminded that Tony Canzoneri knocked him down twice, usually responds, "Yes, but I got up. . . ." Sometimes he says, "I slipped."

CONTENTS

Photo essay follows page 74

FOREWORD

Although I was raised in the film business—where my father B. P. for many years ran the Paramount Studio—my idols weren't the movie stars who worked for him—Maurice Chevalier, Fredric March, Cary Grant, Gary Cooper . . . I knew them well but they didn't get to me as the boxers did. The movie-making that went on all around me, at the studio and on location, was fascinating. But my most vivid, early memories involved going to the fights with my old man.

He was a passionate fight fan, who went to the fights twice a week. In my mind's eye I am with him in the first row at the Hollywood Legion every Friday night. Great fighters came to the Legion, the young Archie Moore, Tony Canzoneri, Bud Taylor, Fidel La Barba, and Henry Armstrong. Boxing has always been an intensely ethnic sport, and so I must confess we had a special *qvell* for the exploits of our Jewish heroes. The 1920s and 1930s into the 1940s were a Golden Age for Jewish boxers, and in Hollywood, my hometown, we couldn't help feeling a surge of pride when the wearers of the six-pointed star on their trunks proved their mettle against the toughest and most skillful of the Italians, Irish, and Blacks who produced so many stars in those star-studded times.

If not only my father but all of the Paramount "family" were fight fans, they came by their passion honestly, with a sense of Jewish tradition and history. The sturdy and inspired little founder of Paramount (originally Famous Players), Adolph Zukor, had been part of the stream of penniless Jewish immigrants who came to America in the late nineteenth century with their pockets empty and their heads full of dreams. Before he was a low-paid, piece-work furrier, young Adolph was hustling to make a dollar here, a dollar there. One of the ways he stumbled into making a buck was to fight for a dollar-a-round in a neighborhood boxing club.

By the time my father was working for Zukor as a twenty-year-old writer and press agent for Famous Players, he was drawn to the pioneer company's enthusiasm for boxing. There seemed to be a natural connection between the movie game and the fight game: both offering a way out of the stifling ghetto on the lower East Side, where nearly all first-generation Jews were desperately poor.

If Adolph Zukor enjoyed overnight success making hit movies with magical discoveries of movie stars like Mary Pickford (whom B. P. dubbed "America's Sweetheart"), the Jewish community had a fistic star in the ghetto wonder, Benjamin Leiner, who fought under the nom-de-box "Benny Leonard."

I still think of Benny Leonard as an early-century counterpart to the latter-day boxing saint, Muhammad Ali. In the early decades of the twentieth century, ambitious young Jews were struggling to break out of the cycle of poverty in which so many saw their parents hopelessly trapped. They became songwriters like Irving Berlin and Billy Rose, budding movie moguls like Zukor and Sam Goldfish (later Goldwyn), furriers, and jewelers, and most notably for me, stellar champions of the prize ring like Joe Choyinski, Abe Attell, and my father's favorite, "The Great Benny Leonard."

That was the only way I ever heard Leonard described in my household. I wish I still had the scrapbook I compiled as a seven-year-old on "The Great Benny Leonard." I remember his picture on the cover, with the trim, athletic body, the look of intelligence, and the slicked-down hair that—so the boast went—never got messed despite fighting in a division, the lightweight, that offered more than half a dozen gifted contenders. As talented young Jews like my father were moving up into mainstream America at the time of my birth, "The Great Benny Leonard" became their flag-bearer, a symbol of their newly-found strength and success. The excitement around those early Benny Leonard fights against champion Freddy Welch, tough Irish Richie Mitchell, and Philadelphia Jewish rival Lew Tendler inspired his Jewish fans in the same way Ali reached out to the Black ghettos from Harlem to Watts in the 1960s and 1970s. Like Ali, Benny Leonard, with the six-pointed star he wore so proudly on his trunks, sent a message to Jewish ghettos across America: "You may think of us as pushcart peddlers and money grubbers. But we can climb into the ring with you, the best you have to offer, and maybe you can knock us down (as Richie Mitchell floored the Great Benny) but you can't keep us down. We've got the skills and the courage to beat you at your own game. Ready or not, we're moving up." Not just in the prize ring with Leonard and Tendler, Jackie "Kid" Berg, "Battling" Levinsky, Maxie Rosenbloom, Ben Jeby, and our host of champions. Their victories in fierce and memorable battles reinforced my father's generation's belief in themselves in their battle in what I've always thought of as the ring outside the ring, the ring of life.

In Hollywood in the 1920s, 1930s, and 1940s we responded with unabashed ethnic pride to the exploits of our local Jewish champions. Mushy Callahan (Morris Scheer), Jackie Fields, Newsboy Brown, and Maxie Rosenbloom were not only sports heroes but personal friends. When Mushy Callahan took the Junior-welterweight belt from Richie Mitchell's brother "Pinky," I proudly hung the winning gloves on the wall behind my bed. And even though Jews had come a long way up in the world from the 1910s when Leonard was in his ascendancy to Mushy's wins over Mitchell and his formidable local rival Ace Hudkins in the 1930s, even though Jews were now leaders in the film industry, the music business, dominant in the arts, and even challenging the WASP movers and shakers in banking and Wall Street, there was still a healthy reassurance that "some of our boys" could fight their way to the very top of the toughest and most demanding of all professional sports.

I've always thought of boxing not as a mirror but as a magnifying glass of our society. It is hardly accidental that out of the poor Irish immigration of a people being brutalized by their British overlords, we had a wave of great Irish fighters. From John L. Sullivan and Jim Corbett to Mickey Walker and Billy Conn. As the Irish moved up into the mainstream, there was less economic need to use the prize ring as their way out and up. The wave of Jewish boxers followed exactly the same pattern, and so did the Italians. The almost total domination of the ring today by African-Americans and Hispanics speaks directly to the continued economic deprivation and discrimination of large sections of our inner-city communities.

But as Allen Bodner reminds us in this welcome work of devoted research, clearly a labor of love, that we have seen in the first half of the twentieth century a Golden Age of Jewish Boxing, score on score of Jewish champions of the world, not to mention fierce and gifted contenders like Allie Stolz, Artie Levine, Maxie Shapiro, Georgie Abrams, Leach Cross . . . the brave boys who made their statement for all of us *When Boxing Was a Jewish Sport*.

Budd Schulberg

PREFACE

When I decided to undertake an oral history on Jewish boxing, I contacted Tino Raino, an Italian middleweight who fought around the time of World War II, and the president of Ring 8, a veteran boxers' association. Its members include former and present prizefighters, as well as trainers, managers, writers, friends and others who wish to join. Since no pension system exists for boxers, Ring 8 provides free medical checkups, eyeglasses, "crisis" money, and a death benefit of $250, and pays the deductible under Medicare. It also arranges for certain medical benefits at the Ray Arcel Medical Center which it helped found. In order to qualify for benefits, one must be a professional boxer (past or present) who fought at least ten professional bouts. All others may be members with voting privileges, but they are not eligible for benefits. Ring 8 meetings are always well attended and include among its former active members Jack Dempsey, the great heavyweight champion, Billy Graham, a welterweight contender in the 1950s, Rocky Graziano, Ben Jeby, Tippy Larkin, and Sugar Ray Robinson, all middleweight champions. Ray Arcel, boxing's most famous trainer, was an active member into his nineties.

Tino invited me to a Ring 8 meeting. There was much hugging as the boxers greeted each other, and a lot of wisecracking and waving. Most of those present seemed to be Italians and Jews, followed by blacks, Irish, and Hispanics. According to Tino, Italians and Jews are the joiners.

After Tino called the meeting to order, one of the most moving ceremonies I have ever witnessed took place. Billy Graham had just died, and as everyone stood, a final ten count (signaling a knockout) was rapped in his memory. I glanced at the faces around me, and I noticed tears streaming freely down the cheeks of nearly every boxer.

To my surprise, Tino called on me to explain my project and offered the help of Ring 8. I told the group of my meeting with Herb Kronowitz at the Coney Island Velodrome in 1948 when I was eight, but could not recall the name of his opponent. Someone piped up, "Eddie Guarino, 2:10 in the third round." I was absolutely stunned to discover it was Kronowitz himself. I had no idea he was alive. From the back of the room, Johnny Colan, a former light-heavyweight yelled out, "He only knows that because it's the only person he ever knocked out." Herbie, who sits in the first row and never misses a meeting, stood up, turned around, put up his fists, and said, "Who said that? I'll kill him." The entire audience, including Herbie, laughed.

That is not the sort of comment to make to Herb Kronowitz outside of a Ring 8 setting. But the feeling among these boxers is one of such mellow acceptance, and even love, that the remarks were appropriate. These boxers, many of whom fought each other, have nothing to prove to one another.

At that meeting I met, in addition to Kronowitz, Al Reid, Oscar Goldman, Sammy Farber, Vic Zimet, and Curly Nichols, each of whom I subsequently interviewed at his home. I was able to conduct interviews with Allie Stolz in Great Neck, Charlie Gellman in Valley Stream, and Bernie Friedkin, Marty Pomerantz, Miltie Kessler, Leo Bodner, Julie Bort and Maxie Shapiro in Brooklyn. I also interviewed Danny Kapilow in Florida, Joey Varoff in Maryland, and Artie Levine in North Carolina. Sigi Ashkenaz (Sidney Ashe) was the only American boxer interviewed who was foreign born (Switzerland). He now lives in Virginia. Several of those interviewed have since passed away.

These boxers represent most of the Jewish fighters then still alive. I would have loved to have been able to interview such wonderful Jewish boxers as Yale Okun, Bob Olin, "Slapsie" Maxie Rosenbloom, Jackie "Kid" Berg, George "Freedom" Abrams, Sid Terris, Lew Tendler, Ruby Goldstein, Abe Simon, Ben Jeby, Solly Krieger, "Corporal" Izzy Schwartz, and, of course, Benny Leonard and Barney Ross. Unfortunately all have died, some many years ago.

Among the nonboxers interviewed were boxing historians Herbert Goldman of New York and Hank Kaplan of Miami; Rose Lewis, for thirty-six years the secretary of the New York State Athletic Commission, which is charged with regulating boxing and wrestling; Harry Markson, former president of Madison Square Garden Boxing; and Teddy Brenner, formerly the matchmaker at Madison Square Garden. For many years there was ill feeling between these last three and Ring 8 over the use of some money that had been collected under the name of the National Sports Alliance. In 1995 Markson was honored by Ring 8, and this helped alleviate much of the bitterness.

I also interviewed Martha Rosenfeld, sister of Ruby Goldstein; Anne Shapiro, Maxie Shapiro's sister; and Rivi Garbowitz, Herb Kronowitz's lively mother.

During the period of these interviews, I met Ken Blady, the author of *The Jewish Boxers' Hall of Fame* (1988) who encouraged me from the time we first spoke. Mike Silver, the boxing writer, was a constant source of information and enthusiasm. Professor Peter Levine, whose *Ellis Island to Ebbets Field* (1992) contains two chapters on Jewish boxing, graciously sent me the footnotes of these chapters months before his book was published. Professors Melvin Adelman, John Hoberman, and Steven Riess were helpful and supportive. Charlie Morrissey, head of the Baylor College of Medicine Oral History Project, rendered continuing advice and friendship. Professor Jeffrey Sammons of New York University made valuable reference suggestions. In many ways, this project was the idea of Professor Dolores Greenberg of Hunter College. She suggested that the story of Jewish boxing might be more satisfying than another paper on the "War of the Pacific." Finally, Professor Deborah Dash Moore helped me maintain focus on the story I wanted to tell.

As the interviews progressed, I became increasingly convinced that the boxers exist more in the parameters of space than in the linear structure of time—not to say that they are unmindful of the discrete events and seasons of their lives. Rather, the boxing experience so defined, shaped, and guided them, and it has dominated all else. It continues to insinuate itself and affect their beings almost as if they lived inside a ring whose core is boxing. However they turn or bounce, boxing is the nexus. The 1920s, 1930s, and 1940s may have been their time, but the 20–foot by 20–foot ring was their space, and that, to them, makes all the difference.

1

INTRODUCTION

When Jewish sports fans are asked to name Jewish boxers, invariably they will mention Benny Leonard and Barney Ross, the famous champions. Sometimes Ruby Goldstein, a contender, will be added, and more infrequently "Slapsie" Maxie Rosenbloom, a great light-heavyweight champion. And there it ends. Even knowledgeable sports fans have no notion that there were many outstanding Jewish champions and contenders, and thousands of Jewish boxers in the twenties, thirties and even forties. "How was it possible?" they will ask. "It is so contrary to Jewish tradition and culture. It is astounding."

In fact, Jews entered the ranks of American boxing in large numbers and by 1928, were the dominant nationality in professional prizefighting, followed by the Italians and the Irish. Ten years later, Jews sank to third place, preceded by the Italians and the Irish. When World War II ended and the G.I. Bill of Rights and other avenues of advancement became available, boxing was no longer attractive to the Jews as participants. By 1950, there were virtually no Jewish boxers, and their number has been minuscule ever since. A similar decline occurred among Jewish trainers, but Jewish managers, promoters, and matchmakers continue to maintain a presence.

On the surface, it seems unlikely that Jews ever participated in such a brutal sport. It is assumed that Jewish pursuits were traditionally more cerebral and that education played an overriding role in the Jewish culture. Who would box when he could go to college and become a professional? But going to college and becoming a professional were not necessarily

options for the vast majority of Jewish youths in the 1920s and 1930s. When
that choice as well as other economic opportunities became possible, after
the Second World War, Jewish boxing rapidly disintegrated.

During the years 1910–1940, there were twenty-six Jewish world champions. This was an impressive achievement, particularly in an era when there
were only eight weight classes, instead of the myriad that exist today (to
say nothing of the multiplicity of sanctioning bodies). But this success must
be viewed in the context of overall Jewish participation in boxing. Throughout the 1920s and 1930s approximately 16 percent of the champions were
Jewish, but nearly one-third of the fighters were also Jewish. While there
were indeed Jewish champions, Jews did not excel out of proportion to their
number of participants and were, in fact, underrepresented at the championship level. In boxing, at least, Jews could be average, a possibility that
was not available in other sports such as baseball.

At the 1907 Chanukah meeting of the Menorah Society at Harvard
University, Harvard's president Charles Eliot stated that the Jews "are
distinctly inferior in stature and physical development . . . to any other
race." Dr. Eliot lamented the loss, since the days of the Maccabees, of the
martial spirit among Jews and thought it would be beneficial if "many of
you joined the militia."[1] Eliot's pejorative description of Jewish physical
prowess ignited some controversy. A considerable number of Jews perceived themselves as Eliot did, agreed with him, and urged the Jews to attain
greater bodily strength and ability. Others were outraged by what they
considered to be thinly disguised anti-Semitism, and argued that Jews were
no different from anyone else physically.

What motivated so many Jewish young men to careers as prizefighters?
Was it a response to the kind of criticism leveled by Eliot? Was there a need
to prove the manliness of Jews who had been persecuted for so many
centuries and who consistently appeared to be physically helpless and
unable to defend themselves? Did the Jews who became boxers believe
thereby that they were representing Jewish people or, more pointedly,
Jewish power?

Most Jewish boxers denied that they were acting for anyone other than
themselves and their fans, and asserted that their only thoughts in becoming
boxers related to the desire to earn money, and had nothing to do with their
Jewishness or other Jews, except as they were fans. But the responses are
really more complex than that and more subtle. From some of the fighters,
we discern a sense that in various ways their ethnicity played a more
defining role than they would admit or have thought about.

The thesis that Jewish boxers represented the Jewish people as a whole is a theme that recurs, with variations, throughout Jewish boxing literature. In discussing the motivation of the Jewish boxer, Jimmy Johnston, a well-known (non-Jewish) promoter of the 1920s and 1930s declared:

> You take a Jewish boy and sooner or later his race is decried. He tries so much harder to fight back for himself and for his people since he regards himself as a representative of all Jews. The knowledge that more than one Jew is on trial when he fights gives him an incentive for training more faithfully and taking greater pride in his work.[2]

This sense of national mission may have been true of a Barney Ross.[3] It clearly was not characteristic of the boxers whom I interviewed. As "Schoolboy" Bernie Friedkin put it, "Who was I to represent the Jewish people?" The boxers interviewed represented themselves and their fans. The idea that they were somehow emissaries of their "race" appears to them as arrogance. And there simply may have been too many Jewish boxers for that. Yet, the boxers' sense of pride as Jews did contribute to a felt obligation to conduct themselves in a certain manner.

It is probably true that the great Jewish fighters such as Barney Ross possessed more of an overt ambassadorial sense. For example, Allie Stolz, who is acknowledged as the best of the surviving Jewish boxers and who came closest to winning a championship (lightweight title in 1942), also came closest to stating that as a boxer he represented the Jewish people. But while some of the boxers had large followings, particularly Jewish fans who took much pride in their fighters, the significance of their ethnic identity was not as powerful as some writers would suggest.

Related to the "mission" theme is the thesis that boxing helped the fighters to acculturate as Americans. While this may have applied to many Jewish fans, it played no conscious major role in the boxers' thinking. They were already Americans. Living as they did among Jews on the lower East Side of Manhattan or the Brownsville section of Brooklyn, the vast majority imagined no broader society into which they were seeking entree. They boxed because they loved it and sought to make money, not because they wished to negate the stereotype of the Jew as weakling or to be accepted as Americans. If they were aware of the stereotype at all, they could not have cared less. Even the boxers who fought in the 1920s, such as Oscar Goldman and Sammy Farber, did not think they had to prove anything to anyone but themselves. Yet, as their testimony indicates, there were manifestations of ethnic pride and identity in their roles as Jewish boxers.

The boxers knew of no fabled Jewish worship of education. To them and their families the choice was not boxing or college, but boxing or work. In the depression days of the 1930s, college was a remote luxury, even for second-generation Jews such as the boxers. It is true that by 1936, 11 percent of the second-generation Jews had entered the professions and the ranks of Jewish boxers were thinning. In New York, where Jews made up 25 percent of the population, they comprised 65 percent of the lawyers, 64 percent of the dentists, and 55 percent of the doctors. But the boxers were not part of the Jewish population for whom it was feasible to enter the professions. Even where education such as at City College was free, the boxers felt they were required to work to support their families. And nothing, to them, was as yet more lucrative than the ring. The boxers did, however, for the most part value education, and once they could afford it, a great number of their children became doctors, lawyers, and teachers.

It should not be assumed from the boxers' lack of "national purpose" that they were not proud Jews. They were and are. Their ethnic identity was never in question. Most of them wore Stars of David on their bathrobes and trunks until religious symbols were banned in the 1940s. Usually, they considered themselves part of the Jewish community, and they participated in major Jewish holidays and rituals. They lived at home until they were married, and contributed to the family's upkeep (as did the Irish and Italians). Like 95 percent of the Jews in New York at that time, they married Jewish women and generally remained married.

Jews in boxing encountered virtually no anti-Semitism either in the ring or outside it. So many of the fighters, trainers, promoters, and managers were Jewish that it would have been difficult for anti-Semitism to obtain a foothold. And no matter how grueling the match, there was very little animosity between the boxers. Professor John Hoberman calls it "The Brotherhood of Arms." The first experience that many of the boxers had with anti-Semitism occurred when they entered the armed services in World War II. Their sensitivity to these encounters is described by mild-mannered Al Reid (see Chapter 7).

If they did not worry about assimilation, anti-Semitism, or ethnicity, Jewish boxers most definitely feared the injuries and brain damage that are inherent in the sport. This fear pervades many of the interviews. Every fighter expressed relief that he quit in time, before he was brain-damaged or otherwise impaired.

The economics of the boxers is another topic often neglected. How did they fare, especially if they were not main-event attractions? When Bernie Friedkin quit the ring at age 23 he had amassed $7,000. That was a lot of money to him in 1940 and the equivalent of three years' wages of public school teachers. Friedkin fought a number of main events but still averaged only a modest $200 to $300 a fight as his net. From the gross winnings, expenses such as gymnasium charges and trainers' fees were deducted. Then the manager received one-third and the fighter two-thirds. If Friedkin's total purse was $500 and his expenses were $100, the manager would receive $133 and Friedkin $267. When Artie Levine, a headliner, fought in Cleveland, his purse was supposed to be $15,000. After all expenses were deducted, he received $300. Most of those interviewed were careful with their money, and when they married, they had established nesteggs that were greatly in excess of what they could have accumulated by working at a regular job. While they were boxing, that was their business, and the boxers usually did not have other employment. The careers of the boxers after their boxing days varied.

In their essay "The Occupational Culture of the Boxer," Weinberg and Arond analyze the jobs of ninety-five former boxers of all nationalities.[4] According to their statistics, one-quarter held blue-collar jobs. Steven Riess, while admitting that he has no scientific data, nonetheless argues that Jewish boxers ended up better than their peers. He claims that only one of the thirty-six boxers for whom he had information was a manual worker and that one-third of the Jews owned businesses or had lucrative white-collar jobs as compared to 2.1 percent in the Weinberg study. A number became cabdrivers, messengers, dispatchers, bartenders, or, like Maxie Shapiro, never really worked. Charlie Gellman was the professional president of a hospital; Danny Kapilow was a high official in the Teamsters Union; Artie Levine was a car salesman and dealer; Sigi Ashkenaz owned a jewelry business; Sammy Farber owned a bar; Marty Pomerantz was in the shoe business; Miltie Kessler sells imported automobiles; and Joey Varoff was a fire chief.

Was the preeminent position of Jews in boxing during its "Golden Era" really so astonishing? Boxing was part of the urban Jew's effort to get ahead. It provided opportunity, and had Jews not played such an important role in boxing during those years, it would have been even more surprising. Howard Sachar, in his book *A History of the Jews in America* (1992), reports that in 1911, 75 percent of the prostitutes in New York and other major urban areas were Jewish; 50 percent of the brothels were owned by Jews. In 1921, 20 percent of the jail population in New York State was Jewish, and practically 100 percent of the bootleggers were Jewish. And what of Murder Incorporated and the pervasive Jewish mob influence in New York and other cities? According to Sachar, Jews dominated prostitution and the liquor trade in major portions of Eastern Europe and continued these activities in the New World.[5] Where the Jews discerned opportunities, they took advantage of them. While boxing was a new activity for Jews, it was no different from anything else that urban Jews were doing to advance their economic position in life.

In 1955, Thomas Jenkins traced the history of the dominant nationalities in boxing, and concluded that the second generation of practically all urban immigrant groups gravitated to boxing.[6] He thereby explained the ethnic succession of the English, Irish, Italians, Jews, blacks, and others. The ascendancy of Jewish boxers was a natural and predictable demographic phenomenon of Jewish immigrants and cannot be attributed to unusual causes. This thesis is supported by the testimony of the boxers themselves. When other opportunities appeared after the war, Jews quickly vanished from the scene as contestants, although they continued their role in entrepreneurial aspects of the sport, which were forms of white-collar business enterprise.

In the precipitous disappearance of Jewish boxers from the ring, the Jewish experience does run counter to that of the other nationalities whose decline in boxing was more gradual. As to their entering the ring, however, perhaps the most unusual aspect of the Jewish boxing experience in this country, especially to a people whose history is so studded with apocalyptic events, is how thoroughly normative it actually was.

2

A BRIEF HISTORY

Boxing was attractive to poor second-generation American Jews who recognized that entry into the sport was dependent on ability alone and that anti-Semitism played no role in the progress a Jewish prizefighter could make. This was applicable equally to Jewish managers, promoters, and trainers, who, like the Jewish boxers, quickly assumed disproportionately prominent roles in all aspects of the sport.

In the history of boxing, there has never been a period of Jewish preeminence, and even dominance, to rival the 1920s and 1930s in the United States, especially New York. But this period did not mark the beginnings of Jewish boxing, which actually had its origins in England in the late 1700s. The most famous Jewish pugilistic name to emerge from this era is Daniel Mendoza, a Sephardic Jew who was English champion from 1791 to 1795.

From 1760 to 1820 there were at least thirty Jewish prizefighters proficient enough to earn mention in the boxing sources of that time. Mendoza, who is credited with introducing a more "scientific" approach to boxing (emphasizing skill and speed, rather than brute force), was the most famous, but others such as Dutch Sam, his son Young Dutch Sam, Aby Belasco, and Barney Aron were also popular heroes to the Jews of London. Their victories were credited with reducing physical attacks on Jews in the city.

Unlike their more dignified and decorous New York cousins of the 1920s and 1930s, the English-Jewish prizefighters were a rougher and more raucous group. After a disastrous fire, the Theatre Royal in Covent Garden reopened in September 1809 with fewer inexpensive seats and a rise in the price of tickets. To counter the loud and threatening audience protests, management hired Jewish boxers to intimidate the crowds, which they did with relish. Among the "enforcers" were Mendoza and Dutch Sam, giving rise to placards such as the ones which read "The Covent Garden Synagogue–Mendoza the Grand Rabbi," and "Oppose Shylock and the Jews." The situation became so alarming that Chief Rabbi Samuel Hirschell threatened the Jewish rowdies with excommunication, still an effective weapon in the early 1800s.[1]

Throughout most of the nineteenth century prizefighting, regarded as a violent and brutal sport, was banned in the United States. To the extent there was boxing in this country, and clandestine contests always existed, it was dominated by the Irish. It was not until the end of the century that a Jewish boxer gained any recognition. When one finally appeared, he was world class. His name was Joe Choyinski, and, contrary to the later stereotype (and reality), his parents were upper-middle-class German Jews from San Francisco. In his career, which spanned nearly eighty bouts, he fought future heavyweight champions Jim Jeffries and Bob Fitzsimmons to a draw and knocked out the great Jack Johnson in 1901.

Although the center of Jewish boxing in the early years of this century was, and long remained, New York City, the first two Jewish champions hailed from other places. Chicago's Harry Harris became the bantamweight champion for a short time beginning in 1901. The more famous Jewish fighter of the era was Abe Attell known as the "Little Hebrew." Attell, a San Franciscan, became featherweight champion in 1901 but had less than a stellar personal reputation. He was a heavy gambler and was suspected of throwing several fights. He was also widely perceived to be gambler Arnold Rothstein's "bagman" during baseball's "Black Sox Scandal" of 1919, when the World Series was fixed.

Boxing was first legalized in New York State under the Horton Act of 1896, making New York the first state to sanction the sport. But the Horton Act was repealed in 1900, and thereafter boxing was technically illegal in New York until reinstated by the Frawley Act of 1911. This is not to say that prizefighting was dormant in New York. To circumvent the prohibition, clubs opened under a "membership" system. By 1911, more than thirty such clubs were operating in New York City.

In 1911, the Frawley Act was passed, legalizing professional boxing to the extent of permitting matches only at licensed associations of clubs and providing for the licensing of the boxers themselves. Bouts could only be "exhibitions," with no decisions and winners unless there was a knockout. This explains the proliferation of "no-decision" and "newspaper decision" results during these years, when designated newspaper reporters rendered a verdict, thereby enabling the placing of bets on the outcome.

In 1917, after a number of abuses, bribes, and a death in the ring, the Frawley Act was repealed by the New York State legislature. Once again, prizefighting was prohibited in New York, although by this time it was permitted in twenty-three other states. New York had become the most important venue by a wide margin, and boxing suffered a serious blow when it was removed from the scene. The old system of exhibitions and membership clubs was revived in New York, but major matches could not be staged there and so boxing in the country as a whole declined.

From the time the Frawley Act was repealed, concerted efforts were made to introduce legislation that would again legitimize boxing. A strong proponent was State Senator James Walker, later the mayor of New York City. He was considerably aided by the fact that boxing had become legal in neighboring New Jersey. Governor Al Smith said he would not oppose a strong bill, and since boxing was used to train soldiers during World War I, it enhanced its acceptance. In 1920, the Walker Law legalizing boxing was passed, and "decision fights" were reintroduced in New York. This structure continues to the present time.

It was in the twilight environment of the early 1900s that the first group of talented Jewish boxers emerged. Joe Bernstein, who fought in the late 1890s as a featherweight, was known as "The Pride of the Ghetto." In a career that ended in 1910, he boxed most of the leading contestants of his weight class. The next "Pride of the Ghetto" was Leach Cross (Louis Wallach), a lightweight who boxed until 1915. Cross studied dentistry at New York University and was also known as "The Fighting Dentist." He first popularized boxing among the Jews of the lower East Side.

The popularity of Cross, as well as Al McCoy (Harry Rudolph), the middleweight champion in 1914, and "Battling" Levinsky, the light-heavyweight king from 1916 to 1920, helped set the stage for the greatest and most beloved Jewish boxer ever, Benny Leonard. Leonard was the lightweight champion from 1917 to 1925 and compiled an extraordinary record. It is practically impossible for a prizefighter to remain morally and ethically unscathed throughout a career, but Leonard came close. He was a model of personal decorum and a visible and committed Jew. Of all the Jewish boxers, Leonard remains the one most admired by both fans and other fighters.

In June 1922, Leonard fought welterweight champion Jack Britton for a title Leonard did not really seek or need. He lost to Britton on a low blow foul that to many observers seemed suspiciously staged. This was the only blemish on his otherwise impeccable record. Leonard retired in 1925 as lightweight champion, but depression losses forced him back into the ring in 1931. He quickly won eighteen fights, but on October 7, 1932, was knocked out by future welterweight champion Jimmy McLarnin, and retired permanently. He later became a referee and died while officiating in 1947. McLarnin gained a reputation as a destroyer of major Jewish boxers, having beaten Benny Leonard, Sid Terris, Ruby Goldstein, "Kid" Kaplan, Al Singer, and Barney Ross. (Ross did beat McLarnin two out of three times.)

Other marvelous Jewish boxers of the Leonard era were Sid Terris, Benny Bass, Charlie "Phil" Rosenberg, "Kid" Kaplan, "Corporal" Izzy Schwartz, and Lew Tendler. Tendler, in particular, gave Benny Leonard fits in the ring. Tendler and Leonard engaged in two epic battles, in 1922 and 1923. Each drew huge crowds and grossed record amounts. Leonard was the victor each time, retaining his lightweight crown.

Ruby Goldstein was universally regarded as the "Crown Prince" of Leonard's throne. He was affectionately called the "Jewel of the Ghetto" but never lived up to expectations. Goldstein was attracted to gamblers and mobsters. In 1926, in a match against Ace Hudkins, Ruby knew that his gambler friends had bet heavily that he would knock Hudkins out in the first round. Goldstein attempted to accommodate them, tired himself, and was himself counted out in the fourth round. He was never the same fighter after that. He later had a distinguished career as a referee which was marred by his unfortunate failure to sooner stop the Griffith–Paret bout of 1962, which ended in Paret's death.

The depression years produced a bumper crop of skilled Jewish boxers, among them light-heavyweight champion "Slapsie" Maxie Rosenbloom; middleweight champions Solly Krieger and Ben Jeby; light-heavyweight champion Bob Olin; Yale Okun; Allie Stolz; and Maxie Shapiro. The star of this class was acknowledged to be Barney Ross, who was the best and most admired Jewish fighter after Benny Leonard.

Ross fought eighty-two professional fights and lost only four. He became the lightweight and welterweight champion. Ross later suffered serious financial reverses and also became addicted to morphine during the Second World War. Despite his problems, he retained the affection of Jewish fighters and fans.

If the years between the wars were a glorious era for Jewish boxing, they were no less a golden time for boxing in general. The Jews did not win championships in proportions greater than their participation in the sport, and in fact may have been somewhat underrepresented. This speaks to the fact that to most Jewish participants boxing was simply a means to earn money and had no other social overtones such as proving masculinity as

Jews, striking a blow against anti-Semitism, and representing Jewish people. These romantic notions were far more prevalent in the minds of the fans than the fighters. But it also demonstrates how high the level of competition was at the time.

Among the non-Jewish champions of the era were Tony Canzoneri, Jimmy McLarnin, Bob Montgomery, Henry Armstrong, Beau Jack, Johnny Dundee, Jack Britton, Fritzie Zivic, Mickey Walker, Harry Greb, Billy Conn, Georges Carpentier, Tommy Loughran, Gene Tunney, Jack Dempsey, Max Schmeling, Joe Louis, Jimmy Braddock, and Jack Sharkey. In addition, there was a plethora of outstanding contenders in all weight levels.

Jews were prominent in other aspects of boxing both during and long after the heyday of Jewish participation inside the ring. Whitey Bimstein and Ray Arcel were the most famous trainers of any ethnic group. Charley Goldman, Heinie Blaustein, and Izzy Klein were also well known as trainers. Frank Bachman (Maxie Rosenbloom), Al Weill (Rocky Marciano, Tony Canzoneri), Sam Pian (Barney Ross), Irving Cohen (Rocky Graziano), and Joe "Yussel the Muscle" Jacobs (Max Schmeling) are just a few of the host of Jewish managers.

Probably in no area of boxing were Jews important for as long a period as in the promotion of matches. Mike Jacobs was long the legendary Madison Square Garden promoter. He was a disciple of the fabled Tex Rickard. Jacobs gave Joe Louis his chance to fight in New York, ensuring Louis's undying loyalty. Louis fought for Jacobs twenty-five times. Following Jacobs was the team of Harry Markson and Teddy Brenner. Other important promoters were Sam Silverman in Boston, Jack Solomon in London, Herman Taylor in Philadelphia, Harry Glickman in Seattle, and Bernie Feiken in Baltimore.

The Jewish presence was also influential in other aspects of boxing. The Everlast Company, owned by Russian-Jewish immigrants, was the leading manufacturer of gloves, trunks, and other boxing equipment. The most popular gym was Stillman's, run by a Jew, and the most important publication was *Ring Magazine*, founded and operated by Nat Fleisher. Fleisher also created the Ring Record Book, the definitive repository of boxing statistics.

During the crucial years of their second-generation experience in America, boxing was a Jewish sport not only in the sense that there were many Jewish participants, but also that Jews were prominent in many of its component parts.

3

THE ALLURE

My father, Leo Bodner, came to America from Galicia, Poland, with his family in 1923, when he was 16 years old. Like thousands of other young immigrants, he gravitated to the Educational Alliance located on East Broadway on the lower East Side. At that time, the Alliance, as it was known, conducted over one thousand classes and programs, with the goal of aiding the acculturation of the Jewish immigrants into American life. Many of these programs were sports based, and Bodner found that he had a predilection, and even something of a talent, for boxing. He therefore spent much of his time in the Alliance gym, some of it when he should have been in school.

For a period of time, my father was an amateur boxer, a natural extension of the Alliance boxing program in which many young men from the area participated. He was employed in the wholesale dry goods business, and, in addition, he had neither the ability nor the desire for a professional career. But he loved boxing and became a fight manager on a part-time basis, never leaving his daytime employment.

It was partially in this world that I grew up. Even in the heyday of Jewish boxing, it was an anomaly for an Orthodox Jew like my father to be part of it, and this was especially so in the 1940s when Jewish boxing was in its death throes. If there was anything unusual about having a father who would take his eight-year-old son to boxing and wrestling matches at the Coney Island Velodrome on a regular basis, the son made no complaint. But then, it might fairly be said that I had a natal connection to the Velodrome, at least on my father's side. That is where he was on the July night I was born. An uncle brought my mother to the hospital.

The Coney Island Velodrome was a wooden outdoor arena with about thirty thousand seats. It was built for stock car and six-day bicycle racing, and was used for other events, including boxing on Monday and wrestling on Wednesday nights. My father had a small "piece" of it. I later learned that this meant a percentage of the profits from the boxing and wrestling shows, which never earned a profit. For several years, I would spend one or two summer nights each week in the company of my father at the matches.

As my father was generally busy at the arena, I had the run of the place and would freely roam the main area and downstairs where the dressing rooms were located. Security was not very stringent in those days, and I would stroll into the dressing rooms of the wrestlers Gorgeous George or Mr. America and have conversations with them. But wrestling was known as an "exhibition," which meant it was fixed, or so the boxing people claimed. Boxing "matches" were the real thing, and it was with the boxers that my heart resided.

There was something about the pitch-dark, open-air arena on a sultry summer night, with the light playing only on the two battling figures in the ring, that captivated me. The roar of the crowd was magnetic, and being in the winner's dressing room after a main event was electrifying.

One June night in 1948, a Jewish middleweight from Brooklyn, named Herbie Kronowitz, knocked his opponent out in an early round. I went down to the dressing room with my father. Kronowitz stood in the middle of the room like some god surrounded by his worshipers. My father introduced me, and Kronowitz grabbed my hand in his, which was still bandaged, although his boxing gloves were off. "Hello, young man," he said. "Congratulations, Mr. Kronowitz," I remember responding. "I hope you become the champ." Two years later, at the age of 27, Kronowitz quit the ring. Neither my wish nor his far greater desire to be the champion was realized. That June night was the last time I heard of or saw Herbie Kronowitz for nearly forty-five years.

By the mid-1950s, Jewish boxing was moribund at the contestant level, and boxing was permanently weakened by the rapid ascendancy of television. Major bouts were now televised, and all forms of entertainment could be found in the living room. Still, several clubs existed, if not flourished; among them were the Eastern Parkway Arena in Brooklyn, Ridgewood Grove on the Brooklyn–Queens border, Sunnyside Gardens in Queens, and of course St. Nicholas Arena on 66th Street and Broadway in Manhattan.

Of these, St. Nick's was the most popular. It was built around the turn of the century as a roller skating rink, and almost immediately boxing shows began to be promoted there. It was second to Madison Square Garden in importance in New York, and maintained a weekly Wednesday night boxing card until 1962. The building still stands and is now a television studio. Once or twice a month, I would meet my father after his work and my school, and we would travel to one of the arenas. My favorite was St. Nick's.

I discovered there is one subculture in boxing, among many others, known as "complimentary tickets." This means that there are those who will go to great lengths and even tip far in excess of the cost of a ticket in order to be admitted free at the gate. At the Coney Island Velodrome, my father's partner was a man named Harry Turner who, fortunately for him, held the lucrative Velodrome parking concession. Turner also printed most of the boxing tickets at that time. Since he usually attended the shows at the various arenas, we never had to pay for admission.

Ticket taking in those days was an art form, not the impersonal business it is today. At St. Nick's, the man at the gate, a grizzled, cigar-smoking old timer, knew my father from a previous life and always waved us in. One time, this man, whom my father called "Smitty," wasn't there, and the ticket taker demanded a ticket. My father is the most mild-mannered of men, but this was outrageous! Pay for a ticket? "Where's Harry?" my father demanded. Harry Turner appeared and scowled at the hapless soul. "Don't you know this man doesn't pay?" How was the poor fellow supposed to know?

The inside of the arena was the paradigm for every smoky black and white boxing movie ever made. I never saw anything there except through a haze of thick cigar smoke wafting slowly up to the balcony which encircled the auditorium. I still think of St. Nick's in a gauzy black and white.

It never failed. After greeting a few of the long time boxing denizens, my father would be enveloped from behind by a bone-shattering hug administered by the burly and boozy Al Buck, long the boxing columnist of the *New York Post*. "Little Leo," he would shout, "how are you? This must be your boy. Come sit with me and dope out a couple of fights." Buck would lead us to ringside, which was under the lip of the ring, and as typewriters clacked away my father would analyze a few fights for him. (On the way home, he would confide to me that Al Buck was a great boxing columnist but knew very little about the intricacies of boxing itself.)

After a while we would ascend a flight of steps to an office. It was occupied by Charlie Johnston, brother of Jimmy Johnston who was one of the best known managers and promoters of the 1930s and 1940s. When

Jimmy died, Charlie inherited the St. Nick's fiefdom. "Charlie, I want you to meet my boy." "How are you, son?" Johnston would say. "I know your father for thirty years. He's a fine man. He never even swears." This script never varied in all the times I saw Johnston.

We would return to ringside and Al Buck. I felt very important sitting next to the famous sportswriter. There was usually a bout after the main event, and when that was over, Buck and my father would embrace and we headed off to the subway.

I have, naturally, been with my father on many different occasions—religious, business, family, social. I have never felt closer or more connected to him than on those smoke-filled magical St. Nick's nights.

4

ES HAYPT ZUCH NISHT UN
(It Doesn't Exist)

Because of its enormous popularity among Jewish fans, especially in the New York City area which produced most of the boxers, it might reasonably be assumed that Jewish boxing was widely reported in the Jewish press of the day. But interestingly, this was hardly the case. Officially, boxing was not quite acceptable to those who presumed to set the standards of Jewish cultural taste, even though their readers comprised the Jewish masses.

Occasional articles appeared in the Anglo-Jewish press, such as the *American-Hebrew*, the *Jewish Tribune*, *The Detroit Jewish Chronicle*, and the *Los Angeles B'nai B'rith Messenger*. But as far as the *Jewish Daily Forward* (the most important Jewish newspaper, published in Yiddish) and the rest of New York's Jewish press was concerned, boxing, and particularly Jewish boxing, barely existed. The first reference to boxing did not appear in the *Forward* until July 22, 1923, when it published a photograph of Benny Leonard and his mother taken just before his fight with Lew Tendler. Two days later, a front-page story was captioned, "Benny Leonard Remains World Champion. 60,000 See Fight."

It was not until 1928 that the *Forward* printed another sports story,[1] and then it did so every Friday for nearly a year. The vast majority of the coverage was about soccer and baseball. There was virtually no coverage of boxing, and when there was, it was usually not about Jewish boxers. Only Al Singer, Joey Glick, Leo Lomsky, Phil Kaplan, Armand Emanuel, and Ted "Kid" Lewis rated even as much as a mention. No further articles appeared until 1932; several appeared sporadically until 1934, when they stopped. *Der Tag* and the *Morgan Journal* had periodic sports coverage in 1928, but none about boxing. Obviously, a kind of disapproval was inherent in this exclusion of such a popular form of Jewish entertainment from Jewish newspaper coverage.

One of the most colorful pieces on boxing to appear in the *Forward* was published on March 17, 1928, but did not relate to Jewish boxers. The previous summer, Gene Tunney had beaten Jack Dempsey a second time and retained the heavyweight crown. Dempsey retired, and Tunney was running out of opponents. The article was entitled, "Where in the World Can One Find a Good Heavyweight?"

The writer in an unmistakably Jewish fashion, laments the paucity of top-flight heavyweight contenders: "A fight between [Jack] Sharkey, who is considered to be as used up as a 'lulav' after Hoshana Rabbah (the conclusion of the Succoth Festival) [an opgeshlogener hoshana], and [Tom] Heeney is not much of a draw. Such a fight would not be popular."

And then: "[Jack] Dempsey has announced that he is retiring from the ring because of his bad eye. But there is conjecture that the story of a bad eye is a ruse. And even if it is true that the former champion does not see everything, it is not out of the question that if [Tex] Rickard (the promoter) offers him a lot of money, Dempsey will forget that he doesn't see and will agree to fight a third time with Tunney."

"If we live that long we will see."

As it happened, Dempsey remained retired, and in July 1928, Tunney knocked out Tom Heeney and finally retired as the heavyweight champion.

The Forward could write amusingly and with knowledge about boxing. It was with the idea of Jewish prizefighters that it had a problem.

There is another odd aspect to the *Forward*'s paucity of coverage of Jewish boxing. The editor of the *Forward* during this period was the commanding Abraham Cahan, who held the position for nearly fifty years, beginning in 1897. He set the newspaper's policy, and the meager sports coverage can be attributed to his fiat. Yet, in 1896 Cahan wrote a novel, *Yek and the New York Ghetto*, in which the character Jake is a boxing fanatic eager to acculturate into American society.

Then in 1914, in an essay entitled "The New Writers of the Ghetto,"[2] Cahan cites a short story by Aaron Wertzman which describes the rift between an immigrant family and its American-raised son who became a boxer. Obviously, Cahan was well aware of the existence of Jewish boxers and fans and placed some importance on their role in the American experience. Yet for some reason this was never translated to treatment on the pages of the *Forward*. Jewish literature, art, and drama, which in some ways may have been less relevant to Jewish acculturation, were widely reported.

At least thirty motion pictures have centered on boxing themes. One of them, *His People*, a silent film made in 1924, is about Jewish life on the lower East Side. The young son of Orthodox Jewish-Russian immigrants finds his place on the streets selling newspapers and fighting rather than in school. The parents are convinced that whatever "nachas" [pride] they realize will come through the older son, who is a law student. One Friday night a gossipy neighbor informs the father that his younger son has been prizefighting. The reaction is swift and violent, as presented in the subtitles:

A box-fyteh!? So that's what you've become? For this we came to America? So that you should become a box-fyteh? Better you should be a gangster or even a murderer. The shame of it. A box-fyteh!

The father expels the son from the house.

While the young son pursues his boxing career, the family hopes are pinned on the lawyer, who is essentially a bastard. First, he leaves home to live uptown, something no Jewish boxer ever willingly did. When he meets a rich uptown Jewish girl, he is too ashamed to admit his parentage, so he passes as an orphan. When the father becomes desperately ill, it is Sammy, the younger son, who fights for the championship and earns sufficient money to care for his parents. Sammy is reconciled with his father, marries his Irish childhood sweetheart (an untypical occurrence then), and the story ends happily.

Much of the film has the ring of truth to it. Jewish parents (and most parents) were usually, though not always, opposed to their sons becoming boxers. The sport was considered a lowly pursuit, and there was the ever-present fear of serious injury. Even the boxers' earnings did little to assuage the fears of mothers, many of whom never became reconciled to it. But throwing a son out of the house was a rare parental reaction. Also, the sons who boxed provided much-needed financial assistance, often turning over their entire purse to their parents. They generally regarded the money as belonging to the household.

In 1949, John Garfield appeared in the classic *Body and Soul*, which is based loosely on the life of Barney Ross. While the main character, Charlie Davis, obviously comes from a Jewish family, there is no specific Jewish content to the film; instead, the film concentrates on criminal infiltration into boxing, a subject that was then very prevalent in the United States. Charlie's mother is unalterably opposed to her son becoming a fighter, but when his father is killed during a holdup of his candy store (similar to the fate of Barney Ross's father), the die is cast for Charlie. His eventual estrangement from his mother has less to do with his boxing, however, than with his disregard for the family and the social values by which he was raised.

Charlie becomes the middleweight champion, but is so mob-connected at that point he is forced to agree to "throw" his next fight. Prior to the fight, he visits his mother, and while he is there, the neighborhood grocer, Shimon, delivers a grocery order. "We're all rooting for you, Charlie, we're betting on you," Shimon tells him.

"People shouldn't bet," Charlie, feeling guilty, admonishes him. "It's not the five dollars," Shimon responds. "Over in Europe, Hitler is killing our people, but here you're the champion. So we bet, you'll win, and we'll be proud." Upon hearing this, Charlie determines to win the fight despite the personal risk.

Jewish boxing has apparently receded from the Jewish historical and cultural consciousness. The existence of Jewish boxing is an irrefutable fact, yet it is still regarded with indifference, if not contempt. Irving Howe's *World of Our Fathers* (1976) devotes hundreds of pages depicting Jewish life on the lower East Side from the 1880s to the 1970s, and includes chapters on Jewish involvement in politics, literature, theater, art, and entertainment. But Howe alludes only once to boxing, a passing reference to Benny Leonard, to the effect that he was "proving [at the time] that a Jew could be the champion lightweight boxer" (p. 473).

In the five-volume series, *The Jewish People in America* (1992), edited by Henry Feingold, boxing is not mentioned. In Howard Sachar's *A History of the Jews in America* (1992), the Jewish connection to boxing is remarked upon mainly to describe what Sachar describes as the almost total mob infiltration of the sport and its Jewish participants.

It is apparent that the arbiters of Jewish culture and history in the United States and those who report it cannot reconcile themselves to the existence, let alone the importance, of boxing in the Jewish experience in America.

5

IN THE BEGINNING

Between 1881 and 1924 more than 2.5 million Jews, mainly from Russia and Poland, emigrated to America. This immigration represented one-third of European Jewry, but was still only 10 percent of the total number of people who came to this country during this period. What was unusual about the Jewish immigration was that it consisted of more families (50 percent) than any other ethnic group, and it was composed of individuals who had no thought of returning to their countries of origin after making some money in the United States.

The year 1881 is generally regarded as the beginning of this great migration because in that year Russian Tsar Alexander I was assassinated and a number of Jews were implicated in the plot to murder him. Over the next twenty years many pogroms took place, the most notorious of which were those in Kiev, Kishinev, and Odessa, where eight hundred Jews were killed. In 1882, the repressive "May Laws" under Tsar Alexander II were promulgated. These decrees further restricted areas of Jewish residency. In 1887, the infamous "numerus clausus" was instituted, sharply limiting Jewish attendance at secondary schools and universities. In 1891, Jews were expelled from Moscow.

These events gave great impetus to Jewish emigration. For the first time, Jews had a viable alternative to the uncertainties of political and physical denigration and economic hardship. They could come to America, which at least was politically free and where anti-Semitism was never institutionalized as an instrument of government policy.

Despite the truly oppressive conditions under which the Jews existed in Eastern Europe, the main motivation for coming to America was economic. As early as the 1870s and before the tsar's assassination, Polish Jews had begun to arrive; in addition, the physical threats to life were not as great in Poland as in Russia. Word of mouth, letters sent home, and return visits to the "*shtetl*" helped convince the Eastern Europeans that a better life awaited them in America. More efficient means of transportation, especially the proliferation of the locomotive and the steamship, facilitated the growth of the migration.

In the majority of cases in the 1880s and 1890s, those who came were from the poorest and least educated classes.The wealthy, the learned, and the prestigious had little reason, despite tsarist oppression, to completely abandon the existing social order. In this respect the Jewish immigrant differed little from the Italians, Greeks, Poles, and others who crossed the Atlantic in search of greater opportunity. They were indeed the "wretched refuse" for whom Emma Lazarus's words were immortalized on the Statue of Liberty. All of these immigrants, coming from areas where caste and religion determined social hierarchy, sought an atmosphere in which change was possible.

From the American perspective, these were the years of tremendous urban industrialization in the United States, and the poor human material from Southern and Eastern Europe was welcome to man the factories during this period of growth. Even though conditions were not ideal for immigrants, who often toiled for fourteen hours a day for minimal wages, and the streets of America were certainly not paved with gold, the circumstances were preferable to the even greater poverty they left behind. Indeed, those who came first to America not only wrote home for the rest of their families and villagers to join then, but also were often able to save enough to purchase their steamship passage.

The Jews from Eastern Europe who came arrived in a country in which there existed an established, accepted Jewish community. This refers, of course, to the "German" Jews, whose previous generation had made a similar voyage in search of freedom and prosperity. By the time of the mass migration from Eastern Europe, the German Jewish community in America had found its niche and felt comfortably at home in America.

The wave of immigration during the 1880s threatened this sense of security, and the German Jews were quick to act to protect themselves. The initial reaction was somehow to attempt to stem the tide of immigration at the source; they hoped that by alleviating the Jews' situation in Europe they would prevent the emergence of a Jewish problem in America. However, the pressure from Eastern Europe was too great, and America's German Jews soon recognized that the Eastern European Jew would be a permanent fixture in America. Given this realization, the German Jews sought to acculturate the immigrants to their new homeland and help them stand on their feet economically as swiftly as possible, thereby eliminating the "foreignness" associated with these Jews and creating a new generation of Jewish Americans in their image.

The period 1880–1920 was one of constant change, even in the backward areas of Eastern Europe. While the earliest immigrants from Eastern Europe were coming to America in the 1880s and 1890s, those Jews who remained behind were moving to the cities of Russia. As they urbanized, they were exposed to the various socialist and nationalist ideologies that were present in the cities of Europe. Thus, the Jew who arrived in New York from the *shtetl* in 1882 was not the same as the one who arrived from Warsaw or Vilna in 1905.

While the experience of New York Jews is certainly not representative of all Jewish immigrants during this period, the sheer numbers of those settling there make it the dominant experience. New York also remained the focal point of American Jewry throughout much of the twentieth century. One of the most pressing problems facing these immigrants was the tremendous overcrowding in immigrant neighborhoods. In 1890, New York was home to 200,000 Jews, 135,000 of whom inhabited the lower East Side. The Jew who had been raised in the *shtetl* was forced to adjust to both American and urban life at the same time. Despite the harsh conditions, America was still considered a paradise when compared to the life left behind. As is often noted, Jews differed from other ethnic groups in that they tended to migrate as family units, with females accounting for almost half of the immigrants from Eastern Europe and children for 25 percent. For the most part, immigrant Jews found work as manual laborers, despite the image of the Jewish merchant peddler. This profile differed from other immigrant groups, because the Jews, with their artisan experience in Eastern Europe, largely wound up working in the needle trades, whereas Irish and Italians generally were employed in heavier industries. Initially, both groups worked long hours for little pay; yet the nature of each industry was different. The Jews sweating in the garment industry could, with little capital, start a business on their own; heavier labor generally precluded such possibilities.

The elite of the American Jewish community stepped in and took an active part in acclimating the immigrants to American life. Individuals such as Jacob Schiff helped establish settlement houses, where the immigrants could benefit from the constructive advice of the German Jews. Although there was undoubtedly a self-serving aspect to the uptown community's sponsorship of these programs, the activities undeniably improved the lot of the immigrant community. The Henry Street settlement, established by Lilian Wald with Schiff's money, initially operated as a combination nursing home, food distributor, and employment agency. The administrators of these establishments soon realized that the most effective means of alleviating immigrants' hardships was to help them to help themselves. Thus the settlements soon began offering classes in English language, home economics, physical education, and many other programs. The program was un-abashedly one of Americanization. The Educational Alliance charter stated, that its scope "shall be of an Americanizing, educational, social and human-izing character."

A further aim of these settlements was to provide both recreation and guidance for the youth of the ghetto. Since the buildings in immigrant neighborhoods were overcrowded and the parents were occupied most of the day with work, an unsupervised street life developed among neighbor-hood youth. The settlement sought to provide an alternative to street life. This took on greater importance as crime became an increasingly prevalent aspect of Jewish immigrant life. And with the growth of nativist movements in America in the years before World War I, Jews recognized that they had to be extra clean in the public eye in order for an open immigration policy to be maintained.

The impetus to analyze Jewish criminality came from a statement made by New York City's police commissioner Theodore Bingham in September 1908, which claimed that immigrant Jews were particularly prone to crime and comprised a disproportionately large share of New York's underworld. While denying the charges, the Jewish leadership was forced to take account of the situation. There was a specifically Jewish criminal element in the immigrant neighborhoods. Jews never dominated the underworld, as the nativists claimed, but Jewish commission of felonies was widespread, confined mainly to crimes against property.

Jewish youths often roamed the streets unsupervised; this situation was ripe for the formation of street gangs. In the community, most such gangs were not seen as harmful, but rather as protectors against gangs of other ethnic groups.[1] Immigrant fathers often remained unaware of this aspect of their sons' lives, and they likely would not have understood. The fathers' vision of America was not one where Jewish youth had to fight against anti-Semitic attacks; that was part of the Old World.

Jewish crime was generally seen as an avenue of getting ahead economi-cally, and therefore socially, by outwitting the system. This theory provides the reasoning for Jewish prominence in insurance fraud, for example. By 1920, as Jewish demographics began to change, there appeared to be a gradual decline in Jewish criminality; the particularly Jewish enclaves of crime, such as pick pocketing, arson, horse-poisoning, and prostitution had virtually vanished. However, with the advent of Prohibition in the 1920s, second-generation Jews saw an unparalleled opportunity for financial gain with minimal risk.

Although the immigrants did assimilate much of American culture, most toiled so long just to get by that they had little time or energy for Americanization, and their lives were still rooted in the experience of the old country. The various *landsmanschaftn*—fraternal orders among the immigrant generation—ensured that their Eastern European heritage would not easily vanish. The great number of synagogues in immigrant neighborhoods, however, did not correlate with a high level of religious observance within the immigrant community. Most immigrants rarely attended synagogue, and many of those who did went primarily to socialize. From their first days in America, many immigrants realized that they would have to work on Saturday in order to support their families. For the next generations, Saturday would take on new meanings as a day of play or even shopping rather than as a day of prayer and rest.

Parents did not want their children to have the same difficulties adapting to and being accepted by America as they did, so they gladly offered their children to America. The children were sent in droves to the American public schools where they learned proper English and were inculcated with patriotism and civic awareness. It is important to differentiate between early and later immigrants. In the 1880s and 1890s, the legal school requirement was only four years of primary education, and due to economic constraints, most Jews were forced to enter the workforce rather than complete high school. The change in education legislation, coupled with the achievements of organized labor, eased the situation in the 1910s and 1920s, but most young Jews still began to work on completing their secondary education.

Eastern European Jews flocking to public universities was a phenomenon of the 1930s. Until then Jews attending university were almost always the children of the elite and middle class. The overwhelming number of immigrant Jews remained working class. It was up to their children to achieve the American dream of stable middle-class life. It should be remembered that generational progress does not correlate specifically with particular points in time. For example, the immigrants in the 1880s would already be in their second generation by the 1910s, whereas the second generation of those who came to America in the late 1910s might not grow up until the

1940s and 1950s. The pattern of economic development conforms more to the generation of immigration than to a specific period of time.

Despite the often strenuous efforts of the German Jewish community, the children of the East European Jews did not conform to the elitist Reform conception of how to combine Americanism with Judaism; rather, they forged various new means of expressing their dual heritage. The religiously traditional autonomous Jewish community of their ancestors held little meaning in their lives, nor did the unemotional, mission-oriented version offered by American Reform Judaism appeal to them. In terms of their Jewish identity, this new generation was still very much rooted in the Eastern European experience. But the modern concept of a Jewish people also defined their Jewish ethnicity. There were a number of ways that one could act and identify as a Jew. Their children also refused to let their Judaism prevent their acculturation into the American mainstream. The success of this generation was measured in the American marketplace, on the American stage, and in national politics rather than in uniquely Jewish concerns. It is this attitude that places the Jewish boxers within the larger framework of the second-generation experience. Thus, the success and celebrity of boxers such as Benny Leonard and Barney Ross should be seen as similar to the experience of Jews such as Irving Berlin, George Gershwin, or Paul Muni.

Although the second generation became thoroughly acculturated to America, this process had a unique aspect. Second-generation Jews most often Americanized within a predominantly Jewish milieu. They were raised in neighborhoods that were mostly Jewish, were taught in school with other Jews by the previous generation of Jews, and secured employment through Jewish contacts in Jewish firms.

The pattern of Jewish dispersion within America actually belied the assimilation feared by many. In New York, as Jews moved from Jewish immigrant neighborhoods such as the lower East Side, Brownsville, or Williamsburg, they created second Jewish neighborhoods, including the Grand Concourse, Coney Island, or Flatbush, which were often more preponderantly Jewish than the initial settlements.

This generation, raised in America, provided what would eventually be the political and intellectual leadership of the American Jewish community in the latter half of the century, replacing that of the German Jewish establishment. Its rapid rise to success was achieved primarily by exploring and exploiting the marginal or untapped sectors of American life. This activity was tremendously broad in scope. It included the performing arts, such as singing, acting, or song writing; advertising and marketing; and new forms of the media, such as the radio, gramophone, and, of course, the creation of the motion picture industry. Jewish participation in the American sporting world as players, coaches, trainers, promoters, and reporters falls within this realm of social history.

For every Paul Muni who made it from the Yiddish stage to Hollywood stardom, there were some who had to be content with a reputation that did not extend beyond Second Avenue and hundreds or thousands, who plied their trade in anonymity. For every Adolph Zukor there were countless movie men whose dreams did not materialize. So too, alongside the great Benny Leonard and Barney Ross, there lived a whole generation of professional Jewish boxers, of all ranks and qualities. This aspect of the American Jewish experience, along with more often mentioned pathways, demonstrates the dynamic growth and opportunism of the second-generation American Jewish community.

Second-generation Jews formulated for themselves how they would interpret their personal connections with Judaism. Traditional historical analyses of American Judaism were frustrated in defining the bulk of second-generation American Jews. When we recognize that Judaism in America consisted of more than a religious component during this period, Jewish identity takes on new meaning.

If such factors as synagogue membership, or even high-holiday attendance, is used to determine Jewish identification, the Jews of this era would not rank highly. But when we take less tangible factors into account, such as political affiliation, social circles, or even eating habits, the story is much different. While these categories were generally determined by a middle-class American outlook, Jewish ethnicity also came into play. Perhaps most significant is the fact that the rate of intermarriage among the second generation was extremely low, and support for Zionism was generally high (especially after the rise of Nazism in Germany). Both of these attitudes reflect a definite commitment to the continuity of the Jewish people regardless of religious outlook.

The Jewish immigrant's family and intrafamily relations were not always simple and pleasant. The immigrant family often arrived in the United States in stages, a situation that led initially to marital problems.[2] Often a Jewish man had no desire to be reunited with his wife from the Eastern European *shtetl* and vanished when she arrived from across the Atlantic. Lower East Side social workers devoted much attention to the syndrome of "deserted wives," and a National Desertion Bureau was created in 1911 as part of the National Conference of Jewish Charities. As early as 1902, the United Hebrew Charities of New York had established a Department of Desertion.

Since Jewish law prohibits the wife from remarrying without a religious divorce, deserted wives were left in quite a precarious position, and great effort was made to track down the missing husbands.

On the other hand, the contemporary literature also recounts story upon story of the husband and father who worked all day long, yet still could support his family, and continued to hold on to vestiges of life in the old world, such as strict religious observance and exclusive use of Yiddish. Such individuals often had great difficulty relating to their wives, who were becoming increasingly aware of the American culture of mass consumption, demanding more and more of their husbands, and to their children, who were growing up on the American street with American values and attitudes. The settlement homes run by the German Jews were little help in this regard, for they instilled within the immigrant families middle-class ideals and aspirations, which few families recently arrived from Eastern Europe were in an economic position to achieve.

As the second generation was on its way to complete Americanization, due primarily to the public school curriculum, the generation gap between parent and child became increasingly wide. This was often the price Jewish families paid for the acculturation of their children to America. The Jewish parochial school or Yeshiva movement was virtually nonexistent on the lower East Side and in the "boroughs" until the 1940s. Until 1920, only the Rabbi Jacob Joseph School existed for the entire downtown population. The lack of these schools was as much an effect as a cause of Jewish religious alienation. In contrast, Italian immigrant families, whose children attended parochial school, tended to remain more close-knit.

The proliferation of Jewish boxers during the 1920s and 1930s was not a spontaneous phenomenon, but was predated by the success of Jewish pugilists in the early years of the twentieth century. Almost all the boxers fit into a similar social and demographic profile in terms of their stage in the immigration process: that is, second-generation Jews, raised in the poor ghettos of America. The prevalence of the Jewish boxer declined in the 1940s in accordance with the virtual cessation of Jewish immigration in the 1920s. As this generation of Jews entered the ranks of the American middle class and left behind the harsh conditions of immigrant street life, their children were not forced to follow difficult roads to success. The way had been cleared by their parents' generation.

Irving Howe writes that the idea of the "New Jewish Character" is the highest denominator of all secular Jewish movements: "active, not passive, subject, not object, erect, not bowed, combative not acquiescent."[3] All such movement shared the dream of making Jewish life normal. These included various strains of Zionism, nationalism, Bundism, and Communism. While of not such cosmic proportions, the Jewish boxer stood securely in this mold, being both agent and manifestation of the Americanization process.

The boxers' families settled in the lower East Side; later, some moved to Brownsville, the Bronx, Coney Island, and parts of northern New Jersey. When the father was a religious functionary, the family often relocated to serve a distant community. Harry Markson, for example, who became president of boxing at Madison Square Garden, was the son of a "*shochet*"[4] who came to Kingston, New York, in 1886, and Markson was born and grew up there. Harry tells of the extent of his Jewish education in the "*Cheder*"[5] in Kingston.

"It was a limited education, because every young guy who just came here from Europe would come up there . . . go to high school, learn how to talk English and he would get the job as the Hebrew School teacher. They would stay one year and leave, so you'd go from the beginning until the death of Moses and they'd start the following year the same thing with another teacher. Over and over and over again, so I never got past the death of Moses. I never really had as solid a foundation in Judaism as I would have liked."

The fathers were employees of various clothing, construction, and other concerns. A few had small businesses of their own. Only one or two of the mothers ever worked, and then just part time. Yiddish was the language most frequently spoken in the home. Like other immigrants, some of the parents never learned to speak English.

None of the boxers except Charlie Gellman graduated from or even attended college.[6] Many did not finish high school; Miltie Kessler never even started. College was not very prominent in their thinking. Most had begun boxing in high school, some professionally, and were anxious to move ahead with their prizefighting careers.

The boxers were proudly Jewish and did not differentiate between Judaism as a religion and a nationality. They were not very observant and are even less so today. Many of their parents were not rigidly religious, but nearly all were traditional and kept kosher homes; a number of the boxers continue to maintain kosher homes. Synagogue attendance among the parents and even some of the boxers was habitual, particularly on the High Holy Days. I am aware of only two Jewish boxers who ever converted: Mushy Callahan, the junior welterweight champion (1926–1930) and Jack Silver. Each became a Roman Catholic after his boxing career had ended.

Of all the aspects of each boxer's history, the family context of their growing up and the Jewish content of their lives had the most similarities.

Maxie Shapiro had a career as one of the most talented and colorful of the Jewish lightweights. Although he began boxing at a later age than the others (he was in his early twenties), the story of his early years is representative of many of the fighters. Their childhoods were not very different from those of their hundreds of thousands of fellow Jews on the lower East Side.

"I was born on the lower East Side . . . that's lower Manhattan. I call it the lower East Side. We used to call it 'the ghetto' at that time. A ghetto is like a gathering of all the, not the wealthy people, you know. And the buildings, the housing there was not what it is today. You know it had bathrooms in the hallways, no showers, no steam heat and we used a coal stove to keep warm. And there was gas light and stuff like that. No electric. I guess that was . . . what it means. A gathering of the poorer people. I was born in 1918,[7] so I guess that goes back into the twenties. And then the depression came on in the late twenties. I had two brothers and a sister and my mother and father. One brother used to come follow me boxing with his friends. He was very proud of me. He was a good fight fan. He drove a bus in lower Manhattan where we lived. And he's gone. So my sister's left and my other younger brother. My parents came here from Poland around 1910. At that time, everybody came from Poland . . . the Jewish people. And a lot of people came to the lower East Side, settled down there. They got off Ellis Island. They came to this country and the wealthier people, or the more financially well-to-do went to Brownsville at that time. Brownsville was a pretty classy section. What do you call it? East New York. By Sutter Avenue. Had an aunt that lived there. Went to visit her and we thought she was wealthy because she had a downstairs bell and stuff like that with a backyard. So the lower East Side and Brownsville were where the Jewish immigrants came to this country from Europe.

"My father had a trade. He was a bricklayer, a plasterer, stuff like that. He used to get jobs plastering broken apartments and bricklaying, which was a pretty good trade at that time.

"I never went to Hebrew school, but we had a rabbi who lived in the tenement building right in the neighborhood and we used to go up to his apartment and he would teach us how to read Hebrew and stuff like that. And then by the time you got Bar Mitzvahed at thirteen years old—there was a Jewish celebration, and that's when you graduate and that's when you quit going to synagogue, ha, ha, ha.

"My father wasn't too, what's the word, pious, religious. He just was a good guy, nice guy, but wasn't too much . . . for going to synagogue. Maybe on holidays, on Passover, Yom Kippur, the holy days. Mother would go, you know. She represented the family in synagogues.

"My mother kept a kosher house. That was a must at that time. Every Passover we had to change the dishes and change the silverware and not burn the gas on Friday at sundown and stuff like that. And there was no eating on Yom Kippur. I used to run to the automat with some of the guys on 14th street on Yom Kippur, when you're not supposed to eat. I wasn't too good at following the rules.

"There was a high school, junior high school where we lived, a block away from the house. We didn't have to take any buses or trains to school. The schools were right there where you lived. On Hester and Ludlow Street there was Seward Park High School. That was a pretty popular high school on the lower East Side.

"All my friends were Jewish. At that time everybody was Jewish. I remember, when I was in junior high school, there was an Italian boy. His name was Calvarado. It was strange to see an Italian boy in the class. The teachers were Jewish, too. David Cohen. Irving Cohen.

"Every neighborhood was a section. The lower East Side where I lived was Jewish people, and a few blocks away there was a boundary line, the Bowery. The Italian neighborhood, Mulberry Street, Mott Street. So we never went there and they never came over to us. Everybody stayed in his own backyard.

"The Chinese were where they are today. In Chinatown. Didn't see any Irish. They were right down by the East River. They had a section there, McAllen Park. The Polish were also in a different section, about a mile away, Avenue A and 10th Street. It seems everybody settled in their own area.

"You could sleep with the doors open. You could sleep on the roof. You could sleep in the park. There was no fear like today that you had to worry about anybody grabbing your pocketbook or people being mugged or something. They were different times. No one had nothing. But that was good enough. They had their safety and their peace of mind. It was easy living at that time."

Marty Pomerantz was one of several of the boxers who never lived on the lower East Side. But his experience did not vary substantially from Maxie Shapiro's. Marty's father was in business for himself, but that did not translate into more money.

"I was born in 1915 and I had a brother and a sister. My father was a dress manufacturer. He owned a toy store, a movie theater. He was a real entrepreneur. I don't remember that he ever made any money, though. And he was born in New York. My mother was born in Europe, and she came here as a very young child. Before we moved to Brooklyn we lived in the Bronx, and there I went to PS 2 on Third Avenue and 169th Street, junior high school on 170th Street, and then Morris High School. I went to Hebrew School with most of the other Jewish boys my age and was Bar Mitzvahed. My parents kept a kosher home. My father went to synagogue, not on a steady basis. He wasn't too religious. But most of the Jews went to synagogue in those days. And I did also."

As far as Leo Bodner knew, he was the only observant Jew who was connected with boxing. His sanguine view of life has not prepared him to think of becoming a plaintiff in a religious discrimination action: "I kept up *shomer Shabbos*[8] and they respected me for being religious. Always they all respected me . . . the Johnstons respected me and all the trainers . . . everybody respected me because I was a religious boy and I kept it up. As far as I know, I was the only one."

While Allie Stolz's boyhood years had very strong religious content, Charlie Gellman's had none. But one thing was universally true: all the families were strong, close-knit units, as they had to be to survive. Whatever their religious observance and that of their families, the boxers maintained deep cultural and ethnic Jewish feelings. As American and acculturated as they felt themselves to be, it would never have occurred to them to deny or hide their Jewish heritage.

The fighters spoke of their parents in reverential terms. The siblings remained devoted to each other throughout their lives. When Allie Stolz recited the names of his five brothers and one sister, he inadvertently omitted mentioning his deceased brother Lenny.

"Oh, Lenny, too. Oh, Lenny. I didn't want him to go. . . . I loved him. Lenny, I'm sorry." At that memory, Allie Stolz, two-time contender for the lightweight championship of the world, began to cry.

For many of the prizefighters, becoming professional boxers was not manifest destiny; nor was boxing the preordained path to earning desperately needed money. That came later. For most of them their beginnings in boxing were a result of the availability of gyms and equipment in community centers and schools, the desire for exercise, and the large number of other Jewish participants. Julie Bort, who had polio, gravitated to boxing because he could not play baseball, his real sports love.

If the boxers showed talent and heart, they often were entered in the Golden Gloves tournament sponsored by the *New York Daily News*. Marty

Pomerantz and a number of others won Eastern titles in the competition, and a few, such as Sammy Farber, believe to this day that they should have won.

Following the Golden Gloves came the "amateurs" and "bootleg boxing," which was an illegal but tolerated hybrid between amateur and professional boxing. For an amateur bout (three rounds) the fighter would receive a watch which would usually be redeemed by the trainer that night for $5 to $10. For "bootleg boxing" the contestant used a different name and could earn up to $50 or more.

The boxers generally had about fifty to seventy-five amateur fights, often fighting one or two each week. Those who showed promise and desire would then turn professional. In New York one had to be eighteen to obtain a professional boxing license. Herbie Kronowitz and many others were underage and assumed someone else's identity to qualify. Kronowitz's name is really Ted. He adopted the name of his older brother Herb so that he could obtain a license.

For the boxers, as a norm, professional fighting was a full-time occupation. They were required to train and exercise constantly to remain in top fighting shape. Most of their matches were in the New York vicinity (there were nearly forty fight clubs in the metropolitan area), but they would travel out of town as well. By the time they were twenty-five years old, they often had two hundred amateur and professional fights. If they were not advancing professionally, it was usually time to quit.

Joey Varoff was one of the boxers who grew up on the lower East Side. The beginnings of his career possess all the earmarks of boxing tradition.

"I graduated Seward Park High School. While I was in high school, I was in the Golden Gloves for New York City and I made it to the finals. Lost in Madison Square Garden.

"Also, incidentally, I was a professional fighter my last year of high school. I fought for a year professionally before I graduated. I was sixteen while I was in the Golden Gloves about 1939. I was seventeen when I became a professional. I lied about the age; you had to be eighteen to be a prizefighter.

"I started as a featherweight and I ended up as a welterweight. I fought about ten years. From 1939 to 1950, or something like that.

"My parents kind of accepted it because I loved it so much as a child and I was in Boys Club tournaments. I was a champion Boys Club boxer, you know, in New York City. As a youngster, I was twelve years old, I was a Boys Athletic League champion. I went into those amateur fights and the

Golden Gloves. And they kind of accepted it. I loved it. I loved to go to the gym and watch the prizefighters. I was thrilled to talk to them and be around them. It was basically my life. I loved it right from the start. I was talented, I guess you'd call it. I was a good boxer as a youngster and people recognized it and I just loved it. There was something about the game I loved."

Charles Gellman was a middleweight. After his fighting days were over, he made a career as president of two hospitals in Manhattan. To Gellman starting to box was a natural adjunct to the general meanness of life in West New York, New Jersey.

"In 1926 I was ten years old. In those days, they didn't have refrigerators and they didn't have steam heat. They were cold-water flats. The people who lived around there were Irish, Italian, and German. All the non-Jewish type people. They were a hard-working blue-collar people. There were what they called "icemen" around in those days. For 10 cents you'd get a chopped piece of ice and he'd bring it into your house and he'd sell coal and they put the coal in the stoves and that's how you kept warm in the winter time. Across the street from where I lived, there was an iceman by the name of Willie DeRazmo. He had three sons. One of the sons wanted to become a fighter when he was about sixteen years old. Somehow or other, the town became a fight town. You know, I was ten years old and the various parks had boxing shows. And the Knights of Columbus nearby had amateur bouts.

"A few blocks away there was a club called the Cosmos Club where they had a ring. They had all the young kids, keeping them off the street, training up there. And a few good trainers up there started to teach people the fundamentals. I was fascinated by it. I always went along, since I was ten years old, to watch offense, defense, how to train, how to develop your stomach, how to develop your body, how to take care of yourself and stuff like that. And I started putting on a pair of gloves with them just to horse around, but I learned how to be a boxer when I was ten years old. And I watched DeRazmo's son go through the various rituals and I went to his amateur fights and I went to his professional fights. I did this until I was sixteen years old. That's how close I was to this guy. And I met the other boxers of that time, with their pushed-in faces, and their battered jaws and things like that. First thing you know, I started to work out with them a little bit, as I got stronger, and I decided to go in the amateurs.

"My parents didn't know. Look, they had enough problems of their own. They made sure I did my homework. They let me go out in the afternoon. Where could you go in those days? I mean, there were no Jewish places to go. There was no temple. So you went on the street and you played with the shoemaker's son or you played with the mason's son or you went into the iceman's house and you talked to them. They paid no attention to what I did. As long as I got good marks.

"I was in the poolrooms. Of course, there was some bad company, too. I was really a street kid. I knew the ins and outs. And I got into street fights. But I knew enough by virtue of the fact that I was boxing in the gym at ten years old, to take care of myself. I came home with a couple, but it was normal. Everybody was in a street fight in those days. I mean, what do you want to do? You want to settle something, you go to the lot. They didn't have knives or guns. There was a guy in the firehouse nearby, he would give you a pair of gloves and he'd watch. Sometimes they used to pick on me. I'll tell you a story about one kid, in grammar school, that had one arm. And he knew that I was boxing. So he challenged me. And when he challenged me, I asked the iceman, Willie DeRazmo, 'Do you think I should fight him?' He said, 'No, you shouldn't fight him.' I said, 'So how do I get out of this?' He said, 'I'll tell you what you do. You're a tough kid. Tell him you're going to fight him. Let him hit you one shot and then you quit.' I said, 'OK.' So we had a fight after school, I remember I was in the eighth grade. So I let the guy give me one shot with one arm and I quit. I said I had enough. And that's how you were taught.

"It took somebody that was streetwise to give me enough common sense to recognize that that was the right thing to do. That's what's lacking today, you see. But that's when you have somebody that has character. Whatever material thing he has in his pocket, it doesn't mean a god-damned thing. You found out later that material things don't mean a god-damned thing.

"When I was approximately sixteen years old, I wanted to fight for the Knights of Columbus, but I was Jewish. It was a little bit peculiar. There was a lot of anti-Semitism around, no doubt about it. You know, in those days, they didn't handle things the way they handle it today. If you were a Jew, you were a Jew. You were Christ's killer. And I felt it. I felt it very strongly. In West New York, Union City, or wherever I went.

"In those days, if I won the first fight, there'd be a semifinal, the same weight, 160 pounds. Fellow that won the first fight would then be matched with me the second time around and if we won, well you get a silver watch the first fight. You get a gold watch the second fight. Then we'd sell it back and we'd get 5 bucks for the damn thing. This was the way we made a few bucks.

"I lost out to Gus Lesnevich in the finals of the Diamond Belt. And Gus Lesnevich became the light-heavyweight champion of the world. I fought Gus Lesnevich half a dozen times in the amateurs. And in the last fight that

I had with him I got raked. Gus beat me four times out of six. But the last one was the one I really wanted to win and I lost.

"First of all, he was a little older than I was, and it was a lot of rivalry. You see, he came from Cliffside Park, New Jersey, and I came from West New York, New Jersey. But the funny part of all these things, all these guys became friends of mine later, and I set up a special fund to take care of them when I was fortunate enough to make it and I ran the hospitals. So none of them were ever left out. I was in school throughout all this stuff. My spare time was involved with boxing. Except I was a good football player. When I was in high school, I played football.

"When my father worked, if he got a few bucks, he was a sport. He would go out and spend it. Take us all to a restaurant or something, and piss it away. But when he didn't work, there were a lot of problems. There were four of us altogether. and when money didn't come in it was pretty god-damned tough. The grocery store, the mom and pop grocery store and the butcher would give them money on credit, but months went by and they couldn't pay. Things were pretty damn bad.

"My father was a carpenter, and he did work for various people around town. Then, certain Jewish people moved in who were in the real estate business. They bought real estate, and he was hired to put up storefronts and a few other things. So when he worked, it was fine. When he didn't work, it was something else. But we were always having trouble. It was difficult. My father couldn't read or write. I mean, he made an X for his name. He was a very clever craftsman. He was an excellent carpenter. But I used to sit and draw the plans for him. He used to tell me what to do. He would tell me how to lay out a piece of wood for him. And I was pretty good with a pen and pencil. And when he would figure a job, for instance, a storefront, he would say, 'Well, I need a few linear feet of this, a few linear feet of that.' So he knew how to order. He wanted me to be an architect. So he sent me to night school, to Hoboken Tech, to learn how to become a draftsman. Architectural drawing.

"I was boxing through everything. Everything. As soon as I got through with my books at school, I would go home. I would meet Louis DeRazmo at the Cosmos Club and I would put on a pair of trunks and I would work out with him and I would watch him. Of course he babied me. When I was a kid, I went to his fights. I got the feel of the dressing room, the smell of the liniments. I got the feel of boxing all throughout. I learned how to take care of myself on the basis of instructions that I got from various trainers. I would listen to a trainer say to a fighter one day, 'Look, you're boxing in this gym. You look good in the gym, but you can't take a punch. When you get in the ring.' And these things stayed with me. He would instruct the guy and say, 'When you go in there the guy you're fighting isn't going to stand still. He's going to hit you back. If you can't take a punch, don't go in there in the first place.' And it sticks in your mind. So when I started to box, the first thing the trainer did to me is put a rough guy in there to throw blows at me, to teach me how to take it. I learned that you got to have timing. You had to have endurance. You had to have guts and you had to be able to take a punch. And you had to learn to control your steam so that you don't run out of gas after three rounds. You learn all these things.

"You have to learn to control your emotions. I learned how to use the tools. I learned how to deal with these things. One of the worst things you can do is lose your cool in the ring. The fighters must know how to think. And I learned this early in the game. The body wasn't made to take a punch. And you got to know how to take it. This is all scientific. Why do you think, I had sixty-five professional fights and I'm telling you, rough fights, and I never got banged up? I got hurt, yes, sure you gotta get hit."

Sammy Farber fought in the Golden Gloves in 1926. It still rankles him that he did not receive the decision he thought he deserved.

"In 1926, I was fighting a guy in the Hudson Guild. That's the West Side. It was the first Golden Gloves. In those years you fought three minutes a round in the amateurs, one minute rest. Now they don't. Now you fight two minutes a round in the amateurs. And when I fought this fellow, three rounds I beat him. And they ordered an extra round. I beat him four rounds! And they gave him the decision. You know why? His father was the referee. His cousins were the judges. So how could I win?

"His name was Terry Roth, and he is the first Golden Glove champion. 112 pounds. He and I had the same manager. I taught him how to fight, believe it or not. I says, 'All right, you go into the 112. And I'll go into the 118.' Because I thought you know, we would take over the lower East Side. I thought that would be great! You know? So he won the championship, and I lost it in four rounds. Which I always have in my mind that I won. In fact, a couple of times they wrote in the paper that I was the champion."[9]

Marty Pomerantz's start in boxing came about as a result of his association with the Jewish Community House (JCH) in Bensonhurst, Brooklyn.

"At some point in the early '30s we moved to 74th Street in Brooklyn, and I started going to the JCH to work out. I played handball there. I had no thought at that time of being a boxer. But while I was there, I met Irving Cohen. Irving Cohen owned a corset shop or brassiere shop. He was actually a boxer. He used to fight amateurs, get the watch and sell it for $15 or $20 and keep the store going. And I became friendly with Cohen. I was a southpaw (lefty). Cohen turned me around to become an orthodox boxer. Southpaws are very difficult to fight. On the other hand, somehow or other they also had difficulty in fighting. They took a lot of punches, maybe because of the way the orthodox fighters fought. And also they used to make for very, very dull fights, because the righty and the lefty would spend the entire fight trying to avoid each other.

"So I became interested in fighting and I enrolled in the Golden Gloves in 1933 when I was eighteen. I was rejected because they said I had something wrong with my heart. A murmur or something. But by 1934, it was all right and I fought in the semifinals in the Hippodrome on 44th Street and 5th Avenue and I lost. In 1935, I won the lightweight championship of the New York Golden Gloves. Teddy Brenner, he became a very famous matchmaker, was very friendly with Cohen. He wasn't Cohen's brother-in-law. The papers used to say that, but he wasn't. But he was friendly with him, and he was a kid. A few years younger than I was. He used to get into the fights by carrying my bag. I don't know if he'd remember that or admit to that today. While this was going on—I was eighteen or nineteen years old—I wasn't in college. Although I think my parents wanted me to go. But I was already in the shoe business as a cutter.

"I also won the Jewish Olympics. I represented the JCH. That was in 1935. The finals were fought in Newark and I won the lightweight division, so that as a result of winning the Golden Gloves and winning the Jewish Olympics, I was supposed to go to Tel Aviv for the Maccabiah games and also to Chicago. The New York Golden Gloves winners were going to fight the Chicago Golden Gloves winners. Well, I decided to go to Chicago. But what happened was, we were put up at a hotel, the St. Moritz at the time, the Golden Gloves fighters, and we were all, believe me, Jews, non-Jews, we were friendly. It didn't matter. And we were all pretty good boys. We came from families where there was respect and there was no rowdyism. But a couple of guys wanted some extra expense money for haircuts and things like that. It doesn't seem like very much. Incidentally, Bernie Friedkin was my roommate at that time. And we were pretty close to each other over there in Brooklyn. Anyway, we were asking for expense money, and as a result of that, the fellow in charge disbanded the whole team and they used the runner-ups to go to Chicago. So I didn't go to Chicago and I didn't go to Tel Aviv.

"In 1936 I turned pro, and I continued to work for a while. And then I stopped working. I was making some money. Not a lot. I never made any really big money. I had a star bout or a main event in the Bronx Coliseum against Lou Kanst. It was on Christmas Eve, and the house was packed. They charged 40 cents general admission. So what did I make? I made a few hundred dollars. All in all I had thirty professional fights, and I think I won twenty-four. My career was from 1936 to 1939. I fought in all the clubs. Never in the Garden except for the Golden Gloves. But I fought in the Coney Island Velodrome, Eastern Parkway and Fort Hamilton, Sunnyside, Broadway Arena, Ridgewood Grove, St. Nick's, and Bronx Coliseum that I mentioned. There were a lot of arenas in those days. A lot of fights.

"I was Irving Cohen's first fighter. Later on he had Graziano and others. He made some money. But he had no connections then. So we had a meeting one day at the Paradise Night Club. I remember, it was Irving Cohen, my father and Frankie Carbo. Carbo wanted to buy my contract. Cohen didn't care. He was a friend. I was really naive. What did I know? I didn't know anything about mob control or things like that. Even then, Carbo had the middleweight division sewed up. He was power. These guys did what they wanted. They bought fights for you. They made sure there was a huge amount of betting. 'Don't knock this guy out. Knock that guy out. Maybe you don't have to win this.' All of that went on. I didn't know what to do. So my father said, 'Listen, you started with Cohen, you make it, you'll be with Cohen.' We shook hands and Carbo left. I had no problem with it. I think I would have made a lot more money with him, and I would have gotten more fights and maybe I would have gotten a shot at the championship. I don't know."

Leo Bodner became involved with boxing so that he could gain some weight. It was convenient for him to go to the Educational Alliance gym. At the time, in the mid-1920s, the Alliance offered more than one thousand courses and programs in support of life on the lower East Side and the process of acculturation. The athletic portion was a small but important part of what the Alliance represented.

"When I worked for Beer Brothers, they had a brother working with them by the name of Harry Beer. They called him Hymie. And he said to me, 'Could you put on any weight?' I weighed a hundred pounds. A hundred and five, a hundred and ten. I was very slim. He says to me, 'Why don't you join the Educational Alliance and you'll do a little training over there and maybe you'll eat better and you'll put on weight.' So I started going to the Educational Alliance, and I met a lot of boys who trained in there, a lot of boxers, like Ruby Goldstein. Yale Okun trained there for a while. The Educational Alliance was on East Broadway near where I worked. It was only a couple of blocks away. I only went twice a week to the Educational Alliance, so those two days I had to skip night school. I enjoyed boxing. I enjoyed skipping the rope. I was very good at skipping the rope. I was good at skipping school too. But I'm sorry that I skipped school. I don't know why my father didn't send me to school during the day. He could have.

"I met Ruby Goldstein and guys that trained up there. They wanted to be boxers, and they weren't good enough or they stopped for one reason or another. But there was a lot of boxing there. They had all kinds of boxing exhibitions. Ruby put on exhibitions so the Educational Alliance could make a couple of dollars. Kids coming from different gyms where they were training, like in Brooklyn or in Long Island, and they put on exhibitions and people came up and paid to watch them box. Especially when Ruby Goldstein was in an exhibition, the place was packed.

"The Educational Alliance was 99 percent Jewish. But the boxers that came for exhibitions weren't all Jewish. They were all different kinds. The Jewish boxers came from families like mine. Very nice families. I met some of the families. Became friendly with a couple of boys who were up there and I met their families. Fine Jewish families. They were mostly from Eastern Europe. A lot of them were Orthodox families. Yale Okun's family was Orthodox. Went to *shul* every Saturday. I think Ruby Goldstein's family was Orthodox, too. Sid Terris's family was Orthodox.

"I think Ruby Goldstein was the model at the Educational Alliance. At that time his trainer, an elderly man, was also his manager. His name was Hymie Kantor. This was a very nice man. When I was boxing in the amateurs, he always came along with me. He was always in my corner. He knew his business. He knew his boxing. But I don't know what happened. He sold Ruby's contract to a couple of guys, a couple of East Side racketeers, and they became Ruby Goldstein's managers. And they ruined him.

"When he fought Ace Hudkins in the Coney Island Velodrome, he got hit on the chin and he went down. They were yelling, 'Get up, get up, get up.' And he listened to them, and he got up too fast, too soon. Had he stayed down until the count of nine, he would have cleared his head. But he got up and he got hit again and he got knocked out.

"Those few seconds could make a big difference. You clear your head a little bit. They were there yelling at him to get up right away because they were betting a lot of money on Ruby. And he knew it. He was afraid that if he didn't get up right away, his life wouldn't be worth two cents. He got knocked out because he got up too soon. He didn't clear his head.

"I never mentioned it to him. It was a sore spot. I spoke to him about something else. At the Educational Alliance in the locker room. He had an exhibition one time, a fellow from Brooklyn was supposed to box with him in the exhibition. And I happened to be in the locker room at that time in the corner, and they didn't see me. And this fellow's trainer who came with him says to him. 'Don't be afraid to hit him. If you can knock him out, you'll get yourself a big name.' In an exhibition, you're not supposed to knock a guy out. You're not supposed to hit him hard. It was just an exhibition. So I went out to Ruby and I told him what I heard. And Ruby knocked the hell out of him. He kept jabbing him and jabbing him. I don't think the guy fought after that. He was finished.

"At that time, I started Amateurs. Going to different places, like the New York Athletic Club, the Westchester Country Club, Newark, New Jersey. My weight class was flyweight.

"I was supposed to be 110 pounds, but I could never make 110 pounds. When I went to weigh in, this fellow Gold, who was the matchmaker, says to me, 'Put some change in your pocket.' And he weighed me in with my pants on. Then maybe I weighed 110.

"I had about twelve amateur matches, each fight was three rounds. I never knocked anyone out. I was just boxing. I was very fast on my feet. And very fast with my hands, and the crowd liked it. I was a good boxer. I used to protect myself pretty good. I very seldom got hit hard enough to get knocked out or to get cut. I never got cut. I never got knocked out either."

It is family lore that Tony Canzoneri who went on to become the welterweight champion knocked Bodner out in the amateurs, or at least down.

"I know you're going to ask me, so I'll tell you, Tony Canzoneri never knocked me out. He won the bout, but he didn't knock me out. I fought him twice and he won both times. Tony was a very clever fighter. Very good fighter. He had a terrific trainer, had a good manager and they trained him like they train a professional. I was down once. I don't know if I slipped or not, but I was down once in one of the bouts. That's about all.

"What did we receive as amateur? Well, we got gifts. We got a watch. We got a medal. I left it in the house and it disappeared somehow. The boxers used to hock them or sell them. But I didn't sell any, I was always working and didn't need the money.

"Because I liked Pancho Villa, I started fighting under the name of Kid Pancho. I used to watch him. I used to go up to the gym and watch him box. He was a terrific boxer, a terrific fighter. At that time he was the flyweight champion of the world.

"I once saw him box a guy, a heavyweight by the name of Jack Grenault. At the gym. He was training with him. They needed somebody for a fast workout with a heavyweight. So they asked him to go in and he went in with him. This Jack Grenault was a pretty good fighter. He came from Canada. And he couldn't lay a glove on him. A beautiful exhibition.

"To me boxing was an art. I liked boxers. I didn't like fighters. I didn't like a guy to go in and just hit anywhere at all. I liked a guy that knew what he was doing and who boxed beautifully. I once saw a fight between Sid Terris and a guy by the name of Benny Valgar. It was at Ebbets Field. It was a ten-round main bout. I don't think there were two good punches landed in the whole fight.

"It was a beautiful exhibition. The crowd didn't like it because they like to see blood. They like to see somebody go in and fight. But as an exhibition, this was terrific. Terris won the fight that time.

"I didn't fight under the name Leo Bodner because, at that time, I don't think any of the kids fought under their own names. They all used different names. Maybe it was because I didn't want my family to know that I'm boxing. My brothers knew, but my father didn't know.

"He knew that I went to the gym and he asked me why I went to the gym, so I told him that I was told that if I do a little exercise, I'll put on weight. I'll eat better and I'll put on weight. I sold him the idea and he fell for it. My father was a sportsman anyway, and maybe he wouldn't have said anything if I told him. Maybe he would have said 'Let me go and watch you. Let me go see how you're doing and be careful, don't get hurt, don't get hit.' But I didn't tell him. I didn't tell my mother and I didn't tell my father. I knew I wasn't going to stay in it too long."

Allie Stolz wanted to become a boxer when he was very young. He was convinced he was talented, and he certainly proved it.

"Well, I wanted boxing as far back as ten years old. I was gifted. Gifted is all right, but the word I want, I think, is 'destined.' I don't even know if 'destined' is the right word. I just had the ability to be able to handle myself as a kid. But the Jewish kid today who has that ability doesn't become a boxer. He doesn't want to because it's not part of him. They choose to go to work or go to school. They do not think about boxing.

"It was more common then. And there were the great Jewish fighters that you have so many of. The great, great Benny Leonard was masterful. I talk a little about him, because there was a love for him. And a great admiration.

"When I was ten years old, I went to see fights at the Oakland Arena in Jersey City, and I was taken there by a fellow who was an amateur boxer, Murray Roth, God rest his soul. He was a good boy, never made it big as a fighter, but to me, he was big because he started to help me learn the trade.

And there, I watched the likes of Lou Lombardi and Joey Costa. They were the local main-bout fighters. Not of any great fame, but they were good fighters. I used to go to the fight, come home, and get in front of the mirror and make the moves that they were making. I was a great imitator.

"Then I went to art high school. I had aspirations to be an artist, because I was a cartoonist—because I was very good with sketching. I'm a jack of all trades. I sing well. I mimic. I do dialects. I was good as a performer. But boxing came first. Because I could mimic, that's why it was so easy for me to imitate fighters.

"I wanted to become an amateur boxer. And I had to wait until I was sixteen. I weighed a hot 102 pounds. And the lowest division is 112. I only weighed 102. One hundred twelve pounds is flyweight. It goes from flyweight to heavyweight. When I went to get my license to box that particular night, the fellow at the boxing bouts said to me, 'How old are you? What are you, about twelve? What did you do, get your brother's license?' So I said, 'No, no.' Some old fellow that knew me said, 'No, he can fight. Don't worry about him. Let him fight.' So I got by to fight that night and I boxed what they call a four-man class. Two fighters fight, and then the winner of that fights for the final prize to get the watch.

"As an amateur, I was approached at Stillman's Gymnasium by one of the fight guys. These are the tough years, you know, the late thirties—from the depression on to the middle and the late thirties. He said, 'How would you like to make extra money?' I says, 'Doing what?' He says, 'Boxing what they call 'bootleg boxing.' Instead of amateur it's called 'bootleg.' You get paid instead of getting prizes.

"It's not pro. But you're fighting a better class of fighters. Not to hurt my standing as an amateur, because I thought I was going to fight in the Golden Gloves, I used a fictitious name. There was a fighter named Julie Kogan who was a pretty good fighter, a Jewish boy out of New Haven, Connecticut, and he took a kind of a sabbatical. He laid off that summer, so they were looking for a Jewish fighter. When I get up to the fights, to fight this first date, the promoter said, 'Let's see, now. Allie Stolz does not sound Jewish enough. It sounds kind of Deutsche. How about something really Jewish? Abie Rosen.' I said, 'It sounds all right with me, as long as I get paid.' So I boxed at that arena, White City Stadium, New Haven, Connecticut.

"After the fight—I boxed quite a fight—I don't like to sound like I'm bragging, but I boxed a tremendous fight—the people went wild. And in came the newspapermen and they said, 'Now, come on. What's your name? Who are you? You got to be a pro.' I said, 'No, I am not. That's my name.' From there, I went on to fight nine or ten fights that summer, at the White

City Stadium. And I won all the fights but one, which they called a draw, cause the guy deliberately butted me and you still could see this one, it was a nasty cut. And as I fought at the White City Stadium, I was then introduced to Hymie Caplin, the famous manager. Hymie had five world champions."

Herbie Kronowitz was born Ted Kronowitz. He adopted his brother's name, Herbie, when he began to box in the amateurs at the age of fifteen. To Herbie, his choice of career was never in doubt.

"I went to a trade school in the late thirties. That was on Flatbush Avenue, Flatbush Extension. It was known as the Brooklyn High School for Specialty Trades. I took up electrical trades—my father was an electrician. I was in school in body, but my mind was out in the sports world, in boxing. I'd be sitting in school with my book opened. I'd have the *Ring Magazine* inside. The teacher would say 'What page are you up to now?' That was really funny you know. I quit when I was in the seventh term. I quit. I didn't finish.

"I went into boxing. I started boxing while I was in high school. In school, the teachers would tell me, 'Write something about what you want to do when you grow up.' I used to write, 'I want to be a fighter. A professional fighter.' And they would say, 'No, no, what do you really want to do?' I met Ben Jeby, the middleweight champ, when we moved around the corner from him in Williamsburg. He lived on Ross Street and Bedford and we lived on Bedford Avenue, around the corner from him. He had won the title at that time. And I used to go up to his house, nearly every day and ring his bell. And Benny would come over and he'd say, 'Whadda you want, sonny?' 'Could I have your autograph?' He says, 'I gave you my autograph yesterday.' 'Could I have it again?' 'Okay sure.' I used to tell Benny about it, you know, in later years at Ring 8 meetings. It's amazing.

"I loved it. I always loved it. In the street, when I went to school there was hardly a day I didn't have a fight. I was a skinny little kid, but I didn't care for nobody. I'd fight anybody. And the kids would come home and they would see my mother and they'd say, 'Hey your son was fighting by the school again.' And she'd say 'You were fighting?' 'Not me.'

"When I was boxing they used to, . . . bring out about the family, about my grandfather being a strongman in the circus you know. It's a great thing for publicity. It was late '37, '38 I went into the amateurs, when I was fifteen.

"In the amateurs we got prizes, no money. Before I used Herbie's name, I called myself 'Joe Block.' I had some job getting to fight until they would put me on. I only weighed about 116 pounds, soaking wet, in the amateurs. I was a bantamweight. I kept growing. I would go down to the amateurs but didn't get called to fight. They wouldn't put me on. The first time I was called, I come in. 'What do you want sonny?' the matchmaker said. I said 'You called me.' 'Who are you, what's your name?' 'Joe Block.' He says, 'Sit down over here.' He had a desk. 'Sit down over here. Don't let nobody see you.' 'Why, what's a matter?' He said, 'I'll get locked up. You know, you should be home in bed.' Everybody in the room got hysterical. I must of gone to about twenty shows until he finally put me on. He put me on once and then I was set.

"I trained on the East Side. I started at the Jacob Riis House, on Henry Street, right alongside the Manhattan Bridge. Then I couldn't get anybody to box with so I moved to St. James House; that was on Elizabeth and Hester. When I was boxing amateurs, I got prizes, I used to sell 'em. Watches, a pen and pencil. Most of the time it was watches when you won. A Waltham. Sometimes I got $18 for it.

"Every one of the clubs had amateur shows. Broadway Arena, Saint Nick's, Ridgewood Grove, or we boxed in the hotels, or in some club somewhere. The amateurs drew pretty well. In fact, the amateurs drew as well if not better than the pros."

Bernie Friedkin was never a world champion, but he assuredly holds the title as the youngest boy ever to aspire to a prizefighting career.

"Born for it. I was born for it, and they all laughed. Two years old. From a Jewish family no one knew anything about it. I wanted to box at two years old. They laughed. Four years old. When I was ten years old, in the Hotel Evans, in Loch Sheldrake—I was standing in a boxing pose. I had my first few fights without them knowing, but then when they found out they did not try to discourage me. They were then my biggest fans. Papa went. Mama didn't go. But Mama made my steaks. 'Bernie, it's five o'clock; time to eat.' She wanted me to quit. 'Bernie, it's nine-thirty, you should be gettin' ready for bed.' She watched me. Six-thirty in the morning they woke me up to do roadwork. Because it was my business! They hated, waited, but it was my business."

It has long been assumed that Jewish parents were unalterably opposed to their sons becoming prizefighters. The stereotype of the distressed mother and father is generally, though not universally, accurate. Whether boxing was "not for a Jewish boy," or simply there was fear of injury or both, varied from family to family. It was not so much either that education was the option preferred by the parents; the choice was boxing or work.

Josephine Colan, the wife of Johnny Colan (Colaianni), an Italian light-heavyweight of the "Golden Era," relates how Italian mothers, too, were not ecstatic about their sons as boxers. "They were not as adamant as Jewish mothers. The fear of Italian mothers was injury. They wanted their sons to be careful. The opposition of Jewish mothers was deeper and more complex than that. They regarded it as shameful."

To the extent that any pattern can be discerned among the Jewish parents, it appears that fathers were somewhat more amenable than mothers. As the European phase of their family's life became more distant, the fierce opposition became more relaxed. Then too, the exigencies of the depression played their role in shaping the parents' attitudes.

Micky Katz has been an avid fight fan all his life. He was born on the lower East Side in 1911 of immigrant Polish parents. He knew many of the great Jewish boxers personally, and he witnessed the proliferation of Jewish boxing.

"Oh, that was a terrible thing. The parents would say, 'Go to work. It is a *charpah* and a *shandah*.'[10] For a Jewish boy to be a fighter, that's a terrible thing. For one thing, it wasn't regarded as, shall we say, a normal way of life. Working in a normal capacity. It's not a trade.

" 'Nit fa a Yiddisheh boy.' It wasn't for a Jewish boy. 'Go to work, get a job,' do anything . . . but fighting? And they made a big issue of it. 'Bom!' You were a bum if you were fighting.

"School meant something. Be somebody of substance. Someone who is making a mark in the world, but not fighting. That's the bottom of the ladder. Except, of course, to most of them, the choice was not boxing or school, but boxing or work. College was great, but they needed the money in the house. They were too poor.

"There was an innate feeling about boxing that the elders abhorred. Izzy Schwartz always said to me his parents told him, 'You can't come home unless you get a job. Go get a job.' He wound up in the motion picture business anyway, eventually. He was a tremendous flyweight champion, but he never forgot how they berated him for fighting. 'So what, you made money? Look at your face! Look at what happened!' And this applied to everybody that was Jewish. The Benny Leonard story is so typical. They accepted the money, but they still didn't like the idea. And Benny Leonard, you couldn't mess his hair up. Because of his boxing skill he didn't get hurt. He was such an outstanding boxer, but deep down that didn't change his parents' opinion of boxing.

"From what I know, and I'm saying, with all due respect, I don't think the Irish and Italian parents made the kind of issue of it that the Jewish people did."

Marty Pomerantz describes how the young boxer avoided maternal scrutiny.

"My mother didn't know I was boxing. She would have been very upset about it. And my father wasn't happy about it, but he did know about it. With respect to my mother, I used to put my grip on the window. I had a black grip and I used to put it on the window sill and I would jump out of the window. Or else I would go out of the house and then retrieve it from the window sill. I know I read that many times about other mothers. And it's true. I assume it's true of the other boxers as well. That's the way I went out to fight."

Anne Shapiro (Maxie Shapiro's sister) remembers Maxie's grip:
"And when Maxie started to box, he, of course, didn't want to tell my parents. So he would walk out of the house with a satchel. My mother would say, 'Where are you going?' in Yiddish. That's all she spoke. Maxie would say, 'I'm going, Mama.' And she would say, 'Where are you going with the satchel?' And he would say, 'I'm a tie salesman. I'm going to sell ties.' "

Roy Arcel, the legendary trainer, was a contemporary and friend of Benny Leonard, the greatest and most popular Jewish boxer.
"Benny Leonard, his name was Leiner. . . . He started boxing on the lower East Side, and, of course, he was always so flashy. I mean his coordination and his reflexes were so sharp, and he had beautiful movement. He could move, he could box, and he attracted crowds. . . . The lower East Side was full of fighters, so naturally they'd all go and see him fight and they used to rent a bus.
"His father, I think, was a tailor, and he probably earned a big $10 or $12 a week, maybe twelve or fourteen hours a day. And one day this bus is standing there and the crowd is getting in there and they got a big sign, 'Benny Leonard, Our Champion.' Now, he was only a six-round fighter in those days, and Benny's mother happened to be there and she asked one of the neighbors, '*Vos tet such du?*' (What's going on here?) So the neighbor said, 'Don't you know? Your son is fighting.' Well, she almost fainted. Her son! What a—a shame! The way she screamed, '*A charpeh un a shandeh!* He's going to disgrace me in front of all the neighbors! A prize fighteh! A Jewish boy, a prize fighteh!'

"She went upstairs and she was crying. The bus left with Leonard, and Leonard didn't know what was going on. Now, she's waiting for the father to come home, and when he came home she called him into the bedroom and she said, 'You know what happened? He's shaming us. Benny is a prize fighteh.' And she says, 'and not even with his real name!'

"And she's telling him the story, and he's worried now. I mean she's saying, '*A charpeh un a shandeh*' and all the neighbors are talking. So Leonard came home and the father called him in. He said to him, 'What are you doing? You're disgracing us. What are you doing? You're a fighter and you're even ashamed of your own name?' And so Leonard, he got a big $35 for the fight, and he took out the $35 and he gave it to his father, and his father said, '*Vos is dos?*' (What is this?) He's angry at him. Benny says, 'That's what I got for the fight.' His father says, 'That's what you got for the fight? One night? You got that for the fight?' He says, 'Benny, when are you going to fight again?' "

Vic Zimet has been a manager, and more especially a trainer, for many years. He is close to the other major figures of Ring 8, of which he is today regarded as an "elder statesman." To Vic, there is no particular ethnic or religious component to parents not wanting their sons to box.

"I would say that 99 percent of the time they disapproved. And that's where the boxers took on different nomenclatures. They changed their names, even changed their ethnic connotation, became Irish, in their ring presence. Some even became Italians. And others, who seemed to have much more ability, were probably almost compelled by their management to retain their Jewish names because it became an attraction to the Jewish fans. I would say that the predominance of fans were the Jews, who supported athletics and this is a known fact. They were great supporters of all types of athletics, particularly when they developed Jewish heroes. They had a tremendous following.

"Most certainly the Irish and Italian parents had the same objections to their sons going into boxing. There are many stories about parents who had found out that their sons were boxing, and took exception to it. And how they had to conceal the fact. There were many Italian boxers who took on different names as well. Took on Irish names and I think some of the Irish even took on the names of Italians, and probably of some Jewish boxers, so that they might have misrepresented to develop a following among the Jewish fans as well. Sammy Mandell, for example, was Italian. It wasn't a particularly Jewish phenomenon, then, to have parents disapprove. It was a phenomenon that existed among all parents based on how they felt. The sensitivity they had about it. Or the way they looked upon boxing as a means of a livelihood, or a sport."

Julie Bort had more fights with his parents over his boxing than he had in the ring. Miltie Kessler, Al Reid, Sammy Farber, Artie Levine, and Curly Nichols hid it from their parents as long they could. According to Oscar Goldman, his parents were not involved in his decision. Danny Kapilow's father had deserted his family and his mother did not care. Joey Varoff's father was very proud of him, and his mother less so.

In some instances, there was tacit, and even overt, approval of the son's fighting ambitions. There might have been something in the family background that lent support to the young boxer's drives. Herb Kronowitz's father had a few amateur fights; Herb's grandmother rode bareback in the Barnum and Bailey Circus; and his grandfather was a strongman who performed under the name "Young Herman."

"Well of course my daddy, he liked it. He loved it. But you know my mother, a typical mother regardless of who they are, I don't care what nationality. Mothers are always against their children fighting. Getting in the ring and possibly getting hurt, or even hurting someone else. But I liked it, I loved it. And that's it. I wanted it.

"It had nothing to do with being Jewish or not Jewish. Because, after all, when you go in that ring you have to expect to get hit, get banged up, at times, you know? And that's it. And you do. Believe me. You catch hell. Which parent wants that?"

Herbie Kronowitz's mother, Mrs. Rivi Garbowitz (she remarried after Herb's father died) lived in Miami Beach until her death. When interviewed, she was undoubtedly the only parent still alive from that era of Jewish fighters.

"No. I did not want him to fight. No mother wants their son to fight. It's not just Jewish mothers. It's not a thing of religion. I was afraid he'd get hurt. It's only natural. But he wanted to fight. His teacher said it for me. He said, 'He's the most wonderful pupil I ever had. He's clean, he's everything. But when I'm talking to him, he's got another book, a fighting book in the book, and he's reading that.' "

When asked how Herbie's father felt about it, she replied, "He's the one that instigated him. Was I happy when Teddy quit? I couldn't be any happier, for G-d's sake. It's rough, rough. Don't ever do it. Listen to me."

Allie Stolz's mother had an unfulfilled dream. She was going to permit Allie to live his dream, even if she couldn't encourage him.

"My mother said to me as a youngster, when I was starting to become a fighter and train, 'I don't want you to fight . . . but in spite of the fact that you could be hurt badly, I still have to relate to my wanting to be a performer as a youngster, and my mother looked upon it as an entertainer and said 'nischt gut,' meaning 'not good.' So she said, 'I never fulfilled my desire and ambition, so I'm not going to stop you from doing it.' "

Ultimately, the parents generally came to accept their son's choice of careers. Unless they were married, all of the boxers lived at home, where their mothers could oversee their diets. There never seems to have been any question that they would not reside with their families.

The boxers contributed all or substantial portions of their purses to the household. They did not hold other jobs; boxing was their full-time occupation. Even the ones who were "club" fighters, and never earned large purses, could earn significantly more than their parents. If a fighter made $300 in a fight, that often represented ten or fifteen weeks' salary for his father. And the boxers fought often. A boxer who had sixty professional fights in a five-year career averaged twelve fights a year.

Miltie Kessler had parents and six siblings. He earned $100 or $200 a fight. "I gave a lot of it to home right away." In Curly Nichols' case, the money was not even that much:

"You know, in those days fighters didn't work much, I don't think. That was our job. I know I used to make the money and give it right to my mother. My mother was my chef. She knew just what to cook for me, you know.

"But if I had quit that very first day, she would have been happy. She didn't care about the money. What money? $25 for the four-rounders. And she didn't want me to fight. What mother wants you to fight? She didn't."

Al Reid never made more than $900 for a fight, but that was big money.

"The biggest amount I ever made, when I fought Mike Belloise up in the New York Coliseum.[11] We packed the house. There was about twelve thousand people there. But the admissions were 50 cents, 75 cents, and $1.15. Or $1.50 or whatever. And I wound up from my end with over 900 bucks. We boxed a draw. That was my biggest take ever. That was, I think 1938. Then we boxed a return match, and I got about the same thing, and with that I put a down payment on a house for my parents. You bought a brand-new house for 6,500 bucks in those days.

"I always put the money on the table, most of it anyway. I'd hold out a little bit you know. I had a girl friend every now and then. I think most boxers of all nationalities brought the money home. A lot of people looked at fellows who got into boxing as no-goods. It's not like that. The average guy goes into boxing and I'm talking about those days, especially in the depression days, it was to help his family. Know what I mean? He put it above schooling. And I was a pretty smart kid in school. But I wasn't making any money going to school. So . . . boxing was our way to get out of the ghetto, although we weren't in that bad shape. My father made a living and my mother worked once in a while. And my older brother was a garment manufacturer."

Bernie Friedkin expressed the values with which he grew up.

"I always lived at home. Mama made my steaks, my lamb chops. Reminded me when it was time to go to sleep.

"Georgie Abrams was a helluva middleweight. And when he came to New York from Washington, D.C., he lived on the West Side. And he was in the gym. But there were a lotta fighters there; they're a little faster group. His manager Chris Dundee, God bless him, didn't want him to play around. He knew I had a reputation of being clean. He says, 'Bernie, look. George is a clean kid. I don't want him to stay up here in the West Side. You know, faster life. Can you get him a room? Near you?' So I got Georgie Abrams a room opposite me boarding with a Jewish family. You know the depression, you rent out a room. And we buddied out for about two years. Georgie Abrams. He was a clean boy.

"He always came to the house, and knew my family. And I watch him like a brother. Georgie was a very clean, shy fellow. Not what the movies would depict a fighter to be. Georgie was very nice. Not terribly aggressive outside the ring. Inside the ring he was. He used to take roadwork with me, and, of course, he wanted to live clean. And I was a very clean kid, you know. And we watch each other.

"I would think most boxers were clean-living kids, not just the Jewish ones. I don't know how they live today. I can't see how a fella can live fast and go in the ring. I just ate two meals a day, by the way. Breakfast. Eight or nineish. And dinner at 5:30. I had to be at the table at 5:30. I was very strict. The rest of the evening, I walked around. Went to my friends. Saw the kids. They played basketball, some of them. And I come up the house at 9:00. I'm in bed at 9:30, 10:00. Mama with the watch.

"I did my roadwork 7:00 to 8:00 in the morning. It's about forty-five minutes. I get up at 6:30 or 7:00. Then I came back. Rest half hour, forty-five minutes. Get dressed. Go to the gym. It was a business. That's the way I made it. No social life. I couldn't have a Coca-Cola. Movies were 10 cents then. That was my entertainment. I was so dedicated. And maybe that's why after so many fights, I think I'm all right.

"If I brought home $300, I would say, 'Hey Mama, please take it, $200, $100, $50, $40.' 'No. Put in bank! Put in bank!' And I put in bank. And I watched it.

"Oh God they really watched me. If I wanted to send them to the mountains—I used to train in a hotel called 'The House of Joy'— in the summer, I say 'Mama I want you to come up for a few weeks.' 'No! No! One week I'll come.' I says, 'Why don't you—' 'No!' She was afraid they'll take my money. 'I'm only gonna come for one week.' Cost too much money. You know what they charged? $30 a week.

"I want you to know that to me, my mother and father are still living. I'm very dramatic now. Where I'd go, I'd use kindness. In the subway, in an elevator, while crossin' the street. And in a bank. Supermarket. And when these people thank me, I say, 'Don't thank me. Thank Mama and Papa. They taught me this.' And I know they're '*kvelling*' 12 up there. That's very important to me. If I didn't give a lady a seat or if I didn't help a lady with a package, I was reprimanded. And I say, 'Where are those days today? Where are those parents today?' No one cares. No one knows about it."

When Maxie Shapiro earned $2,000 for a main event at Madison Square Garden, he bought a house for his mother.

"I bought a two-family house on Ocean Parkway in Brooklyn. Some fight guy was a real estate agent, and he spoke to me about this house and I saw it. I loved it. Two apartments. A two-family house. And I bought it for my mother, but she didn't want to leave the East Side. She didn't want to leave Hester Street. I couldn't blame her for that because she had all her friends and the grocers and the butchers. It was home to her. She belonged to a society . . . the Educational Alliance . . . which was right in the heart of the neighborhood. East Broadway and Clinton Street. I bought the house anyway, and my brother and my sister moved into it. I didn't want to live there either. I still lived on the lower East Side.

"It's funny, I say I bought it for my mother. My father, he was around too, but usually I think of my mother. My father used to love to hang out in Seward Park with all the bricklayers and the plumbers, the little congregation. Every day they'd meet there at Seward Park High. Hester and Essex Street. It was a great neighborhood. Ratner's restaurant, the Loew's Delancey, and the Jewish theaters on Second Avenue and Houston Street, a few blocks away. It was like a community. It was great."

Allie Stolz was one of the boxers who earned substantial paydays. As far as he was concerned, the money was not his.

"Oh yes. My father had access. I loved him. It wasn't 'give him money.' It was our money, because I loved him. Because you see, he was the kind of Jewish papa that was great. He would do without food to give us ice cream in the lean years, in the depression years. The money was 'ours.' That's the way I felt. I brought it home and that was it. He bought me property that I should have had, but unfortunately, a couple of marriages and not the right kind of a woman and the money goes, but it wasn't his fault. I had quite a few pieces of property and went through it. So that was it. But, that's why I say, I loved him. I loved my whole family. Great, great people. And most Jews are like that anyway. Well, I say most. You have some that are not. Yes. But when they are, they go all out.

"When I was boxing, that was my job. Because you can't do it right unless you . . . that's the way you do it. See, when a fighter has to work and then do his roadwork and then go in and box during the afternoon and then come home and lie down and rest, you can't do that with a job. So to be successful, it's better that you don't work."

Artie Levine was another boxer who earned large sums. Unique among the boxers, his parents were "quite comfortable" and did not need the money.

According to Marty Pomerantz, the Jewish boxers were not alone in providing for their families during those depression years.

"I lived at home until I was married, and most of the boxers did and I think it didn't make any difference if you were Jewish or not. I also helped support the family. I tried to be a good son and I know that the Irish did that, the Italians did that. I guess I knew mostly Italians and Irish and Jews, and I guess everybody did that. That's the way it was."

Teddy Brenner, the matchmaker at Madison Square Garden during Harry Markson's presidency, feels strongly that all the ethnic groups were the same in this regard. He recounts the story of Tony Pellone who earned $8500 one night at the Garden. He brought the money home to his father and wanted $15. His father would only give him $12.

This story has an echo in the experience of Leo Bodner. Yale Okun, whom Bodner co-managed, earned $21,000 one night at the Garden in the early 1930s. Bodner's arrangement was 10 percent off the top.

"I told my father, *Alav Hasholom*,[13] 'I got $2100.' He says, 'Give it to me.' I says, 'I'll give it to you if you give me $100.' He says, 'You know what's gonna happen if you have $100 in your pocket? You'll become a bum. You'll become a gambler.' So finally, I settled for $50 and my father got the rest. That was good money for the family at that time, and it was about my largest payday."

6

BENNY, BARNEY, AND THE FANS

Benjamin Leiner was born in New York in 1896. He grew up in an Orthodox Jewish home, and when he began boxing, changed his name to Benny Leonard so that his parents would not know he was fighting. They discovered it anyway when his popularity grew.

Leonard was among the first of the modern-era Jewish boxers. From 1917 to 1925, he was world lightweight champion. Eight years was an exceptionally long period of time to retain a title, especially since the lightweight division had so many talented fighters. Leonard had a truly remarkable record. He was knocked out only four times in over two hundred fights. He never lost a decision, and except for the loss by foul to Jack Britton in 1922 did not lose a fight from 1913 to 1932.

The two fights Leonard had with Lew Tendler of Philadelphia were classics. On July 27, 1922, at Boyle's Thirty Acres in Jersey City, New Jersey, sixty thousand screaming fans, most of them Jewish, paid almost $400,000 (a record for a non-heavyweight title fight) to watch the twelve-round non-title bout between the two Jewish masters.

In the opening round, a rocketing left hook by Tendler crashed into Leonard's nose, staggering him. By the third round, Leonard was bloodied and battered. In the eighth round, Tendler rushed Leonard at the bell and drove him to a corner. A left to the head of Leonard and one to his side, and Leonard sank to one knee. Leonard said something to Tendler which momentarily distracted Lew and changed the momentum of the fight. Benny recovered his equilibrium and went on to win the decision.

Almost a year later, on July 24, 1923, fifty-eight thousand fans packed Yankee Stadium for the rematch: this time Leonard's title was on the line. The gate was a record $450,000.

Leonard, one of the greatest boxers of all time, learned his lesson in the first match and stayed out of Lew's dangerous reach. He won the fifteen-round decision and retained his lightweight crown.

The 1920s produced larger purses for boxers than the depression years of the 1930s. Leonard made considerable money, but when the stock market crash destroyed him financially, he attempted a comeback with mixed results. It did little, however, to tarnish his platinum image as the greatest Jewish boxer and the one most other Jewish fighters wished to emulate. Later, Leonard became an excellent referee. He died of a heart attack while refereeing a bout in St. Nicholas Arena in April 1947.

Barnet Rosofsky (Barney Ross) was born in New York in 1909. His Orthodox family moved to Chicago where his father operated a candy store. After Rosofsky, Sr., was shot and killed in a holdup, Ross decided to pursue his ambition of becoming a prizefighter, an ambition that his father had opposed. Ross held three titles (lightweight, junior welterweight, and welterweight) and was at the tail end of the era of Jewish champions (1938). Thus, he and Leonard straddled the period of Jewish prominence in boxing. During World War II, Ross was wounded at Guadalcanal. He became dependent on morphine and later was generally drug-dependent, but he fought to overcome the habit.

Ross and Jimmy McLarnin fought three of the most thrilling matches ever held in the New York area, and all within one year.

Ross and McLarnin, both welterweights, met for the first time on May 28, 1934 at the outdoor Madison Square Garden Bowl in Long Island City, Queens, New York, before sixty thousand fans. McLarnin had won the welterweight title just a year before and this was his first defense.

Perhaps the long layoff affected the baby-faced McLarnin's pulverizing punch, but Ross was the better man that night. He boxed beautifully, and while he respected McLarnin's greater power, Ross was not awed by it. McLarnin sent Ross briefly to the mat in the ninth round, the first knockdown of Barney's career, but he was up instantly and pressed the offensive against Jimmy.

A hush fell on the huge crowd as the announcer intoned the results: "Judge Tom Parker, nine rounds for McLarnin, one for Ross, five even." A loud chorus of "No's" echoed through the Bowl. Wasn't the fight closer than this?

Then, "Judge Harold Barnes votes twelve rounds for Ross, two for McLarnin, one even." More like it.

And finally, "Referee Ed Forbes votes thirteen rounds to one, with one even for the winner and new welterweight champion of the world, Barney Ross!" Bedlam broke loose, but the vast majority of those present agreed with the results.

There was a particular jinx connected with the defense of the world-weight title, and Jimmy McLarnin was its latest victim. The eight previous welterweight champions were defeated in the first defense of their crown.

Major boxing matches were social and political events then. Among those present were Mayor LaGuardia, Postmaster General Farley, Benny Leonard, Gene Tunney, Bernard Gimbel, Alfred Gwynne Vanderbilt, Tony Canzoneri, Grover Whelan, Bill Terry, and Carl Hubbell.

A rematch was inevitable, and it was held on September 17, 1934 at the same site. Threatening weather and the fact that rain had forced four postponements kept the crowd down to twenty-five thousand. McLarnin brought the fight to Ross from the opening bell and never let up. He boxed superbly on both the offense and defense, while Ross was aggressive only in flurries. Barney swarmed all over McLarnin in the fifteenth round, but it was "too little too late." The split decision went to McLarnin and there were few complaints.

The "jinx of the welterweight title" remained as another welterweight champion lost the crown in his first defense. Another record continued—no champion had ever entered the Madison Square Garden Bowl and left with his title intact, a history which included Max Schmeling, Jack Sharkey, Primo Carnera, Jimmy McLarnin, and now Barney Ross.

When Ross met McLarnin for the third time, on May 28, 1935, at the Polo Grounds in Manhattan, forty thousand roaring fans were present to watch Barney try to regain the welterweight crown. After fifteen grueling rounds, Ross, battered and bruised, emerged the victor.

Jack Dempsey was the referee, and this time the decision was unanimous for Ross. Ross's famous jab won the bout for him as it protected him from McLarnin's storied left hook.

Gene Tunney, who was at the fight, disagreed with referee Dempsey's vote, but James P. Dawson, the boxing writer of the *New York Times* felt Ross had won decisively, ten rounds to five. The "jinx" continued, but it was broken when Barney successfully defended the title against Izzy Janazzo on March 27, 1936.

McLarnin, who was then twenty-eight years old, had become wealthy through the shrewd investments of his manager "Pop" Foster (in California oil) and had nothing further to prove in the ring. Immediately following the bruising match, Foster announced McLarnin's retirement. "I think Jimmy won," Foster said. "But I won't let him fight any more. He's through with the ring."

The retirement lasted one year. McLarnin then returned to the ring, lost and won decisions against Tony Canzoneri, and beat Lou Ambers (both champions) in ten rounds. After that he quit for good. Ross, twenty-six years old at the time of the McLarnin fight, continued to campaign for three years until he lost his championship to Henry Armstrong on May 31, 1938 in a savage fifteen-round battle at the Madison Square Garden Bowl.

Barney was an 8 to 5 favorite in the Armstrong bout, but he was pitted against someone who was the featherweight champion and would later earn the lightweight title to become the only boxer to hold three championships simultaneously.

Ross did well for the first four rounds, but in the fifth round his legs gave out. Although only twenty-eight years old, he was already the veteran of eighty-two profesisonal fights. By the tenth round, Barney was taking such a beating from Armstrong that referee Arthur Donovan wanted to stop the fight. Barney pleaded with him to let the fight continue as he wanted to go out like a champ. He gamely held on for the last five rounds and lost the championship on his feet. It was Ross's last fight.

Barney Ross, an authentic war hero, returned the affection and admiration of the boxing community, particularly among the Jews. He, like Leonard, was gentlemanly and accessible. After Benny Leonard, the fighter who inspired boxers the most was Barney Ross. Both of them were the most popular with Jewish fans, and remain so today.

While the boxers interviewed were sincere in downplaying any differences in boxers based on ethnicity, or the concept that they had a special "mission" as Jewish boxers, their disclosure of their "role models" was rather revealing. Where one existed, it was always a Jewish boxer. To Maxie Shapiro, Benny Leonard and Barney Ross were the standard:

"In my time, there were Jewish boxers like Barney Ross and Benny Leonard. And these fellas were idols. Leonard wasn't even boxing then, but we saw movies of him, we heard of him. They were both very popular and boxing was a big sport at that time. We followed them. Today there are no Jewish fighters around, so the Jewish boys don't go in for it because there's nobody to follow, to imitate. To try and be like them, you know."

To Micky Katz, there was only Benny Leonard: "Benny Leonard was number one to the Jewish boys and nobody, but nobody could compare to him. He was the role model. Number one."

Allie Stolz was a close friend of Barney Ross, but Leonard was his hero: "I guess Leonard was a role model also because he was Jewish. That would contribute quite a bit to it. And Benny Leonard was the model for all that. He set the example of how a Jewish boxer should behave. Also my good buddy, Barney Ross, whom I loved."

Leo Bodner came to this country in 1923, while Benny Leonard was still champion. It is no surprise that his view of what boxers was conditioned by Leonard.

"So many Jews become boxers in the twenties and thirties because it started with Benny Leonard. And if a kid heard that someone is training and he is boxing amateurs, he says, 'Why can't I do it?' So they started that way. That's how Sid Terris became a fighter. His brother Danny Terris became a fighter.

"Every Jewish boy wanted to be like Benny Leonard. He was nice looking. He was clean looking. He was respectable. Everybody respected him. Gentile or Jew. He was a perfect gentleman.

"That was the model of boxing at that time. Then we started getting other boxers—Ruby Goldstein, Sid Terris, and a couple more from out of town. And the Jewish boys came in.

"Barney Ross was a big name, but he didn't command the same respect as Benny Leonard because in his time, he was not the only Jewish boxer. There were a lot of good boxers at that time. But he was a nice gentleman. A nice boy. I was very friendly with him. I used to go up to Grossinger's to watch him train."

Harry Markson remembers Barney Ross as a great hero to the Jews in the late 1930s and 1940s.

"The only one I can think of who would fit into that sort of a category in my time, which goes back to the early thirties, was Barney Ross. Barney Ross was idolized, not only because he was a great champion, but he was a war hero. He was one of the early war heroes. And the Jewish people at the time were very proud of him."

Vic Zimet recalls Barney Ross as impressive professionally and personally.

"Tremendous. Tremendous fighter, tremendous fighting heart. And here too, he fought in a different way. His flurries, how he would trap you and, suddenly he'd throw six hundred punches at you and would box a fellow like McLarnin who could take you out with one punch. And outsmart him and outtrick him. And command respect from McLarnin with his punching power. Ross was not a great puncher, but he could come off the floor with a guy like Ceferino Garcia who could take your head off with his bolo punch. And come on to win the bout. Tremendous boxer and a tremendous person. Tremendous personality."

Bernie Friedkin had no one he looked up to or emulated. How could he?

"I was born for it. Lemme ask you a question. Jackie Mason. You know he was doing comedy. You know he must have been born for it. Or Kate Smith, with these great talents. Didn't you think they were born to have these shticks in them? They're born for it."

In his book, *Story of My Life* (1989), Hank Greenberg, the great baseball star, describes his role as a representative of the Jewish people.

"After all, I was representing a couple of million Jews among a hundred million gentiles . . . and I was always in the spotlight. . . . I felt a responsibility. I was there every day, and if I had a bad day, every son of a bitch was calling me names so that I had to make good. . . . As time went by I came to face that if I, as a Jew, hit a home run, I was hitting one against Hitler.[1]

Barney Ross writes in his book, *No Man Stands Alone* (1957), that before one of his fights with Jimmy McLarnin, "I had never been so keyed up and tense before a fight. The news from Germany made me feel I was . . . fighting for all my people."[2]

There have always been very few Jewish major league baseball players. To box one simply had to excel in the gym and decide to become a prizefighter. There is no limit to the number of boxers there can be. That Hank Greenberg was a Jewish baseball superstar in the anti-Semitic period of the late 1930s was a notable achievement. Baseball was the most popular sport in America. It is natural that Greenberg felt himself the ambassador of his people. It is a role he could not avoid.

Barney Ross along with Benny Leonard were the most recognized Jewish names in boxing. Like Leonard, Ross conducted himself with class and dignity and always seemed to be aware that he had a special role as a Jew in boxing. It is not surprising, therefore, that despite the many hundreds of Jews in the sport, he perceived his responsibilities as special. Herbert Goldman, a boxing historian, has an interesting insight into Benny Leonard's role.

"Benny Leonard had a very distinct and sharp sense that he was representing the Jewish community.

"Abe Attell threw a number of fights, and then later on he got involved in the World Series scam in 1919 with Arnold Rothstein. Maybe because of that, Benny had a sharp sense of this. He was a hero to the Jewish population at large in a way that no Jew before him—no Jewish fighter—and I don't think any Jewish fighter after him—ever was. He was sort of a cross between 'Underdog' and the 'Knight in Shining Armor,' with, I guess, the Star of David as his shield. And he really was very conscious of that.

"A woman I knew named Kitty Donor—I'm telling you something now which very few know—was a headliner in vaudeville. She was a male impersonator, which in those days was very popular. She had an affair with Benny. Went on for some time in the 1920s. But he never came close to marrying Kitty. And she thought one of the reasons was that she was not Jewish. Benny had a very strong sense of what he meant to the Jewish people."

In the interviews with the boxers, there emerged something of a pattern that was fairly consistent with the Ross–Greenberg paradigm. That is, the more accomplished a fighter was, and the more thorough the Jewish background from which he came, the more he articulated a sense that he represented a greater number of Jews than just himself and his fans.

Allie Stolz was the most candid on this subject:

"Judaism meant quite a lot to me, . . . because we were so held back. The people were so anti-Semitic. It was so common. I just looked to my religion and to my Judaism because it meant something. It had a meaning. Because we fought from all the way back when. I mean, back in the dark days, we had to fight. So I think that's what really led to me becoming a real good fighter.

"I really felt that I was representing Jews. Yes, very much so. Because I was very oriented. . . . Jewish oriented. No question about it. At the table, at the *shul*, with people, with cousins and relatives and friends. It was Judaism."

When Al Reid boxed he represented only his fans who had come to see him fight.

Sigi Ashkenaz was born in Switzerland and boxed with the Cologne Maccabees team in the 1930s. Under the Nuremberg Laws, Jews could no longer participate in sports activities with non-Jews, and so the knowledge of who he was was never far from him. This self-identification continued in America. According to Ashkenaz, "When I boxed in this country, I wore a big Magen David on my shorts and on my robe. I was always conscious of the fact that I was representing Jewish people and I wanted the fans to know that."

Bernie Friedkin is a proud Jew and a self-effacing individual. The idea that he was representing a whole race is difficult for him to accept: "I wasn't big enough to represent them. You know what I mean? I was just a fighter.

I was proud of being Jewish and being a fighter . . . but who was I to represent the Jewish people?"

Marty Pomerantz was and is an identified Jew. Being a Jewish boxer, however, carried with it no special role or message.

"So my name was Pomerantz and I was Jewish. I was always very proud that I was Jewish. But as far as it meaning anything of being a boxer, not a thing.

"This had nothing to do with being Jewish. These were hard times. They were depression times. I originally wanted to be a ballplayer, but I was too small. That was my first love. I played in junior high school. And my dream, my fantasy was, that if I made a lot of money I could buy into a team. If I made money, I could buy anything that I wanted. I was a shy kid. I wasn't very aggressive except as a boxer. I could buy admiration and love and houses and cars. Everything that I wanted. And the way to do it since I couldn't be a ballplayer was to be a boxer. You could make money quickly. And you know, I guess I thought I wanted to be a champion. It had nothing, nothing at all to do with being Jewish. I was proud of being Jewish. I wore a Jewish star on my trunks when I was in the Jewish Olympics.

"When I won the Jewish Olympics, I was aware that I represented the Jewish Community House. And there was pride. But as far as being a boxer to show the world that Jews could be aggressive or that they could fight, or they could fight back, that they couldn't be pushed around, that they were as strong as anybody else, that had nothing to do with it."

Hank Kaplan is a retired biochemist. He resides in Florida and is one of the most knowledgeable individuals regarding the history of Jewish boxing. He concludes that the role of the Jewish boxer is the result of a process.

"There was no sense with any of these boxers that they were representing the Jewish people. Most of the guys became fighters because they had some athletic skill and baseball wasn't a prominent sport in their neck of the woods. At least, you couldn't practice it easily—they didn't have the diamonds. Football was kind of out of the question for a lot of them because of their size. Basketball in a sense was also. They came off the streets, and the local gyms were easy to get to. Like the Educational Alliance and other gyms of that nature—city-sponsored and public-sponsored gyms and high school gyms. YMCAs and all that type of thing. So it was easy for a guy, and he learned from the streets that you can walk home with 35 bucks, 40 bucks, after a four-round fight, and that always felt good. You know something? Back in the thirties, when a kid fought a four-rounder, and he got 40 bucks in his hand, that was four times as much as his father made for that week. And he did it in one night. And that was a lot of money to support the family.

"They wanted to spend some money on clothing. Hats and shoes and suits and shirts. You know, it was a big thing on the East Side and Brooklyn to be spiffy. But the rest they brought home. And as he continued boxing, he got better at it. Because, you know, a Jewish kid was always very skillful. Or, in the case of Mickey Farber, it was brawn. He wouldn't listen to skill. He wouldn't listen to Lou, his brother. But very few Jewish fighters were on the style of Mickey. And most of them were clever. They were thinking guys. They became defensive first and then the offense came naturally, which it does, to this day. And they managed to survive. They managed to fight and not get hurt so they could fight ten days later. In those days, you used to fight often. Not like they do now. Today a fighter is looking to fight two, three times a year. In those days, it wasn't uncommon for a fighter to fight twenty times a year, and even twenty-five and twenty-six times a year.

"Now after he started boxing, it could be that to be Jewish came up every now and then because it was . . . he was quite conscious of it because the promoter liked to use him. If you were a good fighter and you were Jewish . . . Jewish people were great fight fans. Great, great, great fight fans. So they were always interested in the Jewish draw, every promoter in town. Especially around New York. And even in places like Portland, Oregon, Seattle, Washington, San Francisco. You know Armand Emanuel, for example, was used and built up because he was a Jewish kid. Especially when he was a Jewish lawyer.

"So, the notion that they were representing Jewish pride or anything like that didn't enter the picture at first. Not at all.

"It was a way to make a few dollars. That's all. And of course, there were some, who, after their introduction to boxing in the gymnasium, loved the sport. It was a thinking sport and a scientific sport. And it suited their temperament and their athletic demands, and they were getting good at it. With each fight, they became better and better, and they enjoyed it. So, why not stick to something you enjoy and make a few bucks at it? When Leonard was fighting, they planted a Jewish star on his trunks, and he was a proud Jew.

"Most of them were proud Jews, but that wasn't the main reason. That wasn't the primary factor. That was a secondary thing. Maybe some enjoyed putting that Jewish star on their trunks and say, 'Hey, look! I'm fighting. I'm a Jew.' But I don't think that ever entered the minds of any. . . . I knew a ton of these guys. And I talked to them. And I hustled around interviewing them, too, when I was a kid. I was a kid in the streets with them who also dreamed of being a fighter.

"Nor was this a way of becoming American. Absolutely not. There was no way, when he took up boxing, that he thought of the Americanization of him or his family.

"Take Joe Bernstein, who was a hungry kid. He didn't start boxing because he was Jewish or because he wanted to Americanize his family. He just fought because he liked the sport and he started to taste the money. Now, if you approach it from this view, how did these kids get started? Did they get started because of the money? Did they go into boxing because of the money or did they first love the sport and then face the money and then stick to it? And only then show pride that they were fighting as Jews. I think that's the answer."

Despite the disclaimers of Bernie Friedkin and others, there was a subtle force in play that made the answer more complex than simply, " I did not represent Jewish people." All the boxers were identified Jews, displayed Jewish stars when it was allowed (until the 1940s when all religious symbols were banned), and would not tolerate any anti-Semitic remarks. There was a part of them that knew they always had to conduct themselves a certain way as Jews. A story told by Vic Zimet illustrates this point.

"There was a Jewish journeyman boxer by the name of Charlie "Red" Miller. He was about eighteen years old and was matched to box in Ebbets Field. And Charlie was told it was a 60 (160) pound contract. He comes for the weigh-in, the manager says to him, he says, 'What are you weighing?' He says, '160.' He says, 'The contract is for 155.' He says, 'You got to take off four pounds.' They allow you one pound. So naturally he was dismayed. And he tried to take off the weight. He takes it off, and he makes the weight.

"That's at the weigh-in in the morning. Eleven o'clock weigh-in in those years. Now he's down into the dressing room at Ebbets Field that night and he gets up to loosen up and his feet give out from under him. Gets up again—his feet give out. He says, 'Who the hell needs this?' He gets dressed and he's gonna leave the arena! And he goes out the gate. And at the gate, where he was recognized, the gatekeeper says, 'Where you going Charlie? Aren't you fighting tonight?' Charlie turns around. He said to himself, 'I'm not gonna let them say that the Jew is yellow.' So he went back and he took his licking for two–three rounds. And that was the end of Charlie's career."

Was there a specific dimension to being a Jewish boxer, something unique in style, approach, ringsmanship? Or was the Jewish fighter simply a boxer who happened to be Jewish? The boxers were about evenly divided. Some even came down on both sides of the question. To the boxers there was no simple answer. Either that or they viewed the issue as having more than one facet.

Marty Pomerantz furnished several responses.

"Benny Leonard once told me, 'He who hits and runs away lives to box another day.' And I will say this. The Jewish boxers—I know this whole time I'm saying there's no difference—I think the Jewish boxers were more clever.

"There were so many Jewish boxers in the twenties and thirties which I'm familiar with. So what did it mean that you were a Jewish boxer? I was a Jewish shoe cutter. I happened to be Jewish. I was a shoe cutter like anybody else. I was a boxer like anybody else. There was no crusade. Maybe if I were the only Jewish boxer or I was one of the only ones. I wasn't. There were so many. It didn't mean anything. Today it would be different. I think that's what you need to understand about those times. There were so many that what did it mean? It was like, you become a doctor or an accountant or a lawyer. You happened to be Jewish.

"I don't want to paint those days as glorious days. They weren't. I mean, at least they weren't for me. I was a club fighter and maybe if I'd gone with Carbo maybe I would have gone somewhere. But they were good days. It may not have been a clean sport, but to the boxers it was. Your body was in shape. Your mind was in shape. You ran, you ate well, you slept well. You had good discipline, you weren't dissipated. You didn't run around. We were part of the morals, the values of our family, and by and large those were good values. And we tried to be good sons and good brothers and husbands and good parents and grandparents. It happened that for a period of time, we were boxers. And that's what it meant."

In the opinion of Vic Zimet, the Jewish boxer was unique in his art.

"To watch the Shapiros and the Stolzes was really a manifestation—I think that only good Jewish boxers box that way. It was a very clever style. It was very enjoyable to watch. The technique, you could see the brains operating. You could see them thinking. And you don't see that kind of boxing today.

"Benny Leonard. Sid Terris. I knew Ruby Goldstein, but I never saw him box. But they tell me he was a tremendous boxer. He just lacked other attributes to make him a great fighter. I think he lacked the will or something. The Maxie Shapiros. Sammy Dorfman. There was a cleverness. They just didn't go out—it wasn't mayhem with them. It was enjoyable to watch. There was no brutality to their actual style of boxing."

The word "clever" often appears in describing Jewish prizefighters. Allie Stolz has another phrase for it.

"Not because I'm Jewish, but I just think we were gifted with more '*seichel*,' with more, you know, knowledge. That we were scientific. It goes back to most of the Jewish fighters. You had some who were rough and tough guys. But there were the ones who were outstanding. Pal Silvers, Sid Terris, . . . again, to name them, Ruby Goldstein, Benny Leonard, Barney Ross.

"Also Jewish boxers know better than non-Jewish boxers when to quit. That doesn't mean all Jewish fighters are intelligent, but I think comparatively, I think they knew pretty much when to retire."

Curly Nichols, who died in December 1992, was a humorous, kind man. His answer pokes gentle fun at the question of whether there was anything different about Jewish boxers.

"Yeah, they were all circumcised. I don't know. Most of them were, boxers are smart. I would say most of them—except Al Reid. He was a tough fighter. He wasn't a boxer. He'd come in and he'd never stop punching. You know, he was just a fighter."

The same Al Reid, described by Nichols as a fighter rather than a boxer, not surprisingly had a different point of view about Jewish art in prizefighting.

"There was no difference between a Jewish fighter and Italian fighter in terms of style. It's the same thing. Many a time, an Italian fighter was trained by a Jewish trainer and managed by a Jewish manager. And a Jewish fighter was managed by an Italian manager and Jewish trainer."

Miltie Kessler effectively summed up the position which holds there is nothing particularly unique in the style of a Jewish boxer.

"There was nothing particularly special about being a Jewish boxer. I think I was just a boxer who was Jewish. There were a lot of Jewish fighters. I was a kid off the street that wanted to box and it just happened to be that I was Jewish. There was no other dimension to it. I saw a lot of good Jewish boxers. And I saw a lot of Jewish boxers that couldn't box that were rough, tough guys. Like Al Reid. He was a strong, young, tough kid, a well-conditioned fighter, but he wasn't a good boxer. Allie Stolz was a great boxer. Tony Canzoneri wasn't Jewish; he was a great boxer. Joe Louis was a good boxer. Jimmy McLarnin was a tremendous boxer—beat Benny Leonard. Beat any Jewish fighter. I would say that most of the Jewish fighters were good boxers. They used to be able to box. Al Davis was no boxer, he was a tough kid."

Note that even as Kessler is developing his thesis, he cannot resist interjecting that "most Jewish fighters were good boxers."

Ethnic identifications were far more relevant to the fans than to the fighters. In his book, *Patrimony* (1991, p. 202), Philip Roth writes of his father's long-time interest in boxing. It was an interest that centered around the Jewish boxers. Roth quotes his father as referring both to a fighter's name and religion. There is very little evidence to suggest that religion played a role between the contestants. but among the fans—that was a different matter. Micky Katz, with a twinge of embarrassment, relates what the ethnic factor meant to the Jewish fan.

"Ruby didn't care too much about it. But he was regarded as if he was a Jewish hero. If you spoke to him . . . and I know he had some good fights. . . . he didn't say he was fighting an Italian or he was fighting an Irishman. He would say, 'Tomorrow I'm fighting. The 14th I'm fighting.' They didn't discriminate. It's the fans that did. I was looking for Jackie "Kid" Berg to beat Tony Canzoneri because he was Italian, while Berg and Canzoneri were looking to produce money and the fight for what it was. For instance, the 'White Chapel Whirlwind,' they called Berg. He had a reputation for being a banger. A great fighter. And a Yiddisheh boy. And back in England, they made a big *tzimmes* out of it. A Jewish boy. But if you spoke to Jack, and he had some big fights, with many blacks, for instance, and came out a winner in many cases, he didn't speak about the ethnic. He had a 'good fight.' He beat him in 'X amount of rounds.' Or even if he lost, that's how he'd talk about it. Ben Jeby was no different, and I was very close to him. He never spoke in terms of ethnic. That's the fighters. But I think I'm right when I tell you that the buffs, us, who followed the game, we said, 'He's fighting that Irishman and I'd like to see him win.' Because he's Irish, or he's Italian. And it doesn't harbor too well with me at the moment when I say it, but it was that kind of thing that filled more seats in the Garden, you know. That kind of ethnic battle. That produced more than you could imagine. They wanted that."

The Jewish boxing fans stood out among other ethnic rooters. Herbert Goldman is certain that "the predominance of fans were the Jews too, who supported athletics and this is a known fact. They were great supporters of all types of athletics, particularly when they developed Jewish heroes among the boxing fans. They had a tremendous following."

The fanaticism of Jewish boxing fans sometimes had a charitable dimension. On October 21, 1929, Samuel Rosoff, the subway builder purchased the entire floor, ringside, and box seat section of Madison Square Garden for $100,000 in support of the Palestine Emergency Fund. The card consisted of five ten-round bouts, and of the ten fighters contesting, five—Yale Okun, Ruby Goldstein, Al Singer, Jackie "Kid" Berg, and Maxie Rosenbloom—were Jewish.[3]

Maxie Shapiro remembers the special flavor of the era.

"They were clannish at that time. You were a Jewish fighter. It was looked up to in the garment center, it was all Jewish people. And they come to watch them fight and they're proud. It seems that Jewish fighters were very popular, because you had a big Jewish population in New York. The garment center, the jewelry center, and whatever, you know. And they followed boxing and the fighters were invited to all the dinners and parties and they came to help their businesses. And so it was very popular.

"They'd come to the garment center, make an appearance. And the big leading manufacturers would advertise that Benny Leonard was coming. . . . Ben Jeby was the middleweight champion on the lower East Side. Lou Kirsch, another boxer, a great lightweight. He fought Canzoneri. He was a popular name."

The role, the art, and the fans of the Jewish boxer combined to create a confluence of participation and adulation that has not existed before or since in the American Jewish sports experience.

7

ANTI-SEMITISM

The second-generation American Jews of the 1920s and 1930s were subjected to an anti-Semitism that their parents did not have to endure. Following World War I, as the country became more isolationist and antiforeign, much of this feeling settled on the Jews already here, who were not regarded as an entirely native element of society despite their intense efforts to acculturate. In the 1930s, the severe economic hardships caused by the depression, coupled with the growing xenophobia in the United States, combined to create an anti-Jewish atmosphere of considerable severity. It was not until World War II ended that anti-Semitism in this country began its deep and continuing decline.

The automobile manufacturer, Henry Ford, through his newspaper the *Dearborn Independent*, was responsible for much of the anti-Jewish feeling during the 1920s. Among the irresponsible rantings of the paper was the statement that Benedict Arnold had "served as a Jewish Front."[1] Ford also distributed the notorious and discredited "Protocols of the Elders of Zion"; this forged pamphlet written in late nineteenth-century Russia purported to elaborate a Jewish plot to control the world financially.

The 1920s also witnessed the famous Harvard Limitations Case in which Harvard University, together with several Ivy League and other colleges, openly declared that they were limiting Jewish enrollment, in Harvard's instance to 10 percent. At some of these schools Jewish attendance had previously been as high as 40 percent. In explaining this new policy, President A. Lawrence Lowell of Harvard disingenuously stated that it was being imposed in order to prevent anti-Semitism: a large Jewish population, he reasoned, would be resented, whereas a smaller one would not be. President Lowell was also a restrictionist in immigration policy. He opposed Louis Brandeis's nomination to the U.S. Supreme Court, and he told a Jewish Harvard alumnus that the solution for the Jews was to abandon their religion, which had been superseded by Christianity.[2]

In the 1930s, Father Charles E. Coughlin conducted an anti-Semitic radio ministry that reached 14 million listeners each week, until it was finally forced off the air in 1940. Very few of the Catholic hierarchy denounced or even attempted to quiet Coughlin. But this was only symptomatic of a larger problem: during this period, there were more than 120 organized hate groups devoted to preaching anti-Semitism.[3]

Historians have several conflicting views regarding anti-Semitism in American history, particularly during the interwar period. According to one school, American Jews have always lived in the shadow of anti-Semitism.[4] Opponents argue that even in the admittedly difficult decades of the 1920s and 1930s, there was no theme of anti-Semitism in this country; that the major strands or events of Jewish hatred were disparate, episodic, and unconnected.

In support of this thesis, historians such as Henry Feingold point out that the United States Congress, which restricted immigration in 1921, also passed the Lodge–Fish resolution approving the Balfour Declaration (possibly because both measures were designed to keep Jews out of this country); and that Henry Ford was successfully sued by a Jew, Aaron Shapiro, whom Ford accused of being part of a conspiracy of Jewish bankers who sought to control the food market of the world.[5]

Harvard and other colleges did successfully reduce their Jewish constituency, but other schools such as New York University were 93 percent Jewish at this time, and the Jewish presence at City and Hunter Colleges was not much lower. As for hatemongers like Father Coughlin, it is Feingold's assertion that for all his audience, he was still part of a fringe element, and such groups were not acceptable to the American mainstream.

Anti-Semitism in this country has never been institutional. Except for the infamous order of General Ulysses S. Grant barring Jews from the Tennessee Territory in 1862, quickly rescinded by President Lincoln, there have been no governmental exclusions of Jews since their enfranchisement in the states. In Europe, Jews were officially excluded from certain occupations and professions in some countries, but that has never been the case here. The major inconvenience of anti-Semitism such as the Harvard case or the refusal of certain firms to hire Jews has been to make Jewish progress more difficult. Jews still managed to attend college and medical schools, and to become lawyers, doctors, and heads of business enterprises. Anti-Semitism may have slowed the Jews of America, but it did not derail them.

The existence of anti-Semitism in American sports is well known. Peter Levine's book, *Ellis Island to Ebbets Field* (1992) is filled with references to these occurrences.

The boxing experience was different because so many of the fighters, trainers, managers, and promoters were Jewish. But even between boxers of different faiths, racial remarks were minimal. Between fans and boxers—that was another story.

Oscar Goldman fought professionally in the 1920s. He is very emphatic about any encounters with anti-Semitic remarks: "No. No. I never had any trouble. Never. Never had any remarks passed or anything." Sammy Farber who fought Goldman in the 1920s, agrees with Oscar: "Never any anti-Semitic incidents while I was boxing. Not even from the crowds. I know they cheered but that's all. Nobody said anything dirty or something obscene or something. Never!"

Marty Pomerantz fought in the 1930s and his experience was similar.

"These were days when things were very difficult for the Jews in Germany. Still, I mean, there were so many Jewish boxers. This is what we did. And I never had any anti-Semitic incidents as a boxer. With any other boxers. They were my friends. Maybe with the fans, you know, in the arena. People would yell and scream things like that. But that didn't mean anything. I belong to Ring 8 now. You go down there and there are Jews and Italians and blacks and Hispanics and Irish. It's like one family."

Miltie Kessler's response has an unusual twist to it:

"Never encountered anything like that, not even among the fans. There was always a big Jewish crowd for the Jews. And there was always a big Italian crowd. So I never heard anything anti-Semitic or anything like that. In fact, one night I boxed on the same card as Frankie Terry boxed. He was out of trunks so I lent him my trunks and when he got into the ring and just before they introduced him he got down on his one knee and he made the sign of the cross. He didn't realize that he had the Star of David on the trunks. And that's a true story. I mean there was really no prejudice."

While racist remarks from other boxers were rare, Herbie Kronowitz encountered them from the crowds and from his opponent in his fights against Frankie Cardinale.

"When people, from the crowd, in the audience, you'd hear them, 'Kill that Jew, Hey beat 'im! Come on Tony, hey beat 'im, make that Jew quit.'

"There was one guy, Frankie Cardinale. He has a restaurant. I boxed this guy three times and beat him. I'm the only guy that ever dropped him. In the fight, in St. Nick's, the one fought before the war, I beat him with a punch, then I dropped him and he got up and wham, I threw another punch at him. I kept punchin' him. He begin to close the eye. 'Ya darn Jew, ya fuckin' Jew, ya cocksucker, ya fuck.' I keep hitting him and bustin' him up.

"I wanted to kill him. I really wanted to kill him. Most of them guys I fought, most of my fights, I had the guy down on the canvas. I had eighty-six pro fights. At least seventy of them, I had the guys on the floor, at least once but this guy I wanted to kill.

"I didn't go for that kinda stuff. The guy insulted me, that's it. 'Ya fuckin' Jew,' I ripped him up. What'd he think, Jewish boxers run? I beat him up three times in two and a half months."

Herbie's statement, "What'd he think, Jewish boxers run?" which extends his reaction beyond himself, has clear overtones of an attitude that he was representing other Jews when he fought.

Allie Stolz's response to this question has a certain echo of Herbie's answer in it. Allie is consistent in his stance that he was representing other Jews. After a boxer had deliberately butted Allie, he said to Stolz:

"Hey, you Jew bastard, now how do you like that?"

"I didn't say anything. I just bided my time, because they wanted a rematch. I gave him again the '*chamalyah*.' You know what the '*chamalyah*' means? The second time out. And when I got through I walked over and I says, 'You know something. That's for all the Jews. Not only me. All the Jews.' So I used to love that . . . because of our being looked down upon.

"Among boxers you had it on occasion. I had fellows walk into my dressing room and say, 'You Jew bastard.' You know. And I said, 'You'll pay for it.' I was not overconfident, but I was a cocky kid, because I could handle myself.

"On occasion you had it from the crowd. 'Kill the Jew' . . . you know, that kind of stuff. But I wouldn't say excessively. I didn't experience it, but I knew about it. It was there."

There have been a number of prominent Jewish trainers, including Whitey Bimstein, Freddie Brown, Manny Seaman, and Ray Arcel. These individuals were among the greatest trainers of any nationality, and of all of them, Ray Arcel was the best known.

In 1983, Elli Wohlgelernter, a journalist, conducted an interview with Arcel on behalf of the American Jewish Committee's project of recording the memories of American Jewish sports figures. Not surprisingly, in view of the general lack of knowledge concerning Jewish boxing, Arcel's was the only boxing interview conducted. It is on deposit at the Jewish Division of the New York Public Library.

Arcel witnessed anti-Semitism in one incident that is classic and in another that was peculiar to boxing.

"In the twenties there were Jewish and Irish and some Italians. Right up until after the world war, then you had all kinds. But the Jewish fighter and the Irish fighter, they ruled the roost and a lot of Italians came down from the Bronx and even from Harlem.

"The main gym we worked at was Stillman's Gymnasium. But it was a funny thing how it started. Grupp's Gymnasium was actually where all the great fighters trained.

"It was at 116th Street and 8th Avenue. After the First World War, in the latter part of 1919 and 1920, Billy Grupp owned the gymnasium. Billy Grupp kept getting drunk, and he went around berating the Jews; he said, 'The Jews are responsible for this war. All the German people got killed because of the Jews.' Well, [laugh] who was training in the gymnasium? Benny Leonard, Benny Valgar, Abe Goldstein, Willy Jackson, Marty Cross, Sammy Good, all of these Jewish fighters.

"So when they heard this, one of the fellows said, 'You know, there's a new gymnasium opened up on 125th Street. Near Seventh Avenue. Let's go over there and find out what it is. Let's look at it.' So a whole gang of us, maybe ten or twelve, you know, a lot of Jews—Benny Valgar, myself, Benny Leonard, Marty Cross, Sammy Good—I remember, the whole gang of us went over there, and we had to climb the steep staircase. We went up on the top floor and we saw the sign in the window. 'Marshall Stillman Movement.' Marshall Stillman was a millionaire in those days, this was in the twenties, and he was the head of this movement which was trying to do some good for the kids of the city, because they had a lot of kids in those days, too, and they figured if they'd open up their little gym and let the kids just work out in the gym, give them whatever equipment they needed, punching bag and everything else, and let them go at it, it would keep them off the streets.

"Now, Marshall Stillman hired a fellow who was a retired cop, by the name of Lou Ingber to run this thing for him; he paid him a nice salary. So we went up there and we met this man, Mr. Ingber, and Benny Leonard and all of them got to talking to him. He knew nothing about professional boxing, but he had heard about Benny Leonard and he was very happy to meet him and he told him the whole story, the history of what this gymnasium was all about. So we asked him, 'When do these kids work out?' He said, 'Well, they work out at night.' So Leonard said, 'Would you mind if we came up here and worked out during the day? Do you have any lockers here?' He showed us, he had some lockers there, they were small. So we started to drift up there. Pretty soon word got around that Leonard was training on 125th Street, you couldn't get into the place. He wasn't charging admission. So when he saw this crowd of people and all these other fighters working out, he started to charge 15 cents admission. Charging 15 cents admission he got so many people, they couldn't get in there. And of course, we told him no smoking and all. He'd walk around, 'No Smoking!' He was lord and master of the thing. Well, we knew it as the Marshall Stillman Movement, so everybody started to call him Stillman, and there's where he got his name, Lou Stillman."

The other occurrence described by Arcel was more traditional.

"Once, when I was training Lou Nova to fight Tony Galento, we went to Atlantic City to train. It seemed like the salt air didn't do Nova much good. It didn't help him any, and he said to me, he says, 'I can't train here, I don't feel right. This salt air is no good for me.' There was a fellow who wrote for the Atlantic City paper; he was the sports editor of the paper down there, and he said that he could put us in a golf club in Absecon. It's right outside of Atlantic City, and there was a big golf club and they used to say Herbert Hoover played golf there, so it made it a big exclusive club. And he said that he could get us in there and I figured if we could live in the golf club, eat in the golf club, we can do roadwork on the golf course, it would be a good spot for him to train.

"So we made the connection and we registered, and before we went upstairs the manager of the hotel–golf course called Ray Carlin over, who was the manager of Lou Nova. 'Mr. Carlin,' he said, 'everything is all set up, but there's one question I'd like to ask you.' He said, 'Are there any Jews in your party?' So Ray Carlin said, 'Ray Arcel is Jewish.' The manager said, 'Well, we can get by with his name.' The majority of people who were not my close friends, strangers, never knew what my background was, and they never knew I was Jewish. I said, 'Let's get the hell out of here.' I said, 'I wouldn't stay here, I wouldn't train.' I said, 'Let's go to Philadelphia, I'll go into the Warwick and we'll train there.' "

Boxing cannot instruct other sports regarding pensions, mob influence, physical protection of the athletes, and many other issues. But its record regarding anti-Semitism, possibly because the Jewish influence was so pervasive, is exemplary.

Sid Terris

Sid Terris, the "Galloping Ghost of the Ghetto, never realized his dream of becoming the lightweight King.

Ruby
Goldstein

Ruby Goldstein was the Jewel of the Ghetto, but his glass jaw and Ace Hudkins kept him from the lightweight crown.

The Great Benny Leonard. His hair was as neat after the fight.

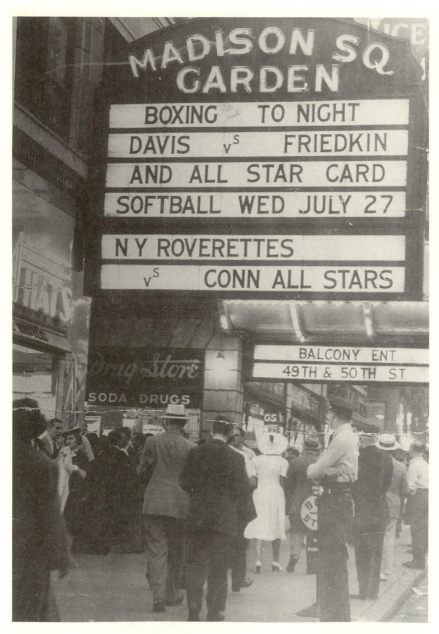

The big night, July 21, 1938.

Julie Bort

Julie suffered from polio as is apparent from this picture. His boxing career is a profile in courage.

Sammy Farber prepares to meet Pete Sanstol. Six-round main event at Tony Martello's Broadway Arena, December 3, 1929.

When Bob Olin met Maxie Rosenbloom in a 1934 light-heavyweight title fight, it was the last time two Jews fought for a championship.

Lew Tendler (at the left) shaking hands with lightweight champ Benny Leonard before their 1923 bout, which 58,000 attended.

Allie Stolz is the "class" of the living Jewish boxers. Most observers agree he beat Sammy Angott for the lightweight title in 1942.

A big 1937 win for Bernie Friedkin over Jimmy Lancaster. Announcer Sam Taub is at the left and manager Frankie ("Jay") Jacobs at the right.

Maxie Shapiro doesn't know why he ever fought Sugar Ray Robinson.

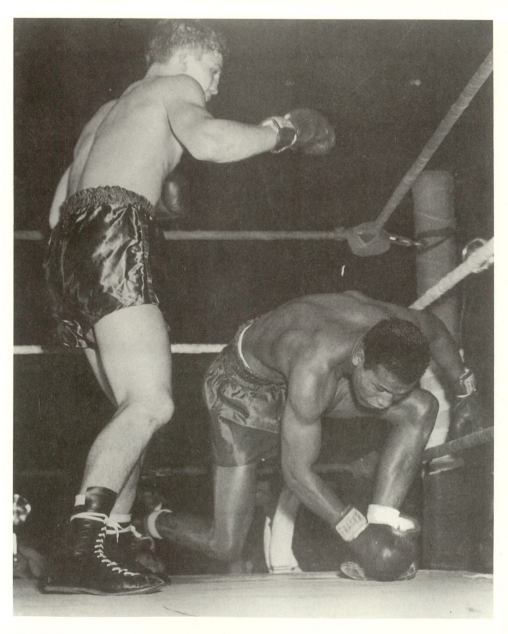

Cleveland—November 6, 1946. Sugar Ray Robinson is saved by a "long count" as Artie Levine nearly knocks him out. Artie had one of the most lethal punches in boxing.

"Schoolboy" Bernie Friedkin returns to his school. Visiting P.S. 190 in Brownsville as a conquering hero.

Yale Okun in 1927. The publicity of the era had no difficulty in describing him as a "Hebrew Heavyweight Contender."

Abe Reibman (his real name) would not tolerate anti-Semitic remarks in the army.

Artie Levine belted Sugar Ray Robinson with the hardest punch Robinson ever felt.

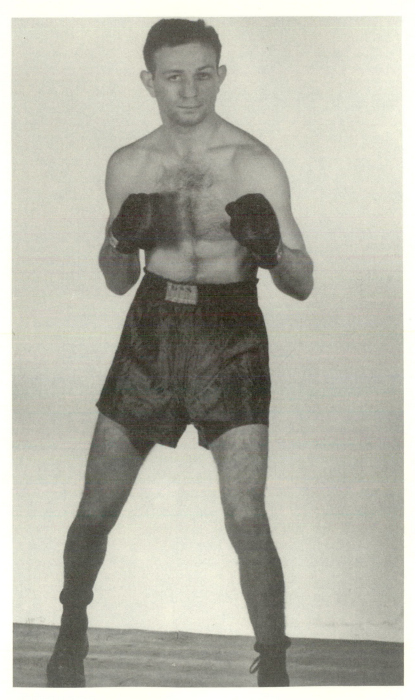

Joey Varoff lived the "Abie's Irish Rose" story as he married his Irish childhood sweetheart.

8

THE WAR

Most Jewish boxers entered the military service during World War II. The Coast Guard was particularly attractive because it had a boxing program run by Jack Dempsey. The boxers' attitudes toward the war were similar to those of most American Jews. Their first priority was winning it; dealing with the Holocaust would come later. While revisionist Jewish history now places a great deal of blame on the Jews of America and the Roosevelt administration for failing to urge and utilize stronger measures to stop the destruction of the Jews, in 1943 and 1944 the policy of the United States government and the majority of the Jews in this country was that all else was secondary to winning the war.

The boxers had another issue. Most Jewish boxers retired from the ring while in their twenties (Maxie Shapiro, who was thirty-eight, was an exception), and the war denied them their most productive years. They show no rancor or regret.

Of the 5 million Jews who lived in the United States during World War II, approximately 550,000 Jewish men and women served in the armed forces. Two-thirds of America's Jews lived within two hundred miles of Times Square. Jewish people lived in Jewish neighborhoods and socialized with other Jews. It was a culture shock for an urban Jew to suddenly be transported to the "foreign soil" of a southern state. One G.I. from Brooklyn wrote, "I was in a strange land among people who hardly spoke my own language. I could not even find lox or bagels or pumpernickel."

The Jews in the service discovered that the United States was a Protestant country and not a Catholic one. They had mistaken the heavily Catholic cities of their residences for the entire country. Wartime service also gave Jews a new perspective on anti-Semitism; the first time many were called a "dirty Jew" or a "kike" was in the military.

The Jewish boxers lived lives that were not different from those of other Jews. They were part of their communities and families, and they similarly concentrated in the large cities. The war provided them as well with the new and unwelcome experience of anti-Semitism.[1]

Bernie Friedkin and Al Reid were Coast Guard buddies. These were two of the most gentle of the fighters, and it must have taken a great deal to get Reid's ire!

"You know my real name is Abe M. Reibman. Bernie Friedkin and I were buddies in the Coast Guard. We were inseparable. And a few guys, every time they used to meet Bernie and myself: 'Hello Abie, ya like this war? Ya getting rich from this war? Puttin' money in the bank?' Always the little digs about the Jews. And I say 'Bernie, I don't trust these guys. They're too anti-Semitic.' 'Nooo! They're nice guys Al!' And we talk about it today. And I say, 'Bernie, I don't trust these guys.' So one day we went to bed. We were goin' to school then. Training school. So it was two in a room. And we stayed in a boarding house. Anyway, I heard them saying 'The Jew bastards are getting rich from this war. We're fightin' to make the Jews rich.' I says, 'Okay Bernie, you believe me, you ready now?' He says, 'Let's go.' You can ask Bernie about this. We run into their room. A small room. And I belt the big guy. The guy on top. We walked out. The next morning the commanding officer apparently knew what happened. I guess he wanted to keep it low-key. So he's calling roll call. 'Jones! Smith! O'Reilly!' He's lookin' at us from the corner of his eye, as if to say, 'You sonofaguns I know what you did last night.' But he's keepin' it low-key. He was smiling. But that's the way it was. Always, 'Jew Bastards.' 'Cause the Jews got money. Ya know what I mean? Unbelievable. I kept noticing it with their digs."

Leo Bodner's boxer, Al Backrow, did not fare as well as Friedkin and Reid. He hit a sergeant.

"A sergeant called him a 'Jew bastard.' Backrow hauled off, knocked him cold, and somehow or other, the bunk, you know, the double bunk fell on the sergeant and hurt him very badly. It didn't kill him, but Backrow goes into the brig. I get a call from his father, 'Leo, we have a problem.' He tells me the problem. He says, 'So what do I do?' I says, 'I'll see what I could do.' I called Al Buck who was the boxing writer, and he somehow had connections with Fort Dix. I knew this and I was close to Al in those days. I says, 'Al, here's the situation. See what you could do.' I think Al either made a call or went down there, but a day later he calls me back and he says, 'Leo, it's taken care of. The kid's gonna get an honorable discharge, and it'll take a few days 'til the unit goes out on maneuvers. They don't want it to happen while he's there, but it'll be taken care of.' And the kid did come out. He was out a couple of months, and his brother called me and he said, 'What do you want for Al's contract?' And I said, 'Al's not going to fight for anybody else but me.' What I meant was I wanted him to quit."

The issue of being Jewish aside, Herbie Kronowitz's Coast Guard career was typical of that of a number of the boxers:

"I went into the service in 1943. I was away for over three years. I had my boot training at Manhattan Beach. Ohhh, what fighters they had there! They had Lou Ambers, Marty Servo, Johnny Colan, Danny Kapilow, Tino Raino, Lew Jenkins.

"The guys fought for the Coast Guard as part of entertainment for the troops. They were known as 'Dempsey's Boys.' Jack Dempsey ran the program there. They didn't draft you for the Coast Guard. You enlisted, at that time. So, Ray Arcel took us down. Ray was our trainer. He took us out to the Coast Guard. And he said he'd get us a racket. Hey, everybody's lookin' for a racket. So, we figured, okay. I didn't stay in Manhattan Beach because they were overstocked with boxers. So they shifted me around. Luckily, I was around the New York area, mostly. When I was supposed to go on a cutter, that's when we got news that my brother was killed. All three of us were in the service during the war. My oldest brother was in the Army, in the Pacific, and the younger one, he was in the Bulge, he was in the Third Army over in the Rhine Valley. That's where he was killed. So they kept me here, because I was the last one. My mother went to the Red Cross to keep me here. And if I'd have gotten my sea duty, I would have gotten out at least six months earlier than I did, but I didn't have enough points to get out at the time, so I had to wait until I had my points.

"I was going to box in the Coast Guard, but I didn't. Near the end I was going to start training, I was going to fight, but then they said, 'Better not, because you're not supposed to fight, not supposed to box. But you can box exhibitions, or box amateur but no pro. You're not allowed to box pro.' Danny Kapilow boxed pro; in fact, he boxed two pro shows and then they stopped him. They wanted to throw him in the brig. Making money, you know what I mean, you're not supposed to. See, if you box for money, the government wants it. So I didn't."

To Herb Kronowitz's mother, the pain and sadness of World War II are still very fresh.

"I had three children. One of my boys got killed. The Battle of the Bulge. At the end of the war. And what right did they have to take three from one family? I should have fought them. I'm stupid. The end of the war. Agh. I cry every day. What a boy! What a handsome kid. He was so tall. He was the youngest one. He was eighteen and a half years old.

"Why did God punish me like that? They took away such a boy, my son. I went with Teddy (Herb) to the cemetery, a couple of months ago. I was in New York. And he cried for that kid. Teddy was like a God to him. He used to say, 'Teddy, don't forget, I wanna carry your bag.' He wouldn't let nobody carry that bag. He was such a nice boy, that kid . . . he used to be afraid to go up in the house alone. That's how scared he was of the dark. You know, he's dead all these years. And all these years I have cried. I cry but I get over it. I have to, otherwise I have to lay down and die."

Julie Bort had infantile paralysis as a child. That he was a boxer is itself a profile in courage. But the Army did not want him.

"First I went to Fort Dix. Then I went out to Camp Bowie, Texas. That's where I stayed. And first they had me in the armored division. This is something. And I was with them for a little while. Then they reclassified me and put me in limited service. They wanted to get me out of the Army altogether, but I said, 'I'm staying!' In fact, they had me before the psychiatrists on account of that, because of my leg. I had no business being in the Army. I wanted to go. Everybody was going, so I went. I was a patriot. They were all going. My brother went. I wasn't making any money as a boxer. In fact, I had lost a fight in the Queensborough Arena, and the doctor told me I'm suspended. He says, 'You shouldn't be fighting.' This was Dr. Schiff, the doctor for the Athletic Commission. And they took away my license for a while.

"At that time I was young, my leg didn't really bother me that much. It didn't help my fights though. I guess it hindered me. It had to hinder me. I couldn't do certain things. But, you know, I could do my share of getting in there and banging. My arms were good. My body was good. I usually was stronger than the average fighter that fought. Except Charlie Fusari.[2] My jaw was wired up! For six weeks. I had to drink through a straw. Baby food. My mother wanted to kill me. In fact, I didn't come home that night. I had to go to the Polyclinic Hospital right from Newark. In the Meadowbrook Ball Park.

"When I first went into the Army, I was in the armored division. Then they took me out of that. They reclassified me. And I was an MP, Military Police. And I did guard duty. And for a little while I did a little train duty. I used to ride from Brownwood, Texas, to Clovis, New Mexico. Just guarding the train. You had to have MPs on the trains. You had a lot of soldiers. And I did carry prisoners. But American prisoners. You know, guys who are fucked-up. General prisoners that went AWOL or something.

"Sometimes, when they brought the German prisoners in, we had to go down and pick them up from the train station. It was like a landing. They brought the prisoners in shackled. We had to take them over there to their camp. Wherever they were going to stay. And then the other MPs took over."

When I asked Julie if he knew the Germans were killing Jews then, Bort looked at me as if I came from another planet.

"What could you do? You were there to guard them, not to persecute them. They would show you pictures of their kids or their mothers. 'We don't know! We don't know nothin'.' Nobody knew nothin'! I don't know how many escaped in this country. But I know that there were escapees. I still don't think they found them. Who knows where they live now. They may be living in Milwaukee. They may be living anywhere.

"After they took me out of the MPs, I was in Special Service. They took me out of there and put me in the field house. I was an instructor. Boxing instructor. And I boxed there too in camp. I did a lot of boxing."

Boxing was never too far from the mind of the boxers even if they were in the service. They could box, of course, as part of a Coast Guard or Army program, but not professionally. Danny Kapilow, who was one of 'Dempsey's Boys' in the Coast Guard, decided to do it anyway, and he is certain it cost him the decision.

"Dempsey was a very nice guy and I was getting—stupidly, I was getting bored in Manhattan Beach and he let me out to fight. And that's when I took on Rocky Graziano one night. October 6, 1944.

"Fought him. Draw. Beat him eight rounds out of ten and got a draw out of it. I weighed 142 at night just before the fight. I could only get out at night to weigh in. Rocky weighed about 152 or 153 in the afternoon. Because he was a full middleweight. We always figured that he came in at about 156 pounds. At that weight, it was a hell of a lot of a difference.

"At any rate, I won the decision easily, but because I was unavailable and Rocky was out of the service at that point, the best they could do was draw. Benny Leonard was the referee that night, and he voted a draw and he came down to me with tears in his eyes and said that he had to do it, you know. Because none of us controlled our own fate. None of us. That began to bother me at that point. Although I realized that there could have been a decent reason because I wasn't around and Rocky was filling up the clubs. So I sort of understood it. Rocky was a hell of a puncher. He was a pretty good fighter. And he was the nicest kid in the world.

"On the way home, back to the base in Manhattan Beach, I heard a rebroadcast of the fight. When I got to the base, I called my mother and my mother-in-law, and I said, 'Don't pay any attention to that. That's shit.' This guy never laid a glove on me. I never had a mark on me. And every time Rocky swung, according to the announcer, I was getting nailed. So even the radio announcers. They're there to do a job. And they get paid to do that job. And they do what they're told."

Joey Varoff was also scheduled to be one of Dempsey's Boys. It did not work out that way, but Varoff was eighteen and he did not mind.

"I decided to join the Coast Guard because other boxers were doing that. So I went down to Manhattan to find out about registering in Whitehall Street. And I met Jack Dempsey there, and he was the commandant of the Coast Guard. And he knew I was a fighter and he said, 'Oh, just register. And when you have to come out for training over at Manhattan Beach, you come see me and we'll set you up. We'll put you in the fighter's unit and put on boxing shows for all of the personnel around the world, wherever they're fighting.' So I did that. I enlisted. I remember going out to Manhattan Beach where the local station was. And I see Dempsey and he said to me, 'Well, all the spots are filled. I'm really sorry. There's nothing I can do.' So I went to the general Coast Guard and that's where I saw all the action that I did. Didn't become part of a fighting unit like the other guys. The truth is that I was eighteen years old and I didn't mind. It was a great experience. I felt I was doing something and it worked out all right. It was very exciting, so it didn't matter."

9

THE MAIN EVENT

After all the preparation, hype, and publicity, boxing is finally two half-naked men pitted against each other, with no one to rely upon except themselves. To Bernie Friedkin and most boxers, the trainer is a very important element in reaching the moment of confrontation.

"Freddie Brown was the best. Freddie Brown had Bob Pastor. . . . Freddie Brown was the best trainer for a kid. Because he was a teacher. Because most trainers stand around, they talk to other fellas—you know they watch ten fighters. Nooo! nooo! nooo! nooo! nooo! Not Freddie Brown. If I threw a left hook from here, Nooo! nooo! nooo! He watched you, like a baby! Freddie Brown, may he rest in peace, was the best teacher for a young kid. Ya know what I mean for a kid coming up? He was there on top of you, he could watch every move. He died very young. He trained Izzy Zerling and a few other fighters. Freddie Brown was the best. And then, Ray Arcel worked in my corner with him, of course. You know the third man.

"And Whitey Bimstein worked my corner once or twice when Ray Arcel was outa town. Arcel was the best corner man. In that fifty seconds he had to work, or less, he was magnificent. Yes, Ray was terrific. With Ray in my corner I'd fight Joe Louis, because I had the confidence.

"I fought under 'Schoolboy' Bernie Friedkin. My manager named me. I was a baby-faced kid. I started when I was seventeen. And I looked fourteen. So he give me the name 'Schoolboy.' And it was good."

Bernie lost the most famous fight of his career. It took place on July 21, 1938 against Al "Boomy" Davis, another Brownsville boy. Davis was called "Boomy" because his name was Abraham. He was often called "Bummy."

"Well, that was a much-publicized fight as you probably know. We came from the same neighborhood. We knew each other. He didn't live actually in the same block. He lived maybe ten, twenty blocks away. I'll tell you exactly what happened. They tell you stories; it was built up as a grudge fight. Makes it look good. For publicity! I respected him. I'm sure he respected me.

"The fight was supposed to be in Dexter Park. It rained! So it was postponed for tomorrow. Rained again. Then they postponed for the next Monday, which rains some more. Again it's rained out! So Madison Square Garden took the match to make it for Thursday. And you heard stories where we met in the street and they almost had to pull us apart. Which never happened. I never met 'im because my manager wanted me not to be in the East New York area. He kept me up in the Hotel New Yorker. Y'know for that big fight. We never met. We fought. He beat me, stopped me."

It was unprecedented for Madison Square Garden to have preliminary matches which were scheduled to last longer than the traditional ten-round main event, but that is precisely what happened on July 22, 1938, when "Schoolboy" Bernie Friedkin met Al "Boomy" Davis in the six-round main event. As Davis was only eighteen years old, the New York law forbade a match longer than six rounds. The semifinal was scheduled for eight rounds (but lasted only one).

The more experienced Friedkin was a close 6 to 5 favorite over the younger Davis, but Davis pounded Friedkin relentlessly with scarring left hooks. Friedkin, a superb boxer, recovered to win the second round, but lost the third round on a foul.

With the sound of the fourth round bell, Davis tore at Bernie with savage lefts to the body and then raised the attack to the head. A left to the jaw and Bernie collapsed in his corner. He got up at eight, slumped again, and the referee stopped the bout at 1:09 of the fourth round.

"The promoter was Mike Jacobs. About four thousand people were there. During the depression. And he stopped me in the fourth round. He hit me a left hook. And of course, quoted in the paper was that he fooled me with a left hook. I went down and he socked me. Which he rightfully did. I got up. I went after him. But I was staggering. So the referee stopped it. He just hit me a helluva good punch and I went down. And after that I fought about two more years. Main bouts. And I beat guys after that.

"That night, the main bout in Madison Square Garden, I made eighteen hundred dollars. Of which I got about a thousand. But! Mama said—Mama and Papa said, 'Put in bank.' So I put it in the bank. The interest stayed. They watched over me.

"After that I fought Pete Scalzo to a draw at the Garden. Al Reid beat me the first time. A very tough fight. They put us back two weeks later, we fought a draw. During the war we were buddies. We palled out together.

"I fought three champions. Kid Chocolate one draw, Mike Belloise two draws, and Pete Scalzo one draw. All featherweights."

No one ever nominated Al Davis for sainthood. On the other hand, to some who knew him well, he was not a sinner; tough but not a criminal type. Vic Zimet remembers him vividly.

"Knew him very well! Al 'Bummy' Davis, when he started boxing was too young of age and so adopted the name of Giovanni Pascone who was a friend of his. He took his birth certificate in order to apply for what was known as an amateur card, which was a license to box in the amateurs. And that was his start as an amateur boxer at about the age of fourteen. As an amateur, he wasn't too successful. Until the very end, after two or three years, he started to show some genuine promise. And then boxed professionally—I think he was about seventeen years of age when he had his first pro fight, about 1938, I think.

"His career, from the start, was meteoric. He was a tremendous puncher. If anything will attract a boxing fan, it's the punching ability of a boxer. They seem to have the greatest audiences. Even in today's market, when you look at a Mike Tyson, the reason he attracts—I don't think his techniques are all that great—is the fact that he can hit you with one good shot and take you out of there. It is something that the spectators always look forward to. And 'Bummy' Davis had that capacity to knock you out with one blow. And did.

" 'Bummy' was a derivation or a corruption of Avrum which was the Yiddish for Abraham, which was his real name, Abraham Davidoff. And we used to call him Vrummy or 'Bummy.' And that's where it was at. Now one of these sports writers, Dan Parker, who wrote for the *Mirror*, at one particular point in time, became very angry with 'Bummy' and the people around him and implied that the name was given to him because he was a bum! Which was not the case at all. While he was a tough kid, personality-wise he had a wonderful personality. He had a very ready smile. He was very ingratiating. And he was a nice kid. He was a tough young man. He was tough on the outside, he was tough on the inside. But he didn't go around manhandling people or abusing people.

"Parker was angry at him because he came down to witness 'Bummy' at a workout at the local gymnasium, which was Beecher's Gym on Livonia and Georgia Avenues in the East New York section of Brooklyn. And after the training session was over, the entire delegation went down below to the local delicatessen. There was a kosher delicatessen underneath the gymnasium. And they ordered the usual cart of sandwiches, and there was a large platter of sour pickles and tomatoes and hot red peppers. And it seemed that 'Bummy's' older brother Willie relished eating these red-hot peppers. And Parker asked him, this was a novelty to him, 'are they really good?' Willie says, 'Try some, it won't hurtcha.' And Parker did! Parker had a bad case of ulcers. And, of course, those red peppers certainly did not agree with the ulcers. As a result, Parker became very indignant. Everybody broke into laughter when they saw he was agonizing, not knowing how seriously hurt he was or suffering. And from that point on, Al 'Bummy' Davis had an enemy in Dan Parker.

"Parker didn't name him 'Bummy.' He misinterpreted how the name was derived. He always used Al 'Bummy' Davis. And the interpretation that he gave was that he was a bum, which was not the case at all.

"His most notorious fight was with Fritzie Zivic. The war had not yet broken out. It was about 1941. July. It was in Madison Square Garden, and it was a ten-rounder. Fritzie Zivic was a notorious thumber and knew how to use his thumbs very well in a boxing match. And the boxing commission under General Phelan was asked to admonish Zivic to be particularly cautious not to employ his thumbs against 'Bummy.' And, with the start of the first round Fritzie, who was always his own man, went right out there and did what he thought he had to do to get respect out of this young whippersnapper who was coming up very rapidly. And maybe he proceeded to use his thumbs. And while he might have been cautioned once or twice by the referee, Major Cavanagh, who was the boxing coach at West Point at the time, and certainly one of the most reputable referees, apparently the round was not taken away from Zivic. When 'Bummy' came back to the corner, he felt that the round should have been taken away, since Zivic had been previously admonished for use of thumbs. So when he learned that the round was not taken away, he says, 'Well, from now on I'll be my own referee.'

"Walked out with the sound of the gong, for the second round, and began to hit Zivic a series of low blows, below the belt. At that point, the referee stepped in to stop the bout. And the police proceeded to jump into the ring as a riot ensued. They grabbed hold of 'Bummy' from behind. Luke Carney who was then the manager of Fritzie Zivic stood behind Zivic and was throwing blows at 'Bummy.' I don't know if Zivic was being held at the time. And 'Bummy' had no recourse. His legs were still free, so he proceeded to kick at Carney and at Fritzie who was also throwing punches. The referee got in the way in attempting to break the whole fracas up, and he got kicked as a result. The complaint eventually was that 'Bummy' intentionally kicked the referee. And as I witnessed it, I didn't think that was the case at all.

"As a result, they suspended 'Bummy' for life. The recommendation was subsequently made that 'Bummy' enlist in the Army and that the suspension would be lifted after about a year or so. The plan was that they'd get 'Bummy' out of the Army—the war had not yet broken—and that he box in a bond show against Fritzie Zivic in the Polo Grounds. A half year out of activity, the match was made. Of course, it was foolhardy on the part of the people that managed 'Bummy' to do a thing like that. They should have at least give him a chance to get into decent condition. Given him some warmup bouts. The responsibility fell on the shoulders of Ray Arcel, who was a world-known trainer. And Ray admitted that it was almost an impossible task. Except that he had to do the best he could do with him. And it went for ten tortuous rounds for Al 'Bummy' Davis 'cause Zivic was in much better shape. He had continued boxing right along. And he gave 'Bummy' a first-class shellacking. And when the referee felt enough was enough, he stepped in and stopped them in the tenth round. 'Bummy' made a pretty good recovery from that particular bout and went on to become fairly successful until he too decided enough was enough, about five years later, and retired from boxing.

"And then he had this most unfortunate incident, where he had sold a bar to somebody. As was the custom, you stayed around to acquaint the new owner with the customers and so forth. Some gangsters came into the bar, and whether they were there to shoot up the place, to rob the place, or to kill 'Bummy' I really don't know what the actual fact was. But at any rate, 'Bummy,' in an attempt to break up the holdup, punched at several of the stickup men and they shot him in return and he was killed.

"The only one who got killed, the only one who got shot was 'Bummy.' He hit the guy, knocked one out. Knocked another one down. And then the third guy shot him. They shot him right in the neck."

In the early Brownsville years, Vic Zimet and Bernie Friedkin were best friends.

"Bernie and I went to elementary school together. It was always Bernie's wish to be a boxer. In the streets he wasn't afraid of a lion. He wasn't a bully type, but he wouldn't let anybody bully him. He was kind of roly-poly built. I got involved with boxing at about the age of thirteen in this local gym that I had mentioned before, Beecher's Gym. And then I introduced Bernie into the gymnasium where he trained for a couple of years and then embarked upon boxing at the age of sixteen and became a tremendous amateur boxer. Eventually he turned pro. And there were some insidious characters that hung around that gym, and they took him away from a fellow whose name was 'Froiky,' or Frank Hane and myself, and he was brought to a manager who was known as Frankie J, or Frankie Jacobs. It created a little hard feeling between the boys who remained in the gym, who felt he should have been a little more loyal."

(According to Friedkin, "at that time amateurs were paid for a fight with a wristwatch. 'Froiky' took every third watch as his payment. Frankie Jacobs was willing to wait until I started earning decent money before he took his one third.")

"Bernie came from a very emotional, very close-knit family. There were four sisters and three boys in the family. When Bernie got interested in boxing, the first bout he boxed was under the name of 'Izzie Baker' because he was too young to box under his own name. And subsequently he got his own amateur card, under the name of Bernie Friedkin, and he was very proud of being Bernie Friedkin. He wanted to box under his own name. The family couldn't believe Bernie, a boxer?! 'Naaah, not Bernie.' I would have to go up every time and sell them a bill of goods. And of course Bernie would come home with the first-prize watches. And the family decided they're going to take a peek at Bernie. By this time his sisters all had boyfriends. So every time Bernie would box, now he had to get his two brothers in, his father—thankfully his mother didn't come—she used to stay home and suffer through the thing—and get the four sisters and their boyfriends into the boxing show. And this was a must every time he boxed.

"And along came 'Bummy,' a year or two later. Now, Bernie lived on Alabama Avenue and 'Bummy' lived on New Jersey Avenue, which was exactly three or four blocks apart. And as 'Bummy' developed, one of the promoters thought it would be a good idea, to make a match between 'Bummy' and Bernie. And they put it into Dexter Park and I think it rained out. And the Garden bought the show. And they put it in the Garden. And 'Bummy' wound up stopping Bernie in four rounds. Which was a creditable feat considering Bernie's experience at the time as compared to 'Bummy's.' And the fact that nobody had stopped Bernie prior to that.

"I kept a neutral stance. I didn't even go to the bout, to be very frank with you. I just had no heart to go. I just didn't want to be there.

"The truth is, I wasn't very friendly with Bernie because of the Frankie J situation. I didn't renew my friendship until we wound up in the service together. But I still didn't have the heart to go to that fight.

"Bernie's married. He's got a very lovely wife. He has two daughters. And Bernie's a very devoted husband and a very devoted father. And a very emotional individual. That emotional strain goes right through the family. Unfortunately, most of his family members are now gone. But he's an upstanding guy."

Allie Stolz expected to be the lightweight champion of the world. He fought twice for the championship, the second time against Bob Montgomery. He acknowledges that he should have lost that fight. But the first time he fought against Sammy Angott on May 15, 1942.

When Allie Stolz and Sammy Angott met at Madison Square Garden on May 15, 1942 for the lightweight crown, Angott had been champion for only five months. This was the chance the twenty-three year old Stolz had been waiting for.

Sixteen thousand fans filled the Garden, many of them rooting for their favorite, the Newark, New Jersey based Allie. Angott was a narrow favorite, but neither Allie nor his supporters cared about that; Allie was ready!

Stolz started strong. He knew Angott's "clutch" style perfectly, and did not permit Sammy to get close, keeping him at a distance with constant jabs and straight rights. Suddenly, in the third, Allie really connected with a right to the jaw and the champion crumpled to the canvas. He barely made it up at the count of nine.

Allie bore in on Angott, but ever disciplined, kept his distance beautifully. In the fifth, swinging wildly, Angott hit Allie a low blow and was penalized the round.

The next four rounds were evenly matched. Allie seemed stronger than ever. He was winning the twelfth and fourteenth rounds, but in each of them he fouled Angott and was penalized the round.

The fifteenth round was a classic brawl. The fighters, no longer boxing, stood head to head and slugged it out. The crowd saluted both valiant gladiators but knew Allie had won.

It was not to be. By a split decision of 2 to 1 the champion Angott received the nod and kept his throne. The usually reticent *New York Times* called the fans at the Garden "irate."[1] Everyone knew Stolz won, including the referee. But, the two judges thought and voted otherwise.

Despite Allie's heartbreaking loss to Angott in May 1942, he did not despair about becoming the lightweight king. Another golden opportunity presented itself when Angott declared he was giving up his title to go into war defense work (he later returned as a welterweight).

Allie was scheduled to fight the up and coming Beau Jack in a ten-round main event at Madison Square Garden on November 16, 1942. It was to be part of an elimination tournament for the vacant title. Stolz, the most highly regarded lightweight contender, a dazzlingly clever and brilliant boxer, was the 11 to 5 favorite.

Beau Jack, a Georgian, had been boxing for only two years at the time, and it was not known yet what a great fighter he was to be. The early rounds were all Stolz's as he gave the 14,250 fans a beautiful boxing exhibition of jabs, hooks, and rights to the midsection. Beau was wild in his attack, thereby aiding the cool, calculating Stolz machine.

But the tide turned in the fourth round when "The Beau" (as he was called) steadied and began to rush Stolz. He opened a cut over Allie's left eye and repeatedly hammered away at it. By the seventh round, the cut was so bad that the New York State Athletic Commission doctor, William Walker, ordered the referee to stop the bout at the end of the round.

In a six-round undercard at the Garden that night, Joey Varoff fought Billy Graham, the future welterweight contender to a draw. Graham had been unbeaten in forty straight fights.

Stolz, always game, never gave up his dream and earned another "shot" at his cherished lightweight crown. That came on June 28, 1946, against champion Bob Montgomery at Madison Square Garden before eleven thousand screaming fans in a fight that James P. Dawson, the *New York Times'* boxing writer, called "one of the greatest lightweight battles."

Stolz was knocked down by Montgomery six different times, but displayed flashes of defense skills, which amazed the onlookers. These were clearly not enough as Montgomery controlled the fight allowing Stolz only four rounds of the first twelve.

In the thirteenth round, Montgomery scored with a left hook and a right smash to the jaw. Allie lay inert and was counted out by referee Ruby Goldstein. It was the end of Allie's quest for the lightweight title.

"The only time my mother ever saw me fight was when I fought Sammy Angott and got to the world's lightweight championship in 1942. And in which they so badly and undisputably stole the decision from me.

"A fifteen-round decision. I had him on the deck in the third round. It looked like he was knocked out. He got off the deck. And unfortunately, the referee gave me eleven out of fifteen rounds, but the two judges voted 8–6–1 identically. Now use your imagination, can you?

"It was in Frankie Carbo days. I'm not going to pinpoint it, because I don't know, but it was a heartbreaker for me because as a kid, ten years old, I had only wanted to be the lightweight champion of the world. I loved Benny Leonard, Al Singer. And this was my dream. My deep dream! I mean, to this day, it disturbs me. It never left me. I was so intent upon winning the lightweight championship of the world—I'm getting very emotional because it was a heartbreaker—it was a heartbreaker. Because I definitely and decidedly licked this man, no question about it. And if those shenanigans did not go on, I'd have been champion of the world. I should have been. I was. I didn't get it from the announcer. But I licked this man. So, this is a thing that was taken from me. A much desired and sought after throne that I wanted so, so badly.

"I didn't get another shot at him, because after that fight the people behind Angott felt that it was not worth it because I would take his title away. So what they did do was go into the welterweight division and deprived me again.

"I was proud my mother was there, because she saw it and she saw a fight in which I didn't get hurt. I won. And she enjoyed it because there was nothing terrible. I didn't get scarred. I didn't get knocked down. So she enjoyed it very much.

"I think I was good that night. I think I could have been better. Not to sound boastful. Angott was called 'Sammy the Clutch.' I don't know if you ever heard that remark. 'Sammy the Clutch' meant that he would maul you and push you. It was tough to fight a guy of that sort because he was very hard to fight. He'd do anything. He'd push you. He'd give you the glove up in your face. He'd do anything, you know, to just maul you. It was very unorthodox. Of course, he's the one who broke Willie Pep's string of sixty-one wins, so it shows you what kind of a tough guy I had to contend with, because Pep was a tremendous boxer. He had like a sixth sense. That's how good he was. That's the type of fighter he was. So that broke my heart, but I didn't get another shot at Angott."

Hymie Caplin was Stolz's manager. He was always rumored to be mob-connected, but Stolz respected and loved him. Caplin went to jail in the early 1940s on a gambling conviction.

"Willie Ketchum then took over. Willie had good fighters after that, because naturally getting the reputation with me as the top-notch fighter, he went to manage some pretty good fighters. When Hymie got out of jail, I had retired, but Hymie called me and he said, and he used to give you that little expression, 'Pally. You got to come back for me. It's rough shape. I'm bad.' And I loved Hymie because I feel he was one of the more honorable managers. He'd tell you how it was, not a swindle sheet or not the jacking up or lowering the prices or whatever. And I looked up to him. I loved him. So I made the comeback, and in six fights I was fighting for the world title, again, against Bob Montgomery. I fought Willie Joyce, who was a great fighter. He was the number one contender in 1946. And I beat him in a decision in the Garden. And then I got the shot at Bob Montgomery. But the boo-boo I made—it sounds like alibi Allie—but the boo-boo I made was I went on a honeymoon to satisfy a girl that I didn't want to marry. Not that she was pregnant or anything, but I married her. We went on the honeymoon, and that was the undoing. Because I won eight of the first ten rounds, ran out of gas in the tenth, crawled through the eleventh, twelfth, and thirteenth. And in spite of being exhausted, I was just moving my head, making him miss, and the place went crazy. That was pretty much it. I just ran out of gas in the thirteenth. He had me knocked flat, but I was on my knees. I'm not going to argue about it, but it's no knockout.

"I was a contender, so I think I made about, maybe, $18,000 that night. 'Cause, again, $18,000 in those years was big money. Well, I made quite a bit of money in my time. You know, I'm talking about hundreds of thousands. But unfortunately, the dream never came through. One night they did me out of the fight. And the second time, I did myself out of the fight.

"I had a fantastic record. And of course, it may sound like old hat, but I have to relate to that I was gifted. I had the ability, I think, to almost carry that out; but the fact is that I had ailments. The *Newark Star Ledger* once had a cartoonist do a sketch of my head and around it medication bottles. 'The hypochondriac kid.' But it wasn't so, it was actual. 'Cause I boxed with an ulcer, not a bleeding ulcer, but an ulcer, a bad sinus condition, an allergy condition, and even the colon wasn't too good. So I was handicapped. If I had a little more energy, stamina, I think I would have lost maybe only a couple of fights.

"Well, naturally, after the forty-odd amateur fights, I turned professional. And then I boxed in the Hippodrome, I think it was. The first main bout I had was with Petey Scalzo in Madison Square Garden.[2]

"I wasn't ready for Petey Scalzo, because Petey Scalzo . . . I loved Hymie, but he made a goof. I backed up like an amateur, like a rank amateur. Because he was a little too seasoned. So I'm going to alibi there. Because, the second fight against Scalzo was no contest. I think that was about a year and a half to two years later. When I had the stamina. . . . Oh, I gave him a bad lickin'. . . .

"I had a big following. I mean, not to boast but, if I had licked Angott, Newark would have belonged to me for a week. Because the mayor at that time was Mayor Ellenstein. And he was a former amateur fighter. Oh yes, a Jewish man. Wonderful man. And he said to me, 'Allie, you win this fight and Newark is yours.' He used to drive me over to New York City in his limousine. He once took me to a doctor to check out this ulcer that I mentioned. So Newark would have been mine, but everything went down the drain. I had a movie contract, had I won the fight. I had personal appearances to make in theaters because they say I was a mimic. I was a singer and I had a talent. Not to boast. I had a talent. And all that went down the drain. That was the heartbreaker. But it was great fun. Great excitement.

"Fortunately, I was never really hurt to be carried out. Because that's one of the real dangers of boxing, God forbid. I was flattened twice. So I know what that's about. The lights go out. I was knocked out with Scalzo, and I was knocked out with Tippy Larkin. I invited him to hit me, and he did.

"I got very cocky. Don't forget, I'm fighting a big, actually, a welter-weight, not a lightweight. He was a welterweight. He came in at 138 pounds at the weigh-in. He weighed 140 like you spit. I weighed the same 133. Now, that's seven pounds. That's a lot of weight. That's almost eight pounds. And it sounds again like I keep making remarks about alibis, but the first few rounds, I'm doing well. I'm outmaneuvering him. And I go like this, 'Come on!' See, and he accommodated me. And I'll never live that down.

"That still bothers me, because, you see, even though I wasn't right with Montgomery, it's not as bad. He still knocked me out, but I didn't do any of that. When I got stopped with Scalzo, I didn't do any of that. It was legit, but this was not. Now I was supposed to be a pretty intelligent fellow. I don't say any kind of a great brain, but I was a pretty intelligent guy as a kid. And to do this, to invite a guy to hit you on the chin—poor psychology. I don't think it was even psychology. It was just stupidity."

Among the boxers, Stolz is unanimously regarded as the best Jewish boxer living today:

Very clever and deserved to be lightweight champion. He beat Sammy Angott one night and didn't get it. I think that he never overcame that.

Harry Markson

Allie Stolz, definitely, definitely could have been champion. In fact, he fought
Sammy Angott for the championship. He was robbed. I remember that. Oh,
what a fighter he was. I loved him. Please send him my regards. I loved Allie.

Joey Varoff

As in other sports, there are a multiplicity of opinions on any issue in
boxing. But the one constant in interviewing the boxers was that Allie Stolz
was robbed of the decision in the Sammy Angott fight. Although the report
in the *New York Times* does not go that far, it does describe the sixteen
thousand who attended the fight as "irate." Neither Stolz nor anyone else
has ever mentioned to me that he was penalized two rounds for low blows.

According to Vic Zimet:

"Very clever boxer. I don't think he was physically weak, but I don't think
that Allie ever really believed in himself. I mean Allie was always complaining that his stomach bothered him or this, that and the other. He always had
something bothering him, and I think he was just a very sensitive young
man. I don't know that he really had the physical requisites to get as far as
he did. But he did. He boxed in a day when there were very good lightweight
fighters. I saw him box Sammy Angott for the title I thought he won! And
so did a lot of other people. And Angott got the decision and I think that
was the crowning point in Allie's downfall. I think after that he sort of lost
heart. 'Cause I think in his heart, he felt that he deserved the decision over
Angott. It was really something to watch."

Maxie Shapiro was one of the more colorful fighters of any ethnic group.
He fought with his arms dropped, and slipped or ducked under his opponents' punches. He began boxing in his early twenties, a much older age
than most boxers begin at, and did not finally conclude his career until 1952
at the age of thirty-eight.

"I started in the fours. I went into the sixes and then eight rounds and ten
rounds. And before you knew it I had thirty-seven consecutive wins. I won
thirty-seven in all the fight arenas, and whoever I met, I came out a winner.
All of them were in New York. I had quite a few knockouts. I was not a
puncher, but at times I had some knockouts. I would say half and half,
knockouts and decisions.

"I wasn't considered a puncher like Rocky Graziano or Lew Jenkins from
Texas. Great right-hand knockout artist. Or Al 'Bummy' Davis from
Brownsville. They were knockout artists, and all the people went to see them
because they were known to be punchers. I was more of a boxer. At times,
I had combinations and stuff. I had somebody going. I had a knockout or

the referee would stop it in my favor. In fact, Bob Montgomery, I had him down for a count a couple of times and the interesting thing is that Benny Leonard that time was a referee and he refereed the bout. He refereed me and Bob Montgomery, who was a future lightweight champion after I fought him. He got a title match and he won the lightweight title from Beau Jack. If you remember Beau Jack, a great fighter. I understand the last I heard of him he was down in Miami shining shoes. That's forty years ago or more. Years ago when I heard somebody died and he was sixty years old, I said, 'Oh my God, an old man. So what?' Today I'm past sixty and now you got me worried.

"I beat some good boys. Patsy Giovanelli. I want to mention the ones I beat. Patsy Giovanelli, there's Al Pennino, great names, you know, good club fighters. And the first guy that came along to beat me was called Al Reid. Jewish boy, tough kid from the Bronx. I see him today at the Ring 8 meetings.

"He just was a bully and I couldn't get to him. It was one of those nights, and he roughed me up and he got the decision. It was at one of the arenas. St. Nicholas Arena or something like that. One of the clubs. It wasn't in Madison Square Garden. I fought him again, a return match, I think it was a semifinal in Madison Square Garden, and I reversed the decision that time.

"When you see Reid, I wish you'd tell him that I want a rematch. I want a rubber match. He won one and I won one. I want a chance to take the rubber match. I think I'm a little older than him. I think by a few years. Because when I started boxing, I was no youngster, you know. I took a little time to make my mind up. I think I was about twenty-three when I started boxing. A lot of people finish then."

Maxie Shapiro and Bob Montgomery, a future lightweight champ fought two battles within two months. In the first, October 6, 1942, nine thousand people in Philadelphia saw Shapiro, the 5 to 1 underdog, give Montgomery a boxing lesson.

Shapiro was all over Montgomery in the third round, battling him around the ring and knocking him down three times. Referee Benny Leonard nearly stopped the fight. He let it continue and Shapiro won a decisive ten-round upset.

In the return match, also in Philadelphia, on December 1, 1942, Montgomery's bobbing and weaving kept Maxie off balance. Montgomery concentrated on a body attack and was the victor in a ten-round decision.

"The biggest win I ever made was Bob Montgomery. All the waiters in Philadelphia made a fortune on me. They bet $10, they took a chance.

"He was a 4–to–1 big favorite, or maybe more. But 1 had a reputation upsetting good fighters, great fighters and losing to somebody who couldn't fight. So this was one of my nights. I had a good fight. I had him down. Benny Leonard was the referee. And people were hollering 'Stop it.' The ones that bet on me were hollering 'Stop it.' But he didn't. It seems he got the job in Philadelphia . . . the referee's job . . . and he wanted to make an impression there and it was the hometown of Bob Montgomery and he let him go on and he took a beating. I'm sorry to say that. But I beat him up, and I got the decision. I got a ten-round decision. I must have won to get it in his hometown of Philadelphia.

"A lot of that stuff went on. You know, your hometown. The crowd, the judges. Everybody's for the native that comes from there. So I must have won it pretty big. They couldn't take it away from me. But the next one was a return match back in Philadelphia a month later. It was a mistake. My manager made a mistake.

"My managers then were Jack Blumen and Willie Grunes. It was 1943, something like that. I was in my prime then. And I should have gone back to Madison Square Garden in New York. And this time, they had a chance to steal the decision. I beat him again, but not as bad as the first time. And they gave it to him. And he went on a few months later in Madison Square Garden and beat Beau Jack for the lightweight title. I should have had at least the match, because with Beau Jack, I don't know. He was great. I didn't want to fight him. He was a machine. He was like you wind up a machine. Punches came from all over. Montgomery had one style. Just to bore in, you know. But Beau Jack, I don't know. But most fighters feel that they could be champion if you gave them a chance. I never gave it too much thought. I was happy to do it as long as I did.

"I also fought Henry Armstrong. He held three titles at one time: the featherweight, lightweight, and welterweight title. But he wasn't a champion when I fought him. He was supposed to be on the way out. He was finished in 1946 or something like that. And my manager felt I could beat him. Which I was beating him for seven rounds. In the seventh round I tired and the referee stopped it."

Even today, Maxie admits the Sugar Ray Robinson bout on September 19, 1941 was a fight he never should have had.

Shapiro's best round was the first. He began with a left to Sugar Ray's head and followed with a "snappy" left to the body. But the tables turned in the second round. Robinson punched Maxie to the side of the ring after a furious barrage of punches, and Maxie fell through the ropes. Maxie came back at the count of three, and Robinson did it again. this time Maxie took a nine count.

In the third round, Sugar Ray "flashed" a right and a left to the jaw and Shapiro went down again. Maxie was wobbly getting up and Robinson belted him with a two-handed body attack. Shapiro went down a fourth time. Just before Maxie fell again, the referee stopped the fight. Robinson extended his streak to twenty-four straight wins, eleven of them knockouts.

Also on the card that night at Madison Square Garden was Bean Jack, another future champion who knocked out Al Reid in the eighth round.

"With Ray Robinson, it was no contest because he was too tall and he was a great puncher, a great boxer and he was too much for me. I didn't know his record. If I saw his record, I would have told my manager, 'I don't want him.' But . . . Madison Square Garden, my name up in lights and Madison Square Garden at that time, in 1941 and I wanted it. And I figured everybody looks forward to fighting in Madison Square Garden.

"The purse wasn't much, but it was an opportunity. I was told it was an opportunity. If I beat him, I could go and fight for the championship. It was an opportunity to get murdered. Because he was too much. He had me down a few times. Don Dunphy was the blow-by-blow announcer, I got the recording of the fight. I run it off sometimes. It's a laugh. Don Dunphy says, 'He's outside the ropes.' I'm on the apron, and the referee's inside the ring counting from the inside. I'm standing outside the ropes, leaning on the ropes, trying to figure should I go back in the ring or stay there after the ten count. Anyway, the people started hollering—the ones that bet on me—they took 10 to 1 odds—and pushed me back into the ring. I got back in the ring, and that's when he finished me off. I went down again and the referee stopped the fight. It was a TKO. I wasn't counted out. The referee stopped it, which I'm glad he did. Well, my manager had said, 'He's a green kid, he's only nineteen years old. And he hasn't been around too much. He's inexperienced.' I found out why. Why he don't know too much. I found out. Before he fought me he had twenty first-round knockouts. How was he going to learn anything going one round all the time?

"This was a funny thing. I was stopped a few times, but not for the full count, except once. Ruby Goldstein was the referee, and I fought in St. Nick's, Chester Jiminez, a great puncher, come from out of town. He was known to be a puncher, and I got into the ring with him in St. Nicholas and I was getting along pretty good. I was winning up to about the sixth, seventh round. And he had me down, you know. And I was on one knee. And I usually take the count. I might as well take the full count of nine. I figured I'd get up at nine. And I got up at nine and Goldstein said, 'It's ten.' And I said to

him, 'Wait a minute. I was ready to fight. It's nine.' He said 'No, it's ten.' I
said, 'Why don't you mind your business? The people want to see me
continue.' After the fight, he told me, 'It is my business.' I said, 'You could
have had me continue. Nobody complained. I got up, didn't I?' Anyway, he
was a good fighter, Jiminez.

"Ruby Goldstein. He was a good referee—he used to run and jump
around the ring like he's fighting himself. He used to move around. He was
a good referee. But I think that was a mistake. He could have let me continue,
because I was ahead up 'til then. Maybe I got up when he lifted his arm up
for the ten. I got up for that, but he didn't come down for ten. But anyway,
I figured he made a mistake in that fight where the fighter got killed. Emile
Griffith and Benny Kid Paret. He was on the ropes. He couldn't go down
because the ropes were holding him up. And he let Griffith continue
punching him. And the poor guy, he died after the fight.

"Paret had fought Gene Fullmer a few weeks before. Gene Fullmer, a
great, great middleweight. Oh yeah. Paret was hurt before. He was in a tough
fight before. Well, that's not the referee's business. The manager's supposed
to worry about that.

"I also fought Phil Terranova. He was the featherweight champion. He
was a great little fighter. He was NBA featherweight champion. And there
was Jackie Wilson who was a featherweight champion. There were five
champions I fought—Terranova, Wilson, Armstrong, Robinson, and
Montgomery.

"The fellow, Willie Grunes, who trained me . . . part manager. He brought
me into the fight business. He was not blind—not totally, but he was visually
impaired. He couldn't see too well. In fact, in the corner, he would advise
me . . . Ray Arcel and Whitey Bimstein were my seconds, cut men, they
called them. They were the ones that refresh you between the rounds. And
Grunes once took out a bottle . . . he felt the bottle from the pail and gave
me to drink. . . . It was peroxide. He couldn't see too well. But he could see
the ring though.

"He was great. He was from the old school. He used to show me how to
do things like Benny Leonard and Canzoneri. And Barney Ross. Fellows
like that. I used to like to imitate them and fight like them. Because they
were great, those guys. They were real classy boxers and fighters.

"When I looked in the book, I couldn't believe it. 140 pro fights. Oh, ho,
ho. Today, if you have thirty fights, you retire. 140 professional fights. It's
in the Ring Record Book.

"I did very well in Milwaukee. I got $3,000 and that was a lot of dough
at that time. And I fought a local boy there twice. Justy Fontaine. He was a

pretty good, well-liked lightweight, and that was my biggest purse. I put down a couple of hundred dollars on the table, and the rest I put in the bank. Yeah. And my mother would say to me, '*Gevournen?*' 'Did you win?' She didn't realize the rough business it was. I would come home without a mark, sometimes a little black eye, but nothing really serious. She thought it was like a game or something. I didn't expect her to say, 'Did you win?' I thought she'd say, '*Geschloggin?*' I forgot my Yiddish. '*Tseclopped? Tseharget?*'[3]

"I was a little afraid of going into the ring, a little concerned . . . a little worried. But not to the extent that you're going to lose. . . . If you're scared you'll get hurt. Once the bell rings, you forget that you're scared. You have to have a little fear in the ring, you know. You can't go in with your chin wide open.

"Near the end Ray Arcel worked about twenty-five to thirty of my fights. He'd been around quite a while. And Whitey Bimstein. They were partners. Great Fellas. I got to tell you a story about Whitey. He was a '*shtarker*,' that guy. One time I'm fighting and he's in my corner. He's usually coming up with the stool at the end of the round. And this time, the bell rings and I'm waiting for him . . . and I don't see him. He's outside the ring fighting with some customer. Some fight fan. He's fighting with the guy. He said something derogatory about me or something. And I'm waiting for him to come up with the stool. Later, when he finally came up with the stool. I gave him the stool. I said, 'Here, you sit down.' I gave him the bottle.

"I mentioned I went down for the nine count. It makes a difference to stay down those extra few seconds. Like taking a deep breath, you know. It's sort of a relief. You may as well take the full count. Because you're going to get a knockdown against you, so what's the difference if you get up at 1 or 2—it's a knockdown—or you get up at 9? It's a difference of a few seconds. It helps. Sometimes a few seconds left in the round, where the guy's getting beat up and he just makes the bell. He gets revived again between rounds, and he's OK the next round. It does help, that few seconds. It means a lot. A second means a lot.

"I didn't get hit in the head. I had a style, I could stand in front of somebody and just move my head. Bob and weave. Just move my head to the side and the punches go over my shoulder. I was very confident about that. I could stand in front of somebody, and he couldn't land a punch on me cause I would just slip the punches with my head. I had the timing for that. That was my one favorite thing. You know, just to stand in front of a guy and make him miss. Grunes used to tell me how to slip a punch."

Maxie's sister, Anne Shapiro (she claims she married a man named Shapiro, because she liked the name so much), attended the Robinson fight:

"I was there the night he fought Ray Robinson. And I'll tell you, I don't know what he was doing in the ring with Ray Robinson. Robinson was taller, had a bigger reach. I don't know what Maxie's manager was thinking of when he put him in with Ray Robinson."

Mrs. Shapiro also describes the way her father determined who was winning a fight Maxie was in.

"In those years when Maxie was boxing, the fights used to be on the radio. My father's English wasn't too good and if I wasn't at the fight for some reason, or if it was out of town, and it was on the radio, we would sit home listening to the fight. My father didn't understand everything, but he would hear the announcer say 'by Shapiro, by Shapiro, by Shapiro.' meaning there was a left hook by Shapiro, a jab by Shapiro. And if the announcer would say 'by Shapiro' more than the other guy, my father would say, '*Er gevint, er gevint!*,' 'Maxie's winning, Maxie's winning!' because the announcer was saying 'by Shapiro, by Shapiro.' And that's how he knew that Maxie was winning."

Among the interviewees, Maxie was a favorite topic of commentary:

Maxie Shapiro was one of the cleverest boxers I ever watched box. He was as slippery as an eel. And he socked pretty good. He was a pretty good boxer and licked Bob Montgomery who was a great champion. Beat a couple of other very . . . he had a terrific record.

He had his own style it was unique. But—the cleverness was so evident. Very slippery style. Just very hard to hit. Boxed with his hands out. Slipped punches very well. And was right there to hit you and he could sock pretty good himself. And I'm telling you, up until the time Robinson knocked him out, he did quite well. But Robinson was Robinson. I mean, there was only one Robinson in thousands and thousands of boxers that come along who could do everything.

Vic Zimet

You know what? In my opinion, Maxie was one of the greatest fighters that ever lived, and don't let anybody tell you different. He's beaten champions. What a fighter he was! He was an excellent boxer. Crafty. He had a style, he fought with his hands completely at his sides, down to his knees. The fact is he fought Bob Montgomery and he licked Bob Montgomery.

Joey Varoff

Maxie was a good fighter. He was a little wacky but—he's still a little wacky. But he gets along. I don't think it was from the punches. I think he was that way before he went in.

Julie Bort

He's a good one. He was a beautiful boxer. A unique style, a great defensive style. He could box anybody and not get hurt. He used to go with the biggest killers and not get hurt. He knew how to handle himself in the ring. He knew all the tricks. And he started late. In fact, it seems to me that he started when he was almost twenty-five years old. That's very late for a fighter. In those days, in Maxie's day, kids were starting at fifteen and sixteen years of age.

Hank Kaplan

Let me just tell you something about Maxie Shapiro. I was very fond of Maxie Shapiro. Rocky Graziano, who had a very troubled background, wrote a book and I walked out of Lindy's with a couple of guys one day, and Maxie Shapiro was standing out in front with Rocky Graziano. And I said, "Hi, Rocky, How you doin'." He said, "Oh, everything is great. The book has sold a million copies. They're going to make a movie. I'm doing great." Then I turned to Maxie, and I said to Maxie, "What's with you?" He said, "What should be with me?" he said, "I was never a juvenile delinquent."

There was a guy in the Garden named John F.X. Condon. Condon was a very successful press agent there from 1955 to 1980. Maxie used to come in and talk with him. So one day as John used to tell the story, Maxie Shapiro came in and sat down and John was very busy. He had to meet a deadline. He was writing a story for *The Daily News* or something, and he was pounding away and he waved at Max. He kept typing and typing. Max sat there for about twenty minutes. Then finally he got up and he went to the door and he said, "John, it's always such a delight to have these conversations with you." He was a funny guy.

Harry Markson

He used to fight with his ass sticking out.

Sammy Farber

Herb Kronowitz still looks every inch the fighter. He was born in 1923, and his career ended in 1950. In the late 1940s he was ranked among the top ten middleweights. Herb has total recall of every fight he ever had (there were eighty-six pro fights) and probably every round.

"I turned pro in '41. When I turned pro, I started fighting four-rounders. And I'd fight whoever they'd put me in with. Many times my friends would meet my mother, they'd say 'Hey, they put him in with tigers, he shouldn't be fightin' these kind of guys, they're too tough.' And I would stand up with them and I'd beat them.

"Oh my God! When my mother sees me, she comes over, she says, 'Teddy, what are they doin'? They'll get you killed, that Nat'll get you killed.' Nat Lehrer was my manager—he made my fights.

"She saw Miltie Kessler. They lived down the block from me, at 29th Street, in Coney Island. He sees me once, fighting a guy Artie Dorrell. This Artie Dorrell was in the picture, with John Garfield, *Body and Soul*, Garfield knocks this guy out; he fights him for the title (in the picture). He was flattening everybody. And he come in to New York, and . . . they match me with him, in the Garden, a six-rounder. A six-rounder in the Garden before the war. Boy, contenders fought six rounds and were tickled to fight in the Garden for six rounds. They took four rounds in the Garden, just to get in there, to be seen. So she sees Miltie, 'Teddy's fightin' in the Garden,' she tells him, and Miltie says, 'but you know, he shouldn't be fightin' that fella. Cause, they wanted me to fight him but my manager wouldn't let me fight him.'

"Kessler's manager was Lippy Breitbart. Nice guy. He'd been around the fight game a long time. He passed away just a couple of years ago. Good trainer, too. He knew his fighters, and he wouldn't put Kessler in. Dorell was one of the fights that they stole on me. I won, but he got it. He got the decision. Six rounds. In the Garden.

"Oh, big thing. I got $600. Ayyy, before the war. I always bring my money home. I always gave money to the house. I was single.

"I would have fought anybody. Anybody. When Johnny Greco came down here, from Canada, that was in 1941, I think. In the Garden. A four-rounder. He was a ten-round fighter. But they bring him in. He fought in Elizabeth, New Jersey, on Monday night, and he fought me on Friday night in the Garden. He had flattened three guys in a row, when they brought him down here. In fact, he flattened Harold Green. I didn't care who he is. I beat him. I beat him.

"I busted his mouth. I banged him with a right uppercut. I enjoyed it all. I never really got hurt in the ring. I was shaken but I didn't get stung. I had ribs broken.

"In the two years from 1941 to 1943, I had about forty fights. I'd fight Monday night, and Friday night I was fighting in the Garden. The following Tuesday I'd be fighting in the Broadway Arena or maybe in Coney Island. And after the service, from '46 to '50, I also had about forty fights, like ten a year. I didn't do anything else, just boxing. I boxed Pete Mead in the Garden. We boxed four times. Four wars. Four wars, man. All main events.

"Ebbets Field was the second time. Beat him. Was the only one I got. And I beat him at least two more, I know. Believe me, they were murderous fights. Man, he ripped me over and under . . . gave me everything he got. Oh, I loved fighting a guy like him. It had to be a great fight with him. You either fought, or you didn't get in that ring. That's the way I fought. And with him, with him you fought, or you didn't fight. And, and just about anyone who fought him, they hated him. They hated him. They said, 'He's the dirtiest bastard.' He was Irish. He was from Arkansas. He called me before my sixty-fourth birthday, to wish me a happy birthday. Can you imagine that?

"I was going to fight Graziano, LaMotta, and Zale, but I couldn't get 'em. Couldn't get the fight. They wouldn't fight me. LaMotta was a tough guy, but there are certain styles, certain guys that some guys won't fight. Or the trainers, the managers won't fight, because they say, 'He's a bad guy for you to fight because, he'll beat you, he has his style. He's too tough. Bastard's too tough.' I didn't have the in. My manager didn't have the in.

"The night I beat Harold Green in Ebbets Field, Jake LaMotta was there. He got introduced before my fight as going to meet the winner. A couple of weeks afterward, Stanley Joss, who was then my manager, was talking with Jake and his manager. But Jake did most of the managing himself. He didn't need a manager. He was a helluva fighter, he could fight anybody, but it petered out, and that was the end of that. But fighting him woulda been like fighting Harold Green. On the same order because he was the same style, short and stocky. But he wasn't as good a puncher as Green. He was tougher and stronger than Green, but he wasn't a good one-punch guy like Green. Green was a good left-hooker. He could flatten anybody. He tagged me but couldn't do nothing with me. I dropped him. And bang a left hook in the belly, he got up and we went to ten rounds. It would have been the same type of fight against a guy like LaMotta.

"Graziano. When I was a welterweight, before the war. I was only about 45 (145) pounds. He was weighing about 50 (150 pounds), 52 (152 pounds). And I nearly got to fight with him. But no, no, Irving Cohen wouldn't take me.

"My record was eighty-six pro fights. I got about, on the record, about twenty-two losses. On the record, I had two draws. Of those twenty-two, I think I really lost about four. I don't say I won 'em all. I lost about four fights. One of them to Pete Mead, and maybe three others.

"I used to train at Jack Barrow's gym in Williamsburgh, but I couldn't get guys to spar with, so I used to box with Miltie Kessler. Miltie was a good fighter. He was better than his brother Ruby. But Miltie became a playboy, he didn't want to train. After he started fighting sixes and eight-rounders, he didn't want to train anymore. So he wound up catching a little hell, and he stopped.

"Then Ruby Kessler came along, during near the end of World War II. He was a good lightweight. But as he started to make money, eight, ten rounds a few dollars, he also didn't want to train. I was supposed to run with him. The Kesslers used to tell me to wake them in the morning to go run with them. On the boardwalk. I used to get up 5:30 in the morning. That's when you run. Not like these guys today 11:00, 12:00 in the afternoon.

"Nice clean, fresh air at 5:30 because then we hadda be in the gym at 11:00, 11:30. To box. That's what I did. I come, I wake him up, couple times, 5:30 in the morning in the winter. The moon was out. Till they opened the door. I sez, 'Come on!' 'Whaddya want?' 'Come on! We'll go and run.' Ruby says, 'The moon is out.' I says, 'Come on.' He says, 'I'll see ya at the gym.' He come in the gym and he says, 'This guy, he comes five-thirty in the morning to wake me up to run. No way. Who the hell is gonna run?' Most of the guys at that time, guys who were really fighters, used to run at that time. You run. And then you come to the gym.

"I'd get to the gym about 11:00. I used to sit there and watch the guys box. Talk with guys till about 3:00. I like that. And then when I was boxing, after the war, when I was a main-bout fighter, I'd say to the guy, 'Make an appointment for 11:30, 12:00 to box in the ring.' When I first started boxing, I'd be sitting there till 2:30 in the afternoon. Then Stillman first put me in. I said, 'You see what time I come in there.' Stillman says, 'Hey, Herbie, you don't like it, go someplace else.' We needed Stillman's, it was the only place really, that you never failed getting someone to box with. You'd always have someone to box with. But then when you're boxing main bouts and you become a top-tenner, top-ten contender, the same guys you boxed with for nothing, they want to get paid. They want $5, $10, for boxing a few rounds with you. And some guys who took the $5 or $10, they're really some fighters. Man, they really give you a good little workout. Make you work. But they still wanted $5 or $10. Because you were fighting main bouts in the Garden, Ebbetts Field, or some other place, ya know what I mean?"

Imagine the excitement at the Madison Square Garden main event bout between Artie Levine and Herbie Kronowitz on March 7, 1947! The crowd-pleasing Jewish boys from Brooklyn were at the top of their form. Artie was twenty-two and Herbie twenty-four. The crowd of twelve thousand at the Garden which paid $50,000 was on its feet the entire match.

They went a blistering ten rounds. Herbie started strong and actually stood toe to toe with Artie for awhile, scoring with his superior boxing ability. But in the fourth round, when Herbie attempted a left to Levine's face, Artie stopped the punch and moving inside he brought a crashing right to Herbie's jaw. Kronowitz sagged. Thereafter, Herbie showed more respect for Artie's power. Herbie showed no signs of flinching or backing away though, and the crowd loved every minute of the fight.

Artie weighed one hundred and sixty-four pounds to one hundred fifty-seven and three-quarter pounds, a large difference among middleweights. Levine, possibly because of his greater punching power, won a close but unanimous decision. The crowd booed lustily, and Herbie was still convinced he won that fight. It was a tribute to Herbie that he wasn't killed. Of his fifty victories, Levine gained 36 or 72 percent by knockouts.

Herbie's was a tall, rangy middleweight. An excellent boxer, his advantage over many of his opponents was that he could best them at long range, fending off their jabs while punishing them with right and left crosses. In his fight against Harold Green at Ebbets Field on June 19, 1947, with fifteen thousand in attendance, Kronowitz's strategy worked well and he was able to thoroughly outbox Green at long range. When Green penetrated, he damaged Kronowitz with powerful jabs to the body.

During the first two rounds Kronowitz kept Green at bay and scored with blistering lefts to the head. In the third and fourth rounds Green moved inside and battered Herbie with short jabs to the body. The fifth round was a donnybrook with Herbie tossing his bombs at Green, only to receive Green's close-range bullets in return. Herbie boxed masterfully in the sixth round, but Green, jabbing constantly, dominated the next two rounds. Kronowitz, in wonderful fighting condition, as ever, came on strongly, held off Green, and won the last two rounds.

Kronowitz was awarded the unanimous decision as the crowd roared in appreciation of the fiercely contested ten-round main event. Herbie always gave the crowd its money's worth.

"I beat Harold Green at Ebbets Field. It was an easy fight, and maybe he won three rounds out of the ten. Artie Levine was a different story. He was, and is, a very good friend of mine. He lives in North Carolina now, and we often talk about this fight. He was a very, very heavy favorite. Maybe 14 or 15 to 5. George Abrams was supposed to fight him. George could have handled himself. George was at the end of his career, and they pulled him. That was a main event in Madison Square Garden, and it was my first main event. He won the decision. There was no question that I won the fight, though. I flattened him twice in the first round. We were very good friends. We never took the fight further than the ring, of course.

"You know, of course that he flattened Ray Robinson in Cleveland. He won that fight, but they took it away from him. When Robinson went down, the referee took Levine to a corner and then started to count. Robinson stopped him in the ninth or tenth round. And there was no way that Robinson was going to lose that fight. But I tell you that Levine had knocked him out early in the fight. Levine is a hell of a guy. A great guy. "There was talk of me fighting Robinson. But they were afraid of me.

"After the Green fight we were showering together at Ebbets Field. Harold had beaten Graziano twice, but the last time he took a dive. Everyone knew it. 'How come you didn't go into the water for me like you did for Graziano?' I asked him. Green didn't say a word. He knew I was right."

Herbie Kronowitz is convinced that if he had had the right opportunities, he could have been the middleweight champion of the world. Fights with Graziano, LaMotta, and Marcel Cerdan never materialized. Herbie was not afraid of anyone and would fight all comers. Leo Bodner, for one, did not think this was such a terrific idea.

"One thing about Herbie Kronowitz, he had fights that he never should have had. He's a wonderful person. And he's still saying, 'I would have fought anybody.' Well, that's not too smart. I don't know what his manager was thinking. You don't just fight anybody. If you have a career as a boxer, and you want to move up, then you have to plan your spots. Your next fight should be with somebody who can help you if you beat them. But Kronowitz, I don't know. He fought in places like the Fort Hamilton Arena. It was an awful place. There was no control. There were riots there. And he fought people that ended in brawls. And if he would fight somebody who wasn't going to help his career, and if he didn't do well, or if he lost, that set him back.

"A manager is worth as much as a fighter. Because if he's good, you plan, you project, you see where your fighter is going, who he should fight. Maybe there are some boxers who may not be as good and he could beat them, but he's not going to look good against them. Southpaws, the left-handers, some people just couldn't fight them, so you stay away from them unless you absolutely must, but you don't look to fight them.

"But Kronowitz was a crowd pleaser. He could punch. He could take a punch and he was a good boxer. He was a clever fighter, and he had a lot of stuff goin' for him. He looked like a boxer. Herbie Kronowitz was a great name for a Jewish boxer. It was the end of the forties and there weren't so many Jews in boxing and he was a local boy, a Brooklyn boy. He had some followers and he had some main events in the Garden and Ebbets Field. He fought Harold Green, knocked him out. I don't know whether he could have gone all the way, but I don't think he was managed well."

> Herbie was a good boxer. Dead game fellow. But didn't have extraordinary talent, I didn't think. A good fighter, don't misunderstand what I'm saying. But you had Solly Kriegers around and you had a lot of other great boxers.
>
> *Vic Zimet*

Joey Varoff loves Herbie Kronowitz. Perhaps living two hundred miles from Herbie allows him the objectivity of safe distance.

"Oh. Herbie and I met when we were young amateurs. We knew each other. We were both like up and coming kids. He was from Coney Island. I was from New York. And we boxed each other in training. We got to know each other. And then, coincidentally, Ray Arcel trained us both. Herbie he was a wonderful guy. We had a lot of fun. We went in the Coast Guard together.

"I love Herbie, but he was not going to be a champion. Now don't tell him. He was an excellent fighter, but no. He had all the attributes. He had courage. He was strong. He was tough and he would take on anybody. No doubt he could take on top-level fighters. But to be the champion, I don't think so. I could be wrong. This is my opinion. He was not championship caliber. If I was a student of boxers, I would not say Herbie."

In evaluating Herbie Kronowitz, his own description of himself is soundly based. Every other boxer would agree that it is an accurate one: "I was tough. I'm a stand-up guy and I was tough. See? They knew, if they fight this guy, you gotta fight. You gotta kill this guy, if you wanted to beat 'im. This guy don't quit for nobody."

When Leo Bodner came to the United States in 1923, at age 16, he gravitated to the Educational Alliance on the lower East Side where he took up boxing. After several amateur bouts he left the ring to become the co-manager of Yale Okun together with the Johnstons. Okun was a light-heavyweight who fought in the late 1920s and 1930s. Bodner also managed several other fighters.

"I was more or less aligned with the Johnston brothers. There were four of them. The oldest was Nat Johnston, who was a trainer. Then Jimmy Johnston who was the real power. Then there was Billy Johnston and then Charlie Johnston. Jimmy had his office in the Paramount Building. And Billy and Charlie had their office across the street, for some reason, on Broadway. They had come over from Liverpool when they were very young. They used to tell me stories how poor they were when they lived on the lower East Side, and that on Saturday, they'd go around to the Jewish homes and turn the lights on or off, whatever, and there would be a penny or two or three, maybe a piece of cake, honey cake or sponge cake or a piece of challah. And how they made a few cents which in that time was money. I asked them if they resented it, if they resented the Jews for that. And they would say, 'No,' they didn't resent it. That's the way it was. They performed a service and they got paid. Some of the Jews were too poor, they said, so they told them not to pay them. That's how they got started. Then they went into boxing, and they were managers and then they took over clubs—St. Nick's, Ridgewood Grove. For a while, Jimmy was the matchmaker at Madison Square Garden. A lot of boxing people resented them, because if you were managing and a promoter, then you'd want to promote the fighters that you managed. Others couldn't get fights there but they were good to me. I never had a problem. My fighters got fights. Of course, we co-managed Yale, so I had some business, some partnership situation with them.

"Jimmy was the best judge of fighting talent that I ever saw, and he would judge a boy in the gym. Jimmy always told me to look for four things: 'How the kid blocks a punch.' 'Cause you don't want him taking too many punches. 'How he jabs,' because you got to keep jabbing, jabbing to keep your opponent away, and jabs count, they count as points. Balance, 'how he was on his feet,' could he move? Was he graceful? And 'was the kid in shape?' He had to always be in shape. If you had those four things, Jimmy felt he could be a boxer. You didn't have to have a great punch. Of course, you had to have the desire. That goes without saying. You had to want to be a boxer.

"Anyway, one time, I had this Jewish kid, Al Backrow, nice boy. I said, 'Jimmy, come on up to the gym and have a look at him.' Jimmy says, 'OK, I'll be up there.' I think it was Stillman's or Pioneer. Jimmy looks at him for about three minutes, he says, 'Leo, he's not gonna be a fighter.' And once he would say that, I knew that he was 99 percent of the time correct. But I had him. I was his manager. And I felt, listen, we'll have a couple of fights and we'll see where he goes. And I watched him carefully. I didn't over-match my boys. And you had to be careful, because, if the other side, including the Johnstons, were promoting somebody on the way up, they would want to use your fighter as a guinea pig, and you had to be very careful of that. But then there were a lot of boxers and you had to know who they were. And you had to ask the right person about somebody else.

"I put him in one four-rounder, and he does well. I think he knocks the guy out. Now he's scheduled for another four-rounder, Ridgewood Grove, it's on a Saturday night and of course, I couldn't be there for the weigh-in, which was Saturday morning at 11 o'clock or 1 o'clock in the afternoon, so I needed someone to go to the weigh-in. I asked Birdie Briscoe who was going to be in his corner that night, to be there. And the plans were to meet him at Ridgewood Grove after *Shabbos*.

"I get to Ridgewood Grove and somebody says, 'Leo,'—Charlie Johnston had Ridgewood Grove—'Leo, Charlie wants to see you.' OK, so before I see Al, I go in to see Charlie and he says, 'Leo, we have a little bit of a problem.' And I says, 'What's the problem, Charlie?' He says, 'Well, the boy that Al was supposed to fight tonight couldn't make it.' I'm looking at Charlie and I had an idea what was coming then, and I said, 'Who'd you put him in with, Charlie?' 'Well, look, we couldn't get anybody, and we didn't want to lose the fight, so I put him in with . . .' and he named somebody that I knew and I said, 'Charlie, that kid has ten knockouts. Ten fights, ten knockouts. My boy's had one fight. How could you do that?' So Charlie said, 'Leo, what am I supposed to do?' So what could I do? The fight was set. The fact is that I never would have permitted it. Because I would never permit a boy of mine to be overmatched.

"I was on my way to the dressing room to see Al. I had to pass the back where the gamblers were. They used to hang out in the back. And in back near the gamblers was the whole Backrow family, and they're listening to the odds on this fight, 10 to 1, 12 to 1, 15 to 1. They stopped me. The Backrows . . . wonderful people. They owned a grocery store, I think on 16th Avenue and 39th Street in Brooklyn where Al used to work. As a matter of fact, when I first came to see him, he showed me how strong he was, and he picked up one of these huge milk cans. Picked it up with both hands and brought it to his lips to drink from it, you know. These tin or copper cans that they used to have. They used to ladle milk out of it. So they said, 'Leo, Leo, what did you do? What did you do to Al? 10 to 1, 15 to 1.' I said, 'Take it easy, take it easy. Don't worry about it, not a problem.' 'Leo, he's gonna get killed.' If they weren't sitting near the gamblers, they wouldn't have known about this, but there they were.

"I walk into the dressing room, and there's Al sitting with his hands over his face. I said, 'Al, what's the matter?' He says, 'Leo, I understand this kid has had ten straight knockouts. What's he gonna do?' I said, 'Al, let me tell you something. Those ten knockouts don't count.' He looks at me and he says, 'Why don't they count?' I says, 'Every one of them was bought.' We never used to use the word 'fixed.' We used to say 'bought.' 'Just don't worry about it,' I said, 'You go in there, you're gonna knock him out.' I rarely said that to a boxer, but I figured he's a big strong kid. He could take a punch. I wasn't worried about that. He could really take a punch, this kid. And he had a punch. He was just clumsy, and that's why the Johnstons didn't like him. And eventually, he couldn't go too far because he was clumsy. So I said, 'You just don't worry. Everything's gonna be all right.' So when I got through, Birdie Briscoe says to me, 'Leo, you better sit right near the ring, because we're gonna need help carrying this guy out after the first round.' I look at Birdie and I said, 'Birdie, weren't you there this afternoon.' He says, 'Yeah, I was.' I said, 'You knew what's going on.' Birdie kind of shrugged.

"Look, he wasn't the manager, he wasn't the trainer, you know; we just hired him to be in the corner that night. Anyway, the fight starts and my kid comes out swinging and punching and he really gives the other fellow what for. I mean, the other guy didn't know what hit him because he just . . . they felt that this was an easy match. Al comes back to sit down at the stool, and I says 'Al, this round you've gotta knock him out. Just knock him out. Go in there, don't worry about a thing. Just knock him out. You just swing and hit,' and he looks at me cause he knows that I was kind of a defensive manager. I thought defensively, you had to protect yourself, and here I am just telling him to go for broke. Al looks at me, doesn't say anything, 'cause I'm the manager. Comes out the second round, and the crowd is loving this fight. Sure enough, he knocks the kid out. Al's the winner, a knockout. Oh, and the place went wild.

"Even though it was a four-rounder, some of these four-rounders were terrific. So now Al is excited, and I'm feeling a little bit better but still annoyed at Charlie, a little bit at Birdie, but, listen, what could I do? The kid goes to the weigh-in by himself. What could he do? He was twenty years old. He wants to fight. He wants to make the 100–150 bucks that they got. I passed by his parents, they're ecstatic. They're full of joy. The father says to me, 'Leo, I'm really sorry. I apologize.' I says, 'Mr.' He must have been fifty. I was thirty, so it was 'Mr. Backrow.' 'Don't worry about it; everything's OK. I knew. It was one of those things.' Well what am I gonna tell him? And they were very, very happy and they always thought highly of me.

"I go in to see Charlie Johnston, and Charlie looks at me. Nothing happened. You know, that was Charlie. Nothing happened. He says, 'Leo, the kid is a crowd-pleaser. He's not going to be a fighter. Jimmy told me that. But he's a crowd-pleaser. I'll put him in next week if you want.' I said, 'Sorry, none of my boys fight two weeks in a row. You can't put him in next week.' He said, 'But Leo, you know, we'll pay him $250, put him up to six rounds, the whole business.' I said, 'No.'

"Now one thing about the kids in those days, when a manager said something, that was it. And I don't even know if I told Backrow this, but I said, 'No.' A little while later, he enlisted and he went into the Army and was at Fort Dix. If I had agreed to the match and I put him in, Johnston would eat him alive. You have to be careful about those things.

"Now Yale Okun, I was his co-manager. I had 10 percent with Johnston, off the top. A manager usually got a third after expenses, but I didn't want to know about that. So my deal, which was approved by the Athletic Commission, all deals had to be approved by the Athletic Commission, was that I got 10 percent. Yale was a terrific guy. He could have been the light-heavyweight champion, but he was lazy. You know, to be a champion boxer, a very good boxer, you need a lot of things. You need skill, you need desire, you need the right manager. The manager's so important to get you the right fight. To keep you from fights when you're not ready, not just put you in there because it's a big pay night. And even to tell you when to quit. Most boxers don't know when to quit and that's why . . . they get hurt, they can't defend themselves and they get hurt. Benny Leonard, when he quit in 1925, he was a genius. He came back in 1931. He needed the money. The depression wiped him out.

"It was a terrible mistake what happened to Benny Leonard when he came back. He could have gotten seriously hurt. I enjoy watching Foreman and Holmes but they shouldn't be boxing. Years ago the Commission would not have sanctioned these fights. You can't box if the reflexes aren't there, especially if you've had a layoff.

"Anyway, Yale was a terrific boxer, a sweetheart. Wonderful, wonderful family. I used to go up to his apartment and his mother would say, 'here you can eat. She meant her house was kosher.' I says, 'Mrs, Okun, I know I can eat here.' She was a special lady. She loved Yale.

"You know, the fathers worked. They were busy, they were tired. But none of these mothers worked. They couldn't work. They didn't speak English. Where were they going to get a job? Their whole lives were their husbands and their children. She loved Yale. They had a brother who was a dentist. She knew Yale was boxing. She didn't like it. She used to say, 'Leo, as long as you're taking care of Yale, I'm not worried.' What she meant was, I wasn't going to put him into matches where he didn't belong. Especially in the early years. You've got to get seasoning. Today, a fighter has ten matches and he fights main events. In those days, you had to have thirty to forty fights. You didn't just go into the main event. You weren't ready. Maybe you had a hundred amateur fights before that. I think they probably got hurt a lot, too, because, you had a lot of fights. And there was training.

"Yale, he liked to play cards. He used to play in one of the stores that was on East Broadway. And I'd go out to my lunch and I'd say, 'you should be in the gym.' It was the day before a fight. He should be doing loose sparring, loosening up. He's sitting there playing cards. I said, 'Yale, you're sitting on your butt, they're going to knock your butt in.' He says, 'Leo, don't worry.' I said, 'Yale, I'm worried,' because you cannot . . . it's not possible, you have to train. Even "Slapsie" Maxie Rosenbloom . . . he was a nut and had the craziest training schedule. But he trained. He trained 10:00 at night, but he trained. He was clever. Yale was a terrific, clever fighter. He didn't like to hurt anybody and he didn't like to get hurt. He didn't like to take a lot of punches. He said, 'Leo, don't worry a bit.' Well, I was worried, because I didn't want him to get hurt. You know, we used to worry about that all the time. You didn't want your fighter to take a lot of punches and get hurt.

"There are two parts to boxing. To punch and not to get punched. You cannot take too many punches. I don't care who you are. Muhammad Ali is the way he is . . . they don't call it Parkinson's, they call it a syndrome or Parkinsonian or something like that, something fancy. He took too many punches. He permitted himself, especially after he laid off for three and a half years, he permitted himself to get hit, and it takes its toll.

"Another time, Yale had a match at Ridgewood Grove and it was on a Saturday night, so the agreement was that I was going to pick him up after *Shabbos* and we were going to go over to Ridgewood Grove together. It was in the winter. So *Shabbos* was over about 5:30. I didn't show up 'til 6:30 and one of Yale's friends says, 'Leo, we just wanted you to know, Yale went to weigh in today, over at 80 Worth Street, but the rest of the time, he's been playing cards.' So I went over to Yale and I says, 'Yale, what are you, crazy? I understand you've been playing cards all day.' So he says, 'Leo, stop worrying.' I says, 'Well, I am worried. Couldn't you just stay home?' 'You can stop worrying, Leo, I'm going to knock the bum out.' I said, 'I think he's going to knock you out, Yale.' So we went over to Ridgewood Grove and sure enough the guy hits Yale a punch, the ends of his hair stood on end. Sends him reeling. Boy did Yale get mad. I've never seen Yale as mad as that. Yale comes up, hits him a right uppercut, sends him flying right through the ropes, and knocks the guy out. He said to me, 'Leo, I told you I was going to knock the guy out.' I said, 'Yale, you're more lucky than you are good.' I knew in my heart that Yale wasn't going to be a champion. He had great heart, but he didn't have the desire. He was too nice. There were other things that were important to him.

"Yale was a clever boxer. He didn't like to get hit, and he had a punch, and he was always on his toes, so even when he hit the guy, there was no power behind it. Because he was always on his toes. He didn't stay still to hit a guy.

"He was no crowd pleaser at all. In fact, they used to write that the hot dog stand was making a lot of money because Yale Okun fought. Everybody went out to buy frankfurters. But he was clever. He protected himself beautifully. He knew just what to do.

"He never got a shot at the championship because at that time Maxie Rosenbloom was the champ and they started bringing up Bob Olin. And

Rosenbloom gave the title to Bob Olin. But we tried to get Yale a shot at the title. Rosenbloom's manager was Frank Bachman, and I spoke to him many times. Bachman says, 'No, we don't want Okun.' I says, 'Why don't you want Okun? He's a good fighter.' 'Well, we don't want him.' Why? Because they were bringing up Bob Olin. They thought he'd be more of a crowd pleaser.

"Olin was a nice boy. He lived in Borough Park. He had the Borough Park crowd with him. In those days Borough Park wasn't religious, you know. It was mixed, Italians and Jews, all different kinds. He had a nice crowd from Borough Park, especially when he fought in New York. Finally, we decided we're going to see Maxie Rosenbloom himself. So we went up to his hotel, Yale and me. Yale wanted to fight him in the worst way. Yale had it all figured out how to fight him. One time Maxie Rosenbloom fought in the St. Nick's and I was sitting next to Yale. Yale says to me, 'Boy! Give me that man. I'll cut him to ribbons!'

"Of course they knew each other. 'Boy, give me that man!' He always wanted to fight him. First of all, he wanted the title. He wanted the light-heavyweight title. He fought long enough and he beat many a heavyweight.

"We go up to his hotel room, and there he was with two girls. They were all stripped, all naked. The three of them. Maxie Rosenbloom says, 'What do you guys want?' So we said, 'We want to talk to you.' So he got out of bed, all stripped and he knocked on the table with his pecker and he says, 'We hereby call this meeting to order.'

"We told him what we wanted. He said, 'It's up to my manager, not to me. That's why I have a manager. I can't do my own managing.' And Okun never got the shot."

Actually, Okun previously had a chance at both Rosenbloom and the light-heavy weight title. when Tommy Loughran, then the champion, vacated the title to fight as a heavyweight, the New York State Athletic Commission held an "elimination" tournament to determine the new champ.

Rosenbloom was originally declared ineligible by the Commission, as his noctural activities and haphazard conduct offended the straight-laced commissioners (this when the partying Jimmy Walker was Mayor of New York City). Cooler heads prevailed, and on December 9, 1929 (after the stock market crash), a crowd of 17,000 was on hand at Madison Square Garden to witness Rosenbloom dispatch Okun handily in twelve rounds. Six months later Maxie became the light-heavyweight king, a title which he held until relinquishing it to Bob Olin in 1934.

The Rosenbloom–Olin light-heavyweight title fight at Madison Square Garden on November 16, 1934 was the last of ten title matches between Jewish boxers. Of these, Benny Leonard was a contestant in three and "Slapsie" Maxie Rosenbloom in two. From any standpoint the bout was a disappointment as only eight thousand fans showed up to witness one of the dullest championship matches in memory.

Rosenbloom had long stated his desire to move to California to try his luck in the movie business, and Bob Olin was an up and coming attractive fighter with a large following in the New York area, where he was born. No one has ever accused either of a "fixed" match, but it was taken for granted that the title should remain in the New York, and that Rosenbloom's effort would likely be half-hearted. Still, all in all he was so much the superior gladiator that he nearly won the match.

Rather than the roar of the crowd which could normally be expected at a title fight, most of the noise was the loud "boos" from the fans who recognized a "stinker" when they saw one.

Olin gained a split decision in the fifteen-round bout, but only because what little action occurred was initiated by him, as the majority of the crowd thought Rosenbloom had won, as did the *New York Times* writer Joseph C. Nichols. But nobody much cared—it was one of those nights.[4]

Of equal interest to the fight itself was the recent promulgation of the New York State Athletic Commission rule that hitting with an open glove (or slapping), which had earned Rosenbloom the nickname "Slapsie," would no longer be tolerated. Maxie conducted himself in exemplary fashion and was not even warned by the referee.

The caliber of boxing in general during that period was extraordinarily high. In the Rosenbloom–Olin eight round semifinal, James J. Braddock defeated John Henry Lewis. Six months later Braddock became heavyweight champion of the world by beating Max Baer (Braddock later lost his crown, by a knockout, to Joe Louis). A year later, Louis captured the light-heavyweight title by outpointing Olin.

Rosenbloom moved West and never fought in New York again. Boxing mostly on the West Coast he proceeded to win an impressive forty more bouts, losing only four. For his part, Olin, much the inferior fighter to Rosenbloom, compiled thereafter a record of ten wins and twelve losses before retiring. Olin died at the age of forth-eight in 1956. Rosenbloom, who fought an astonishing two hundred and eighty-nine times was seventy-two when he died in 1976.

Harry Markson's recollection accurately depicts the proceedings: "It seemed evident to a lot of people that Maxie was trying awfully hard to hand

Olin the title that night and Olin was having difficulty knowing how to accept it. Olin was a pretty good fighter, but he was not in the class of Rosenbloom."

Two of the greatest trainers in boxing were Ray Arcel and Whitey Bimstein. Arcel died in 1994 at age ninety-four, and Bimstein died in the early 1970s. Most of the Jewish boxers had one or both of them as trainers at one time during their careers.

We used to call them the "Gold Dust Twins." They were partners. The others became jealous that they were garnering . . . all the boxers were being brought to them to work with. And they complained to Stillman. So Stillman concocted some story. And he got them to get into an argument. And they wound up bitter enemies. Bitter enemies? They just didn't talk to each other for a lot of years. And I happened to like Whitey. He was a nice guy. A fun guy. Ray was much more serious and much more trustworthy—now don't imply that I'm saying Whitey was a thief. Whitey was a playboy. Whitey liked to play. But if you had to send a fighter out of town you'd send Ray. You know, years back you had enough boxers so that you couldn't be all over the place. You might have a fighter in Jersey. You might have a fighter over in Holyoke. You might have one boxing in Brooklyn. So you sent a trusted person to go with the boxer to collect the purse after the fight.

I've known boxers who could not perform without Ray Arcel in the corner. Billy Soose wouldn't box unless Ray Arcel was in the corner. "Boom Boom" Mancini went into a blue funk—because Jacobs, Frankie J, who was his manager and Ray had a falling out. And so Ray didn't work the corner with him. And he went into a slump. And when Ray came back, Boom! That was it. Picked his spirits right up and he became a winning fighter again. So there were a lot of them who depended upon Ray.

As far as being a corner man, he was supreme. He was super. Clean. Neat. His hands were like a surgeon. I'm in Washington, D.C., I have a young Jewish boxer by the name of Marvin Dick. And Ray was running the Saturday night fights, and he puts Marvin Dick as a favor to me on the show. And Marvin is doing very well. Boxing Herb "Biff" Jones. And in the fifth round he gets cut. So I patch up the cut and he goes through the sixth round. He gets the decision. He was far enough ahead. So now I have the doctor come over and look at the eye. He says "You better call Mr. Arcel. He knows more about these things than I do."

Vic Zimet

Joey Varoff was never knocked out. But the one time he lost on a TKO remains etched in his memory.

"I fought in Madison Square Garden and there was a semifinal under-neath the Beau Jack–Tony Janiro fight. Tony Janiro was in the same stable I was in. I'll never forget that night because Ray Arcel had to take care of Janiro for the main bout, so he didn't work my corner. Whitey Bimstein worked in my corner that night. And it was a packed house. Even though I was never a top-notch fighter, Ray Arcel used to tell me, 'nobody wants to fight you.' I was considered a very clever fighter and with my style, I made everybody look bad. They couldn't hit me. I'd dance around, jab and all that stuff. So the only guy I could get to fight me was this guy, Waylan Douglas. And they said to me, 'Joe, this is your big opportunity. Make a big hit here and maybe they'll fight you, all these big guys.' Because I had a very good record. Very few guys had beaten me.

"Anyway, the first couple of rounds was the worst fight for me. It was a stinking fight. It was a terrible fight. He couldn't hit me. I couldn't hit him; he was six foot tall, long arms, you know, one of those long fighters. It was a terrible fight. I went back to the corner after round three. The crowd was booing and they were stamping. You know how they get. And Whitey Bimstein said to me, 'Joey, you're stinking out the house.' I said, 'I can't hit this guy. Too big. He's got long arms, he doesn't want to fight.' He says, 'Joey, go out there and make him fight.' So I was so excited and mad, I went out there like a slugger, instead of a boxer and voom, he hit me on the chin and I went flying through the air. I hit the deck and—you know at that time they didn't have the three knockdown rule. He knocked me down three times and I got up. The fourth time, just as he was going to hit me—if he had hit me one more time he would have killed me—the referee stopped the fight and I got up. And that was the only fight I ever got stopped in, in all the sixty-five fights. Never happened again."

Artie Levine was one of the hardest punchers in the middleweight division. Levine had thirty-six knockouts out of fifty wins. This was very unusual for any fighter and extraordinary for a Jewish boxer, most of whom did not score many knockouts.

"I'm looking at my record book. And I had a lot of straight knockouts. In 1945 . . . I had come out of the service and I had a lot of knockouts, and then in 1946 I knocked out Jimmy Doyle, who had beaten Tommy Bell who fought Robinson for the championship. At the time, Tommy Bell was a great fighter. I don't know whether you know anything about Jimmy Doyle. He was also a great fighter. He was taught by Jack Johnson. And he was really a perfectionist as far as a fight was concerned. He was one of the best I have ever come across. And I knocked him out in the ninth round, and he almost died in the ring on me. They had to bring a respirator in the ring to keep him alive. It destroyed me in boxing. I lost my killer instinct after that. That was in 1946, March 11, 1946." A year later Sugar Ray Robinson fought Doyle. He knocked Doyle unconscious again and Doyle died.

In Ray Robinson's last fight before he won the welterweight championship from Tommy Bell, he boxed Artie Levine. The date was November 6, 1946. Robinson won the fight, but there was a disputed "long count" reminiscent of Dempsey–Tunney.

"Yes. I was the first guy to knock him out. They gave him a long count. Ray Arcel himself was working in my corner that night. I knocked him out, but they gave him a 20-second count. There was a riot at ringside. They protected him at Cleveland. The referee walked me back to my corner and then he picked the count up at 'one.' He was supposed to start the count immediately upon him going down. He's supposed to start counting then, provided I started going back to my corner, which I did. In other words, I was in the opposite corner when it happened, I was going at a pretty fast pace with Robinson. It was in the fifth round."

Twelve thousand fans paid a record of $83,000 to view what promised to be a thrilling match. By then, Robinson had won seventy-two of seventy-four professional fights and eighty-nine straight in the amateurs (losing only to Jake LaMotta and drawing once in the pro's), and Artie's punching power was legendary.

In the fifth round he pushed Robinson into his own corner, and unleashed a left hook to the jaw, that Robinson would recall, "flopped me like a fish." He fell on his face. The referee walked Levine to a neutral corner and did not pick up the count until he returned to Robinson. He should have began the count when Artie started walking to the corner. Had he done so, Robinson would have been knocked out. Robinson was gifted with an additional seven seconds and was able to struggle to his feet.

In the eighth round, Levine staggered Sugar Ray again with another left hook. But in the ninth round, as they slugged it out to the wild roar of the crowd, Robinson caught Artie with a left to the midriff and Levine sagged to the ropes. Robinson followed with a machine gun-like barrage and Levine fell back hanging onto the top strand of the ropes. He refused to go down, and was counted out at 2:41 of the tenth round with only nineteen seconds remaining in the fight.

It was the only time Artie was Ko'ed in his seventy-one fight career. Robinson later acknowledged that Artie's left hook to the jaw in the fifth round "was the hardest punch I was ever hit."

"It was the largest crowd they ever had in Cleveland at that time. Any fight. I got $25,000 for that fight. It was a lot of money in that time. I got half of the money. $12,500. The manager paid the expenses out of my share. This was an agreement we had. Isn't that terrible? I got half."

Al Reid died in January 1993. He was the treasurer of Ring 8 and a long-standing member of the boxing brotherhood. Al consistently positioned himself in favor of benefits for the boxers and against "outside" people benefiting at the expense of the fighters. Vic has very fond memories of Reid.

"Al Reid was from the Bronx. I became very friendly with Al Reid in the service. I had known Al briefly prior to that, just casually. And he was responsible for my becoming the boxing coach on the Coast Guard recruiting station, which was on Ellis Island. And a more loyal, a nicer fellow than Al Reid, you won't find anywhere. He's a delightful guy and was a helluva good fighter, too. Terribly mismanaged, by the way.

"He was thrown in with everybody. He was a rough, tough, game, game guy. And you know you don't go through walls, you go around walls. And seems that he ran up against a lot of walls. The Chalky Wrights and Mike Belloise and a lot of others. He boxed Bernie a couple of times, I believe.

"His manager was Sammy Goldman. And Sammy was the manager of Tony Canzoneri. And Sammy thought that every fighter he had was another Tony Canzoneri. He threw Tony Canzoneri in with everybody, and he did the same thing with the boys that he was bringing up. Canzoneri was a great fighter. Look at his record. You see how few losses he had? Al was a good money fighter. But he didn't take the precaution. His record does not bespeak—Look at Canzoneri's record! I saw Canzoneri box. They talk about Duran doing this, being the greatest fighter since Benny Leonard. He wouldn't have licked one side of Tony Canzoneri. In his heyday, Tony Canzoneri was a great fighter. Courageous. Could punch. Could box. Terrific fighter."

Whoever the Jewish fighter was, he generally was not a heavyweight. Abe Simon or Art Lasky as heavyweights were not the usual Jewish boxers. There have been few Jewish heavyweights and no Jewish heavyweight champions. Marty Pomerantz's theory as to why there were so few Jewish heavyweights followed that of most of the boxers:

"Jewish kids just weren't as big as . . . they still aren't. We certainly weren't in our day. You wanted to know why there were no Jewish heavyweight champions. There were no Jewish heavyweights. Abe Simon wasn't really a boxer. He was like Primo Carnera. He was a big Jewish kid, and they tried to make him into a heavyweight. But he really wasn't. Art Lasky. I guess he was Jewish. But I don't know if he was from New York. You know, I can't think of any others."

Harry Markson believes that Art Lasky came nearest to becoming a Jewish heavyweight champion.

"The closest was Art Lasky. Art Lasky fought Jimmy Braddock for the right to fight Max Baer. And Braddock and Lasky fought a very close fight in which, at one point, Lasky lashed at Braddock with the back of his glove and he was penalized. He was penalized that round and it cost him the vote of the judges. And the championship. That was the closest we had ever come."

Although Max Baer, heavyweight champion in 1935, wore a Jewish star on his trunks, he apparently was not Jewish. At least, not a single interviewee believes he was. Leo Bodner claims proof positive on the subject.

"There weren't too many Jewish fighters in the heavyweight class. Most of them were light-heavyweight, middleweight. A lot of lightweights, featherweights. There weren't many heavyweight Jewish fighters. Except for Baer. Well he wasn't Jewish. And his brother Buddy was no fighter anyway. He thought he was a good fighter but he wasn't.

"Max Baer was a good fighter, but you know, he wasn't even circumcised. I was in his dressing room many times."

Maxie Shapiro carries the image of the small Jewish fighter to the next level: "Even the comedians are small, Jackie Mason, Eddie Cantor, and Georgie Jessel. I guess it's just inherited. Just inherited. Max Baer was big, and I think he passed off as Jewish. He wanted to be Jewish. I don't know why."

Mike Silver, the boxing writer, believes that there was nothing specifically Jewish in the paucity of heavyweights. Sixty years ago, according to Silver, the average male was 5'6" tall and weighed 140 pounds. The heavyweight category begins at 175 pounds. It is Silver's contention that there were not many heavyweights of any ethnic background.

Harry Markson, born in 1905, was president of Madison Square Garden Boxing from 1959 to 1973 and is now honorary president. He and Teddy Brenner, the Garden matchmaker, were two of the best known figures in boxing. Markson, a graduate of Union College in Schenectady, got his beginning in boxing by reciting a poem.

"I guess you would call me an anomaly in my business. Mike Jacobs hired me. I worked for the Bronx News and Mike had his office in the Hippodrome and a circus came in. They had with them a young clown named Emmett Kelly. And a boxing writer for the *New York Journal,* in those days, before it became the *American Journal,* was assigned to do a feature story on Emmett Kelly. I happened to walk into the Hippodrome office one day, and Hype Igoe, which was a funny name, but that's what he was called, was sitting behind a typewriter. He's typing, turning out one page after another, one lead after another, and he was cursing, and I said, 'What's the matter, Hypie?' 'I'm trying to write a lead on this Emmett Kelly story and I just can't get the right kind of lead. I don't want that silly business, you know, 'laugh, clown, laugh.' So I said, 'Hype, when I was a kid, I knew a poem. It was called 'The Fool's Prayer,' and it went, if I can remember, something like this':

> The royal feast was done.
> The King sought some new kind of sport to banish care
> And to his jester cried, "Kneel now, and make for me a prayer."
> The Jester doffed his cap and bells and stood the mocking court before.
> They could not see the bleeding heart behind the painted grin he wore.

"I remember when I said that he jumped six feet up in the air and said, 'Type it out, type it out!' Mike Jacobs was sitting nearby and he walked over to me and he said, 'Jesus, can you do that for me?' And I was making at that time, $36 a week. We had just lost our first child. My wife had a child that lived only ten days. So for the first time in my life, I had gone into debt and I'm making $36 a week. Mike offered me $90. To me, that was a fortune. $90 a week. That's how I came to work in the boxing business.

"I really feel that the only time I actually enjoyed being the head of boxing at Madison Square Garden was the night that they gave me a party and elected me to the Hall of Fame when I retired. I had so much heartache in that business. I have to tell you that I was too cowardly to quit. Because I had a wife and I had a child, and I just didn't know where the hell I would go to get a job. I'd have taken a job as an office boy at any newspaper in town.

"Nobody should go into the fight business. You've got to be very, very careful. Because, something is going to rub off. You know the expression, 'If you lie down with pigs, you're gonna stink.' I remember one time, it was also in the old Garden. One day, just before I retired, who comes to see me, but Norman Mailer and Pete Hamill. And they said, 'Harry, we got a fighter that we want to . . .' I think Gus D'Amato gave them a fighter and he was busy, he couldn't handle him. And they were going to handle this fighter.

" 'We got a fighter we want to handle. Are you going to give us a match? Will you give us a bout at the Garden?' And I said, 'Not as long as you're handling him.' And they said, 'Why?' And I said, 'Listen. Go next door. If Teddy Brenner will give you an opponent, I'll give you a match. Because I trust Brenner 100 percent. You don't have any idea what you're doing. You're going to go to New Orleans or to Las Vegas. Or to any of these other places. They're gonna put your guy in with somebody, they're going to overmatch him. You're not gonna know. He's gonna get hurt. Maybe he'll get killed. You'll find yourself in front of a grand jury. What do you know about it? What kind of answer you gonna give? You didn't know? You're responsible, you have to know.' I said, 'Just stay away from this. You want to write a book, Norman? You want to be a fan? You want to write about boxing? Do that. But you cannot get in where you are on the level of running fighters unless you grew up with it. And you didn't.

"So if anybody wants to invest in a boxer, I would say, if you want to invest, you can't have anything to do with that boxer's career, and even that is very, very tenuous."

10

THE MONEY

The manager had sole control of the money, and it was he who decided whom his boxer would fight next. He negotiated the contract, collected the purse, determined what the expenses were and paid them, and then divided the balance with the boxer. The standard procedure was that expenses (which included the trainer's fee) were deducted from the fighter's gross purse. Of the balance, the manager received one-third and the boxer two-thirds. It requires little imagination to figure out the number of ways in which a boxer could be exploited.

Some managers were scrupulous in their actions and accountings; others less so. Why stay with a manager who you knew was cheating you? First, there was a three-year contract. And then, this manager may have had connections for lucrative fights that others did not. The boxers were usually in their early twenties and totally dependent on their managers. Their job was to train and fight.

How much were the purses of the boxers? Oscar Goldman fought professionally in the 1920s. He was a "club" fighter and never earned more than $500 for a fight, of which he kept about $300. To Oscar it was good money.

"But it was a lot of money. I mean it was, but things was bad . . . it started getting very bad. People were broke and all . . . it was the depression . . . what did you pay in rent? $10, $15 a month rent? You go in to have bacon, I don't mean bacon, I mean eggs and potatoes. What did it cost? 15 cents. With coffee, a quarter? Now it costs $2 to $3. You could get a good nickel cigar, a dime. Now you pay a dollar you get a lousy cigar."

Goldman participated in several "ticket shows," which were popular in the 1920s. The boxer would sell tickets to friends, relatives, or customers of his local candy store. He would keep half the proceeds; that was his take, which he then split for expenses and with his manager.

Oscar also fought at the Garden. He received $150 for four rounds and $250 for six rounds. At the smaller clubs he earned $40 to $50. But when the depression began, these clubs reduced payments to $20.

New York had many boxing arenas in those days. In addition to Madison Square Garden, there were, among others, the Broadway Arena, St. Nicholas Arena, Sunnyside Gardens, Ridgewood Grove, Eastern Parkway Arena, Fort Hamilton Arena, the Bronx Coliseum, the Coney Island Arena, and the outdoor Coney Island Velodrome (in the summer). Friday was fight night at the Garden, but on the other nights there was boxing in at least one place. On Sunday night no bouts were scheduled.

Although Yale Okun may have earned $21,000 at the Garden in the 1930s, this was not a typical night's pay, even for a main eventer. The Garden was in its own class, Leo Bodner recalled:

"If Yale Okun was fighting in St. Nick's, in the main event, he would bring home maybe $500, $600. That's all. There was no television. Radio they had. They didn't get anything from the radio. Just the promoter got from the radio. The fighter didn't get anything. Today the fighter gets from television, and he gets from cable and he gets from this and he gets from that. Years ago there was no such thing. The four-rounder, he got $20, $25, $15."

Julie Bort believes that managers are similar to agents for entertainers and should be limited to a compensation of 10 percent. No other boxer expressed this opinion. They did not seem to begrudge the manager his share; they just thought that they should have earned more money and gotten better fights. Bernie Friedkin built his money up slowly:

"My brothers were playing baseball and punchball. I wanted to be a fighter. At a main bout in the Broadway Arena, you got a big 500 dollars, of which you wound up with maybe a little better than half—300. I used to come home to Mama and Papa, 'I want you to take so much or so much.' 'No! *Leg im bank. Leg im bank.*'[1] I says, 'Mama take so much. I want you to have so much.' 'No, *leg im bank! Leg im bank.*' So Bernie, legged im bank. So I took $25 for myself for the next fight three to four weeks away. Because I was a clean kid. I didn't smoke, drink.

"When the fight came, I still had $15 left over. I quit the ring after almost one hundred fights with almost $7,000. That was a lot of money; $7,000 in my whole career. The economics of boxing those days was not great. If you were Dempsey or Armstrong or Canzoneri and fought at the Garden, then you could make out. But for the others, it was mostly the clubs. I fought a main event at the Broadway arena, the gross could be maybe $3,000. If I got 20 percent, that was $600. Expenses were maybe $100, trainer and so forth, and then my manager took one-third of the $500, and I got the rest. So when I retired at the age of twenty-three, twenty-four with $7,000, it was a lot of money. Movies were a dime, doctors' visits were $2. A man fights today makes a million dollars. But, thank God, my wife took care of it, secured my money."

Allie Stolz, Danny Kapilow, Herbie Kronowitz, and Artie Levine, who fought after the war in the forties, had the largest paydays. "When I quit," Kapilow recalls, "I had about $60,000 in the bank, which you have to understand was a lot of money then. It's like $600,000 now. So I thought I had some money. But in three or four years, it was all gone.

"My biggest pay night was in Chicago with Johnny Bratton, and $18,000. He was once a champion. But that purse had nothing to do with me. That was in Chicago. He was a big name in Chicago and I had retired already. And they only offered the fight because it would be a good win for him, and I took it because I was just looking to put some money together. I knew I was going to quit.

"I thought I beat him, myself. He was a big boxer in Chicago and he was filling up the arena. It was a record that night. So what the hell are they going to give me the decision for?"

Artie Levine had a number of high-grossing fights (he did not always receive what he was entitled to). Kronowitz also had years of significant earnings. He once fought Levine at Madison Square Garden.

"Levine was my biggest payday. I got $15,000. Gross. I wound up with about $9,000, for myself.

"I always saved. I always used to come home and give money to the house. After that fight I bought my mother a coat. You know a guy gets a big fight, if he's living at home or if he's married, he gives his wife or his mother a fur coat or maybe he buys something. I always did that. First main bout in the Garden . . . I bought my mother something."

Many boxers who earned large sums in the ring were ill-prepared to handle these monies and lost them through poor investments. The following story about Yale Okun told by Leo Bodner played itself out countless times with other boxers.

"Yale once had $75,000 and he says to me, 'Leo, I'm going to buy a golf course.' I said, 'What are you doing buying a golf course? What do you know about golf?' So he said, 'Well, they're building this golf course on Long Island and it's gonna be the greatest thing in the world.' And I said,

'Yeah, it's gonna be the greatest thing for them. What do you know? Put
your money in the bank.' At that time, 3 or 4 percent interest. 'You'll be able
to live. You won't have to worry. You're making some money. Put some
money together.' 'No, this is my chance. I'm gonna . . .' He put in the money.
It was sold for taxes, and Yale became a waiter.

"There's nothing wrong with being a waiter, but he didn't plan. He wasn't
able to do things. Most guys didn't make much money in boxing, or if they
did, it was gone and no careers. Some of them, even Benny Leonard, bought
a restaurant, but the restaurant failed. Some of them had bars and grills. I
think if you look around, not very many were able to have careers and have
businesses and things like that. So I'm very happy the way it turned out.
And I loved it. But it was good for me the way it turned out."

During the period Okun was a waiter, he often worked at weddings and
Bar Mitzvahs held at the Yeshivah of Flatbush, which was located across
the street from our home in Flatbush, Brooklyn. Yale frequently stopped by
to visit. It was obvious that he and my father loved each other, but something
else struck me.

By this time, my father was living a life that was totally removed from
boxing concerns, except for our occasional forays to St. Nicholas Arena or
other boxing venues. I did not realize how much a part of my father's earlier
boxing existence my religious, education-addicted, no-nonsense, almost
puritanical mother had been. It seems that most of their courtship and much
of their early marriage were spent at matches where my father "had a
fighter." My mother, Esther Bodner, developed an empathy and affection
for his boxers, of whom Okun was the most prominent, which was difficult
for me to reconcile with her present life.

When Yale came over, my parents reminisced and joked with him like
the lifelong friends they were. It was just so incongruous to see my mother
engaged in lighthearted banter and sometimes serious discussion with a
prizefighter. In discussing Okun, my mother always said, "Yale is a gentleman." I am still amazed.

Alone among major American sports, boxing has no pension or health-
care system, and never did. Even in its years of glory, no meaningful attempt
was made to institute one. The greed and mistrust were just too great. And
so boxers who have had many fights and who may be injured or brain-damaged, and who have very little money, are required to depend on organizations such as Ring 8 with its minimal resources.

Approximately seventy years ago an organization called the National
Sports Alliance was formed. Its guiding spirit was Nat Fleischer, and its

purpose was to aid distressed boxers. To raise funds, a 50-cent surcharge was added to each complimentary ticket issued at Madison Square Garden. It is estimated that between $100,000 and $250,000 was raised. There has long been a sharp dispute over the use of these funds, and the animosity between Ring 8, for example, and the Alliance continues to this day. Harry Markson was one of the prime movers in establishing the Alliance:

"I heartily disapprove of a federal boxing commission. I think that there are enough bureaucracies in Washington. I think that boxing is not in the national or the world scheme of things, to necessitate a bureau in Washington which would undoubtedly be headed by some political appointee. I don't approve of it at all. It isn't like baseball or football where they have this czar. This is the way boxing has been for a hundred years or more and it should continue that way with its ups and downs and its good guys and bad guys.

"How do you handle pensions? Who's going to handle it? A pension fund? Who's going to contribute to a pension fund?

"We had something called the National Sports Alliance. We have a few thousand dollars left. We are now reduced to four members, of which Rose Lewis is one. We're doing our utmost to dissolve it because we don't have enough requests for monies except from the same few, maybe ten ex-fighters every year. And we no longer have any income. When I was in charge of boxing at Madison Square Garden, on every free ticket, I would put a 50-cent assessment. But they don't permit that at Madison Square Garden any more. That was where the money came from. Now there is no money being put in the treasury, and it lies dead and we're trying to dissolve it. And Rose Lewis came up with an idea about seeing if we cannot give it to the Olympic Boxing Committee. But we are prohibited by the terms of the charter under which we operate by the state. We've gone to the attorney general's office about this to try to give us the release that we need to get rid of this money. We don't want to give it to Ring 8. I'd rather not discuss why. I would rather not discuss it."

Herb Kronowitz has a different perspective on the Alliance's activities.

"I have been very disappointed in Harry Markson. 'Cause the Sports Alliance got money from sports, from events, and they hold money for times when fellows are in need, former boxers or former wrestlers. The Sports Alliance is supposed to give them money. Help them. And it's only recently that we were able to find out how much money the Alliance had in the treasury, through Danny Kapilow. Thanks to him.

"At the time they admitted to finding $90,000. But the fellows who were in need went up there, they threw 'em $50, $40. Guys who were topnotch fighters. Guys like I don't want to say went up there. $40. You don't give a man $40. What's he gonna do with $40? Know what I mean? Give him $500, give him $1,000. And no one knew how much money they had in there until Danny Kapilow found out.

"They wouldn't give it, and any time the subject would come up about, 'Hey how much money is in the Sports Alliance?' 'That's none of your business, you're not supposed to know. Who are you?' 'We're the ones, if not for us fellows you wouldn't have no Sports Alliance, you wouldn't have any money there.'

"Ring 8, on the other hand, has been trying to get a pension for boxers. Former fighters but mainly fellows who are boxing today.

"The money is going to come from fights. From boxing. Every show. These multimillion-dollar shows, $20, $30 million, $100 million-dollar gates. Take 1 percent, take half of 1 percent.

"In the twenties, thirties, forties, and fifties, when there was a lot of boxing, nobody, nobody would speak up. We had fighters who needed money in those days. No one looks after the former boxer. The retired boxer. They just want to use you, while they can."

Rose Lewis was the secretary of the New York State Athletic Commission for forty-six years, from 1937 to 1983. She became one of the trustees of the Alliance fund. "Oh we helped those fighters that were sick. Disabled. Hospital bills. Medical bills. Doctor's bills. We did a lot a work." Rose insisted it was time to dissolve the fund. When I suggested Ring 8 as the recipient, she had a two-word answer: "God forbid."

Teddy Brenner has his own notion as to how a pension plan should work, at least for the Garden main eventers:

"As far as pensions are concerned for boxers, Harry Markson and I came up with a plan that we thought would work. You know in those days, in addition to their percentage of the gate we would give fighters $4,000 for TV money. So we came up with a plan that the boxers would get $3,800. The fighter puts $200 into the pension. Gillette (the sponsor) would give $500, and MSG (Madison Square Garden) would give $300. And they were gonna have a thousand dollars from every main-event fight. That was going to be set aside for the boxer. And they would have a pension. And it was all set. The boxers agreed, and we were gonna put this kind of money in. And guess what—the managers resisted. Not the boxers but the managers. They didn't want any money off the top, I mean, you're talkin' about your one-third cut of $200! And we said to them—I remember Harry and I said to them, 'Listen, you guys—what about us? The Garden and Gillette are putting in $800!'

"But imagine—imagine that shortsightedness! Selfishness! When here's a chance for the boxers to have something finally put aside. So they could have a pension! And what did the managers care? We said to them, 'Boxers have a very short lifespan in terms of boxing. You guys go on forever. You could make more money. You can have fifteen boxers, if you get a third of each, you make a lot of money, if they're good. A boxer has only himself. Who's he going to make money from?' He's uneducated. Usually. This was a terrific thing. And the managers were selfish and stupid!

"As far as a preliminary fighter is concerned, nothing's going to help a preliminary fighter. I mean, who helps the minor-league baseball player? This was at least a beginning. It was a good start. And the managers killed it."

Danny Kapilow has spent his adult life as a union organizer and also worrying about boxers. He is convinced the solution to the pension problem lies in organization: "Today with the money that is generated and advertising, there's no reason why fighters shouldn't have a pension or in-depth medical coverage because of the danger from the injuries in the sport. But you can't get these people to voluntarily come up with the money to do it."

Kapilow has special animus against the Alliance for Sports establishment.

"Well, you can have Harry Markson. I have a particular dislike for those people. They had a boxer's organization where they collected money off the tickets. And no fuckin' boxer, maybe one or two guys ever got anything out of it. They did their own mess with it. They gave each other the money.

"Nobody in the controlling aspects of the sport gives this one thought, and the minute you express it to them, they run like you got the plague. The only thing you can do—and I keep telling these guys—the next time there's a big fight in Atlantic City, all of us come out. We have the big names in our organization, although some of them are dead now. And we march around the casino with big signs. And the TV will pick it up, and the public will pick it up and you'll get something going. That's the only compulsion you have. Nobody's going to do it because you present a good story to them or touch their hearts. But these fighters are so prideful. When I said that, they say, 'I'm going to carry a picket sign outside Caesar's Palace?' I said, 'Listen to me, my friend, I did it for thirty years and I know how effective it can be. That's our only power at this point.' But they're too proud.

"None of them have really made it. OK, that's one thing. But there should be some income they should have today for what they brought into the box office in those days. It's too late for us, but kids today should be getting more, because the money is so much bigger. But they're not and they won't.

"Listen, I found out one thing in the labor movement. If you can't exercise compulsion, nobody's going to give you anything for nothing.

"If you can't effectively call a strike and effectively use your power to gain your way, nobody's going to do it out of a moral sense. This is, I have to share with my brother human being. What they do is, how much can I steal from him? You know how much money TV and the purses and hotels throw off from boxing? It's the easiest thing with a minimal contribution and a fair standard of who's entitled to it and who's not. People can do very well. Forget about $400,000. How about if a guy gets $12,000 a year? You know what I mean? And he matches that up with his social security, at least he doesn't have to come in shamefaced. And he's carried himself. And nobody's giving him a handout. I get morose talking about it. I think of some of these guys and they're such nice guys."

At the beginning of March 1993, the formation of a new organization was announced. It was called BOX and its stated purpose is to raise funds to assist retired boxers. It was headed by Randy Gordon, the former chairman of the New York State Athletic Commission, and Bert Sugar, the publisher of Bert Sugar's *Boxing Illustrated*. The members of Ring 8 were wary of any organization professing to aid fighters which is not headed by boxers and which in its publicity material described itself as having been established to "help the down and out fighter." Two years later it disappeared without a trace, and boxing remains the only major sport that has no system or plan for pension and health benefits.

11

THE WISE GUYS

The year 1919 was the year of the "Black Sox Scandal." Eight members of the Chicago White Sox baseball team were found to have conspired to lose the World Series that year to the Cincinnati Reds. Parenthetically, it was widely assumed that Arnold Rothstein, the Jewish gambler, was behind the scheme. It is known that Abe Attell, a Jewish bantamweight champion of the early 1900s, was the "bag man." During his career, Attell was often suspected of throwing fights. The scandal made sensational headlines. Baseball reorganized itself and federal judge Kenesaw Mountain Landis was hired as commissioner, a post he held until 1945. The legitimacy of a major league baseball contest has never been questioned since.

From time to time, and particularly in 1950, "point shaving" has come to light in the world of college basketball. But these have been discrete occurrences and do not seem to indicate a pattern, although recruiting abuses in college basketball are endemic. Professional basketball, football, and hockey have never been tainted by scandal.

Professional boxing, on the other hand, has a long and undistinguished history of mob infiltration, control, and fight fixing. It is the most unregulated sport. In his book, *Beyond the Ring* (1990), Professor Jeffrey Sammons devotes long sections to various congressional investigations into mob activity in professional boxing. *The Set Up*, a 1949 film starring Robert Ryan, may be one of the best boxing movies ever made. In it, Ryan, a journeyman fighter, is instructed to throw a fight. The film is a riveting depiction of the seamy underside of prizefighting.

Into the 1930s, Jews dominated prostitution, gambling, rackets, and bootlegging.[1] Meyer Lansky, Dutch Schultz, Waxey Gordon, Bugsy Siegel, Arnold Rothstein, and Lepke Buchalter were all Jewish. The gamblers who did business in the rear of each fighting club were Jewish, as were many of the managers and promoters. It was a logical step for the Jewish racketeers to move aggressively into boxing.

It is well known that Ruby Goldstein's contract was partially owned by Waxey Gordon. Abe Attell, as mentioned, was long suspected of throwing fights. Yet, it would be incorrect to assume that "barely any Jewish fighter avoided such temptation or threat" from criminals and gamblers, as Peter Levine states[2] and Howard Sachar[3] implies. The majority of the respondents professed no personal involvement with unsavory characters. Certainly, however, the Jewish fighters acknowledged that the mob element existed. How they were affected differed from boxer to boxer.

According to Leo Bodner, the serious infiltration of the criminal element did not begin until the 1930s.

"In the 1930s, all the racketeers got into boxing because there was money in it. They got into anything there was a dollar in. Prohibition was over. They couldn't make any more money on the beer and liquor and all that stuff, so they started with boxing. They would have grabbed anything to make money with. Not only boxing. I would say that that's a big reason that a lot of Jews got out at the end of the thirties. A lot of the fighters, if they were any good, they knew that the racketeers were going to come in and try to buy their contracts."

Bodner had his own experience with one of his boxers. It demonstrates a certain ad hoc form of Athletic Commission justice.

"I had a boxer. Pretty good guy. I think he was a baker during the day. His name was Gus Rotenberg and he was pretty good. He was a heavyweight, and they weren't that easy to come by. I had him with Red Wald as trainer. And he was up to fighting six rounds. We made a few dollars. He had a fight, it must have been '34, '33 maybe. Around Christmas time, in the Prospect Hall in Brooklyn where they used to have boxing. It was against a guy the Brooklyn racketeers had brought over from Italy. I couldn't get out there in time for the fight because, it was the season and I had to work late. But I was going to finish and then go over to the Prospect Hall. So I told Red to handle him.

"When I get there, the fight was over and he had lost. He was knocked out in the fourth round, and the place was in an uproar. I asked Red what happened, and he said Leo, it was the damnedest thing. This guy comes back—it was a six-rounder—this guy comes back after the third round and he says to himself, 'I forgot, I forgot.' So I said, 'What did you forget.' He said, 'I forgot, I forgot.' The fourth round, down he goes without taking a hit, like a shot. 'Must have been,' Red said, 'that he had promised to go down in the third round.' But he took the dive in the fourth and he didn't even get hit. He must have been scared. He was kind of upset. 'But the dope,' Red says, 'at the end of the fight he crosses his hands on the ropes and jumps out of the ring like nothing happened. The crowd went nuts.'

"Next day, I'm in the store, 53 East Broadway, and as I expected, around 10:30, it's Bert Stand. Bert was the executive secretary of the Athletic Commission. 'Leo?' 'Yeah, Bert?' He says, 'When you have a chance, I'd like you to stop by the office.' They were on 80 Worth Street, kind of right down the block. I knew what Bert wanted and I figured I'm not going to wait, so on my lunch hour I walked over to 80 Worth Street. I go right in and he says, 'Leo, what happened last night?' I said, 'Bert, I was working late. I don't know anything, except when I got there, it was all over and I only know what Red Wald told me.' Bert believed me because I always leveled with him. He says, 'Leo, we're gonna have to lift his license. Do you have any problem with that?' I says, 'No, Bert, I don't. I just want to ask you one thing. Pay him for the fight and then lift it.' The payments were always on the following Thursday. Bert said, 'Okay, Leo. I'll do that, but then his license is gone.' I says, 'OK, Bert, that's fine.' And that was the kind of guy he was. I mean, he knew he had to lift this guy's license but he didn't want to deprive me, or the guy of the last payday. It was a couple hundred bucks the guy made me. It certainly came in handy to me, but there was no way they were going to let him fight again. I think if the guy objected and they had to have a hearing, they probably would not have been able to pay him for that fight. But he didn't object and that was the deal."

The phenomenon of racketeers moving in to take over contracts was a real threat to the managers and fighters. This is how Bodner handled it.

"Abe 'Callahan' Lipschitz was brought to me by his brother. His brother said that he has a brother that goes to college, plays football, and he looks like Schmeling. He did look just like Max Schmeling. I took him up to the Educational Alliance, and Red Wald was training him at the Alliance. He never saw a fight before. We got him a fight in Brooklyn. They had a baseball field in Brooklyn. Bushwick Stadium. He knocked the guy out. First round, second round. Then we got him a few bouts. I spoke to Johnston. I got him one bout in the Garden.

"He did quite well 'til Schmeling was training to fight Sharkey, I think. The fight never came off. I don't remember the reason why. But he was training to fight Sharkey. Yussel Jacobs was Schmeling's manager. I think they told Sharkey to pull out so Louis could fight Schmeling, the second match. Jacobs came over to Red and asked Red if he'd send Abe to train with Schmeling. So Red called me up. I said, 'Why not?' I says, 'He'll learn.' But I told him, 'Tell him to make sure he doesn't hit him. Because, you know, some of those kids, they see an opening with a hook or a right hand, they're bound to hit him and then they'd fire him.'

"He was going to earn $30 a day, which at that time was good money. Thirty dollars a day with room and board. So we sent him up. Sure enough, second day or the third day, he hits Schmeling with a left hook and knocks him down. And that was the end. It happened at that time Al Smith's son-in-law, John Warner was his name, was the head of the state troopers. He was up there on that day and he saw it. So he told some of his state troopers about it, and a lot of them came up to watch it the next day. But the next day, Lipschitz was walkin' around already, he was fired already, he was just walkin' around. So they saw him, and they called him over, 'What happened?' He says, 'They told me to go home.' So this Warner says to him, 'You're a nice looking kid. Why don't you become a state trooper?'

"Meanwhile, I get a call from a guy by the name of Ziggy, which I knew his name but I never knew him. And he says to me, 'Your name Leo?' I says, 'Yeah.' 'We want to buy Lipschitz's contract.' I says, 'It's not up to me. First of all, I'm not his manager. Red Wald is his manager.'

"I says to myself, 'Hey, that's no good. I'm gonna get involved with those guys. They'll give me a couple of dollars and take the whole thing and at the end I'll get nothing but trouble. And they're going to ruin him like they ruined Ruby Goldstein.' I spoke to Red Wald and he agreed.

"I called up Lipschitz. He was still in the camp, and he told me on the phone about this Warner. I said to him, 'Abe, take it.' He says, 'Why?' I said to him, 'Look, I have a good reason why. You'll be better off as a state trooper than as a fighter.' So he took it. And he said, 'I had an idea to take it too.' And I says, 'Good.' And he went up to Malone, New York. That was their headquarters. And he met this girl and her family. The only Jewish girl in town, in Malone. And he married her."

Herbert Goldman is a boxing historian. For many years he has been associated with Bert Sugar's *Boxing Illustrated*. (There is also a *Ring Magazine*.) To Goldman, originally a definite dichotomy existed between gambling and gangsters in boxing.

"Until 1920, when the Walker Law came into effect in New York, decisions were not permitted in professional boxing contests. For instance, in New York, under the Frawley Law, you could have a bout up to ten rounds.

But you could not have an official decision. The reason for that was to discourage gambling, which existed in boxing to such a great extent in that period before World War I. However, people gambled, and in those days, gambling was much, much more prevalent than it is today. A lot of things were much more prevalent because you had no TV. If a man wanted to do anything, he went out at night. There was this whole nocturnal male culture, you know, that disappeared in the fifties. But anyway, these guys and professional gamblers and so forth would rely on newspaper accounts to determine who won. They would decide as to which newspaperman they would go by or maybe two out of three or three out of five newspapers, or whatever. There was one newspaper, I think it was the *Brooklyn Eagle*, which for many fights would actually start off its column with a rundown of the other papers and what their decisions were in the fight. So that was the no-decision era, or the newspaper-decision era.

"In the 1930s, gangsters moved into boxing. There's no doubt about it. I would attribute that to the depression in large measure. And there was money in the fight game, that a lot of gangsters could see. And of course, a lot of it was the repeal of Prohibition where gangsters had to look for other sources of income. And that really stepped up quite a bit at that time when Prohibition looked like it was going to be repealed. It was repealed in '33. And certainly, Primo Carnera, was very much mob-controlled."

Beginning in the 1940s, Frankie Carbo and his henchmen, including Blinky Palermo, ran boxing. Jim Norris, one of the wealthiest men in America, was the promoter at Madison Square Garden. Through the International Boxing Club, he was part of a group that controlled the fighting in every major area in the country. Was it not strange that Jim Norris's president at Madison Square Garden was the professorial Harry Markson? Markson describes the era as follows:

"Jim Norris was immensely wealthy. Someone asked Frank Hogan, the district attorney at the time, why he thought Norris, who certainly did not need the money, associated with the kind of characters that he did. And Hogan's answer was. 'This is his cup of tea.' He didn't need these people, but he got a kick out of associating with them. Frankie Carbo and his group managed to ingratiate themselves, and they made their way into boxing where they had a piece of almost every noteworthy fighter. Norris had two contracts, one with the Gillette companies which called for fifty-two fights a year, and one with the Pabst Blue Ribbon Beer people, which called for fifty-two fights a year. It would have been impossible for him to fulfill those contracts without the cooperation of these mob guys who had all the good fighters. You had to do business with them or you couldn't stay in business.

As one columnist wrote, I was the 'conscience' of Madison Square Garden. I had many arguments with Norris about this. I would say, 'Jim, you gotta get away from this. You can't go on like this.' And his answer was always the same, 'Harry, we can't fill our cards if we don't do business with them.' And so I struggled through. I was in charge of 'The New York Office.' Madison Square Garden was the New York Office. We operated here. Norris operated in Chicago, Detroit, and St. Louis.

"I would say that he was very scrupulous about this. When he was going to meet with these people, I never was there. And I was widely disliked by these people. There were a few occasions where the district attorney assigned bodyguards to me because he felt that I might be in danger. Because the minute I suspected that there was something off color, a little bit fishy. I would run to the boxing commission and ask them to change the officials at the last minute. They would put entirely different officials in. I used to do that, and this was especially during the time of Commissioner Christenberry, when he had his office in the Astor Hotel, of which he was the manager. And I would say, 'Commissioner, I can't tell you what's going on. I just feel that something is not right here and I don't want to know who your officials are' . . . they never announced officials until just before the main event . . . 'I don't want to know who they are, but would you put three different officials in there?' And that happened on several occasions. On a few occasions, it was Norris who stepped in and said about me, 'Leave him alone. Don't touch this man.' Because, I think he felt, and I feel as though this is self-serving, this is what I'm telling you now here, but there were occasions when I felt that if they got me out of there, they would be in real trouble.

"Hymie 'the Mink' Wallman was a guy who was on the edge of the mob. I'm not saying he was a part of the mob, but he was kind of connected. He could have done their bidding. Anyway, he was always being investigated by the District Attorney's Office. I remember one time, I was at the old Garden, meaning the one at 50th Street and 8th Avenue, and my mother or father had just died. And every day at 4:15, I would rush out to go to the Actor's Temple on 47th Street to daven 'Minchah' (pray the afternoon service). I had it timed perfectly, and I would just race. . . . Wallman once said to me, 'You know the D.A. doesn't know where you're running every day at 4:15. He's got you tailed, but they can't keep up with you.' I just had to laugh, because that's where I was going. Not only that, he told me that Hogan said that I was 95 percent honest. Wallman said, 'Well, what about the other 5 percent, Mr. District Attorney?' and Hogan said, 'Nobody in the fight business can be 100 percent honest.' "

To Danny Kapilow, mob influence in boxing is only the most prominent manifestation of a system that robs the young boxer of any control over his destiny.

"Before the war, Joe Gould had been my manager. He got into some trouble during the war. I don't know if you remember. He had gotten a commission in the Port of New York, and there came a time when a lot of landing craft sank in the attack in Salerno in Italy. And when they traced it back, they weren't properly inspected in the New York Port before they were shipped overseas. And he was one of the guys implicated; they threw him out with a dishonorable discharge, and he couldn't get a license after the war. And I wanted to keep him in because I liked him, so he turned over half the contract to Al Weil. And Al Weil then handled it for me from that point on, and he was the biggest thief in the world and it didn't take me long to find it out and that's when I quit.

"I found out you have no control. Yeah, you start out thinking that if you're good, you're going to get fights and you'll make your way, kind of. But that's not completely true, either.

"The implication is that if you don't do certain things, you're not going to get certain fights. And if you holler or you complain that you won't do this or you want to see a statement after the fight was over, or how much money came in and what your percentage was, forget it; you were almost blackballed at that time. Lots of those kids at that age didn't even have the know-how or the sense to ask those questions. They became totally controlled and absorbed by the people that were controlling them and they did whatever they had to do.

"They took whatever they had to take. Beau Jack never got more than $50 in cash a week and three new suits a year, and he thought it was all the money in the world because he came out of the backwoods of Georgia and never got any education at all. You know what Sandy Saddler told me once? He had 160 pro fights. Over two hundred amateur fights. And he won the title in his sixtieth fight. And he told me, 'Danny, I never got more than $1500 after any fight I fought.'

"Rigging was part of it. I was told to take a fall once and I didn't do it, but by this time I was getting ready to quit. I had the guy out in the second round when the bell rang. And I wouldn't go back to the corner for fear of what they might do to me in the corner till the bell rang in the third round. I knocked him out in the third round. And after that, I was persona non grata. But I didn't care because I was quitting anyway. I was too young to be really afraid. I really found out about what could have happened later on. I guess I wasn't personally important enough at that point.

"I had no say in who my manager picked for me. None at all. As a matter of fact, I used to complain, 'Why ain't I getting this guy and why I'm not getting that guy?' and they used to give all kinds of crazy excuses.

"The fighters get nothing. The fighter is the cattle in this situation. All the deals are made way over his head. You see a little of it now with someone suing King for misappropriation of the money. And here, at least you got it on the books. You got records. In those days, you had nothing. There was never a record. You met somebody—when I boxed Rocky Graziano, I came up with my sailor suit to meet Joe Gould under the stairs in Stillman's Gym and somebody gave me $700. And that was the whole thing. And if you are overmatched in a fight, isn't that the same thing as rigging it?

"When Ray Arcel ran the Saturday night fights on TV in the 1950s, he tried to buck the IBC [International Boxing Club]. On Yom Kippur in Boston he was nearly killed by them. Ben Jeby was another guy that they jobbed left and right in those years. There was a guy in those years that was a pretty good fighter—his brother was a featherweight champion—his name was Steve Belloise. And with Steve, there came a time in the 40's that he started to talk around the gym about the fighters' organizing. Somebody quickly put a piece in his ear. That was the end of that. They're not going to talk about it. Ray Arcel was not as talkative as I am. He knew all these things, but he wouldn't say it, because he figured, you know, it's the code. But you know me, I tell all these fuckin' bums, 'You're all thieves and you're no fuckin' good.'

"I got to tell you something. Those were wiseguys. Those were tough guys. This was their baby, and they had their own code. These guys we're talking about now are all college graduates, respected businessmen, TV executives. They're the same fuckin' guys. They're no different. They're worse than those wiseguys used to be. The wiseguys, in the old days, if you came and you needed it, they'd put their hand in their pocket and they'd give it to you. These guys are worse than those guys were in my opinion."

12

A DANGEROUS SPORT

The fear of death in the ring was not a major concern to the boxers, but the fear of brain injury, or punch-drunkenness, was. It was never very far from their minds. A number of boxers expressed gratitude that they had quit in time. Broken limbs heal, but damage to the brain, *dementia pugilistica*, is permanent. It is evidenced by memory loss, slurred speech, tremor, and abnormal gait.[1]

Most books on boxing avoid the subject of brain damage entirely. It is as if silence is the equivalent of nonexistence. One of the exceptions is Jeffrey Sammons' book, *Beyond the Ring* (1990). In a chapter entitled "The Physical Aspects of Boxing," Sammons thoughtfully discusses the medical literature on the subject. Over the years, a number of articles on brain injury in boxing have appeared in scientific journals and popular magazines. Their conclusions are frightening.

The Journal of the American Medical Association directed attention in its January 14, 1983, issue to "Brain Injury in Boxing." According to statistics presented to the AMA's Council on Scientific Affairs, the fatality rate for boxing has been calculated at 0.13 per thousand participants, whereas for college football it is 0.3, motorcycle racing 0.7, scuba diving 1.1, mountaineering 5.1, hang-gliding 5.6, sky diving 12.3, and horse racing 12.8. This is not surprising since boxers are generally in excellent physical condition and are trained to protect themselves in the ring. The statistics for the other sports are created by accidents or injuries that rarely occur in boxing.

The more serious problem, however, as addressed by these articles, is the effect of repeated blows to the head, which are a normal and expected part of boxing. According to one study performed on 224 boxers, 17 percent of those who had boxed for six to nine years displayed brain damage. Another study concluded that the incidence rate may be as high as 55 percent for some form of brain damage.

The June 12, 1983 (Sunday) *New York Times Magazine* contained an essay by David Noonan entitled "Boxing and the Brain." The piece was a layperson's review of the *JAMA* articles and some others. It pointed out that there were 423 ring fatalities in amateur and professional boxing between 1918 and 1961, but also emphasized that far more prizefighters are disabled by brain injury.

On March 10, 1993, the Permanent Subcommittee on Investigations of the United States Senate conducted hearings on Corruption in Professional Boxing. Among the witnesses was Dr. Barry Jordan, the medical director of the New York State Athletic Commission. Dr. Jordan reported that 20 percent of retired professional boxers experience "chronic brain injury." This manifests itself by any one or more of slurred speech, memory loss, personality changes, difficulty with walking, and Parkinson's disease. Dr. Jordan concluded that a long exposure to boxing or a long duration of career contributes to the condition.

By the time I concluded my interviews, I was aware of the dearth of boxing-based (rather than medical or journalistic) material and thought it would be a good opportunity to question the boxers themselves. Except for Bernie Friedkin, who flatly denied that the punch-drunk syndrome exists, the boxers felt that it was indeed a pervasive problem. This is what Bernie had to say:

"If I didn't get hurt, then no one will. You know why? I was a game kid, would take crap from nobody. My career meant everything and I was courageous. And if you hit me or called me a 'Jew bastard,' I went after you. And I forgot my boxing skills. They used to do it to upset me. And I'd make a war out of nothing. All my fights were wars 'cause I had a lotta heart. When you don't have heart you don't make wars. And I got out, okay. I used to get in a hot tub. My Mama would say 'Lay in there ten minutes.' And I'd take a hot glass of milk before I went to bed, so I could sleep better. So maybe that saved me."

Allen: But Bernie you were twenty-three when you quit. What about the guys who were thirty-three? What about George Foreman?

Bernie: But they're not in tough fights are they?

Allen: What about taking a lot of punches to the head; doesn't it affect a
          boxer?

Bernie: I don't see how, 'cause I would imagine most managers and trainers,
          after they see a fella's lost his ability to protect himself he's not goin'
          any further, they would tell him to stop before he got hurt. I don't
          believe there is any such thing as a punch-drunk fighter. I resent very
          much when they show a fighter like Rocky. Why do they make a
          fighter degraded? Why do they do that to an ex-fighter? Or I'll go to
          the mountains, someone will say to me, "Oh Bernie Friedkin, you
          were a fighter? How many fingers do I have up there?' or 'Did you
          ever win?" Why do they make degrading remarks when they see you?
          Or, "Are you punchy?" If you met a movie actress, from show
          business, would you say, "How many times have you been laid?"
          Would you say that?

Julie Bort has a less sanguine view:

"Those punches around the head don't do anybody any good. Around the
kidneys. Around the liver.

"I took them, too. I took a few. Maybe it didn't affect me, but I don't
know if it advanced me any. Let me put it that way. I don't know if it helped.
It's got to affect every fighter. It's got to."

Marty Pomerantz, like many of the others, stressed the importance of
getting out of boxing "in time," before getting hurt.

"The Jewish boxers were clever boxers. They knew what they were doing
in the ring. It was a science. They didn't want to get hurt. They didn't want
to get hit. And I would say that, generally, for a Jewish boxer. If the Jews
could get out, they did. It was common sense. Boxing was not a sport that I
think you should stay with. Look at Muhammad Ali. They call it Parkinson's.
They can call it what they want. He took too many punches. Joe Louis also.
He was incoherent. Maxie Shapiro the same thing. I mean, look at him. That's
too many punches. The body—you can't take that many punches. Boxing
is a wonderful, entertaining sport, but you have to know what you're doing,
have to learn to defend yourself, learn not fighting, but boxing, learn not to
get hit. Then when you've made it, you've made some money, you get out.

"Let me tell you that most boxers don't even fight ten years. That's a very,
very long time. I think that if you look at the careers of most of the boxers,
and I would say, for sure, most of the Jewish boxers, they did not fight ten
years. Including the amateurs. Two, three years amateurs, three, four, five
years in the pros. That was it. They got out."

The boxers were very concerned to demonstrate that they had avoided
the effects of too many punches and are coherent and normal in every way.

Artie Levine, who was interviewed on the telephone, made a special effort to be understood clearly:

"Muhammad Ali was a very, very glib person until it started to catch up to him. He stayed in boxing too long. When he would stand there and let them people hit him. When he would stand there and put his hands on both sides of his head, he would get hit in the head and things like that. These things would hurt you, no matter how strong you are. And eventually, it caught up to him. There are many fighters years ago that were hurt very badly, and they didn't realize they were hurt . . . but I think I was very lucky.

"That was the reason why I quit. I was around. I saw these people and I didn't want to be in it. But I was in it for ten years. I was in it until I was twenty-five years old actually."

Oscar Goldman kept returning to a particular theme:

"But I got my senses. I wasn't hurt in any way. I'm living a normal life. I never had any pains in my fights.

"Listen, your head could take so many punches. If a guy keeps taking punches and punches, like that, you've gotta get hurt. I was a boxer. I didn't punch for punch. I was a good boxer. I avoided getting hit."

Sammy Farber, like so many of the boxers, still relates his boxing experiences to the reactions of his parents:

"My father used to say, 'Remember, the other man has a pair of hands too. You have to watch yourself.'

"My mother never said nothing. The only thing, she worried that I didn't get hurt. After most every fight, I never came home—I always went to the steam baths. And my ears would hurt, I would get antiprogestine. That's clay. And that brings down the heat, so you wouldn't get no cauliflower. Believe it or not. You know what antiprogestine is? You never heard of it? Well, you were never a boxer.

"Anyway that's what I used to do. With hot towels. And overnight the swelling went down."

Sammy wasn't overly concerned that taking a lot of punches would affect him mentally.

"I just told you. My hands used to be swollen from stopping the blows. I was a boxer. A good boxer. Very clever. I told you.

"Never got hit very much. I never got knocked out. You know, a lot of fighters get knocked out. I never got knocked out in fifty amateur fights starting in 1929 and seventy-five professional fights." Farber obviously had a keen sense of the physical danger of boxing, however. His professional career lasted five years and he relates his leaving the ring to the possibility of getting hurt, especially as he was not making much money.

"I had to get out. I didn't want to get hurt. I made up my mind. I'm not going to fight for nothing. Absolutely for nothing to get my brains knocked out? So I quit. I made up my mind that it didn't pay for me. Maybe I was too intelligent. You can get hurt. And get nothing out of it. And wind up in a bughouse or somewhere."

Allie Stolz has definite opinions about the dangers inherent in boxing:

"You know. Like they say, I got away. I got some marks like all fighters get. But I luckily, didn't get hurt permanently. There's a term, 'punch drunk.' It doesn't do you any good. The brain cells can't be helped by it. But, if you don't stay in too long, and you get out of there, you got a shot to be able to speak properly.

"Boxers had a lot of fights then. Many more fights than they have today. It was common for someone to have 100 amateur, 150 professional fights.

"You take all that training and all that punching and all that amateurs and all that professional fighting, it's a lot of punches. It's too much.

"I possibly would do it again. Because I had a love for boxing. But I still wouldn't do it to any great excess, more than I did. You take fellows like Tommy Hearns and Sugar Ray Leonard, the middleweight champion. They stayed too long. I think what they should do is to be more strict in cutting down on the duration of time. There should be no fifteen years and twenty years and eighteen years. I think that a fighter should be allowed to fight so it gives him a chance at least to be kept from being severely hurt. But as you get older, the brain cells and the system start to break down.

"I don't think George Foreman belongs in there. No matter what he does. Because he's fighting stiffs and it's a shame. You see the guys he's knocking out? He made such a great stand against Holyfield. What great stand? What did he do? Holyfield's not that great a fighter. He's a good fighter. But he's not great. And Foreman, what did he do?

"He's much more likely to get hurt now. And he didn't fight a great fight. He's got no leverage left. He's got no power left. He's gonna knock out the 'tuna-fishes.' Come on. Those guys can't fight. It's ludicrous to watch the opponents."

Stolz would let boxers fight for approximately ten years.

"I'd say the most, I would say about eight, professionally. I think so. Because after they were in there ten, eleven, twelve years, then they started to look hurt. Then they start to talk rusty.

"I think I lost eight or nine out of seventy some odd fights. Something like that. I feel better about not having fought that many fights. I didn't need it. That's not a negative view of boxing.

"I could love something and not go to an extreme of getting hurt. I think you have to use intelligence. I think you can't get lost in it and say, 'Well, no matter what I'm going to fight,' and wind up a little bit 'fachatted' or hurt. What good is your money? What good is your popularity? There are many fighters who don't sound too good. There are many fighters that are hurtin' pretty bad. For what? Did you ever see some of these poor souls that have been used as punching bags? I mean, so who needs it? For what?

"Hymie Caplin was my manager, but he never told me when to quit. It was me. Thank God that I had enough of an intelligence and an awareness. That was just my own thinking. Nobody ever told me these things. I just came to this conclusion.

"You know, Ray Robinson stayed too long. Robinson definitely got hurt. Absolutely got hurt.

"Take Mohammed Ali. Ali took too many punches, especially the last two years of his career. He dropped his arms and challenged the opponent to hit him. Like I did with Tippy Larkin. Ali doesn't have Parkinson's. Or he might but its really a result of taking too many punches."

Herb Kronowitz, who was a referee after his fighting career ended, is critical of both Ruby Goldstein and the New York State Athletic Commission in connection with the Griffith–Paret fight held on March 24, 1962. Paret died as a result of the punishment he received that night from Emile Griffith.

"And in the twelfth round, I'll never forget, Griffith had Paret on the ropes, and he was bangin' away, bangin' away, and really the fight should have been stopped, right then and there. But Ruby let the fight go into the thirteenth round. The bell rings and Griffith has him there, and Griffith wasn't a one-punch guy but a good, well-conditioned fighter. He was hitting with a lot of punches. And he was goin', in and out. And Paret, was just standin' there, and standin.' Bang bang bang bang bang bang bang.

"Paret was the champion, and Ruby said, 'Well, this was a championship fight, and you don't stop a fight on a champion.' Never mind championship. I don't care what fight it is. Whether it's an amateur fight or a championship fight. If that fight has to be stopped, I don't worry about nobody. I'm worried about that kid, see, and that's it. There were a few different times when I was refereeing that writers put in their article about it, that the referee wisely saved so-and-so unnecessary extra punishment by stopping the fight.

"You know that in his previous fight, a few weeks before, Paret got slaughtered by Gene Fullmer. Wow! Gene Fullmer murdered 'im. Out in Utah. Paret was welterweight champion, and Fullmer was a middleweight.

It was a nontitle fight. After that beating, that he got stopped by Fullmer, he shouldn't have fought for almost a year after. The beating that he took. Ask anyone who saw that fight who remembers the Fullmer and Paret thing. That wasn't a fight, that was a slaughter. And then, I think it was three weeks later, he goes and defends his title against Griffith. They should have postponed the fight. The New York State Commission should never have let the fight go on, but the Commission's a joke. They let it go. You don't okay a man like that."[2]

Kronowitz is extremely proud of the fact that he was only knocked down twice in his career and never was knocked out.

"I was only down twice, in two different fights. Never flattened. No, thank goodness. No. It could happen though. But if a boxer is knocked down, he should always take an 'eight' count and not get up after two or three seconds. Those extra five or six seconds give you a chance to clear your head. To try and gather your reflexes, come to yourself. A friend of mine, Ruby Kessler in Ebbets Field, we fought in the same show that night. And Pete Scanlon dropped 'im. And Ruby jumped right up, and he was shakin' and they were hollerin' from the corner, 'Get down, get down, take the count, take the count.' He went down and the referee started the count again. And that extra five or six seconds helped him gather himself. He wound up stopping Scanlon. And that was a tough fight."

Charles Gellman was the only boxer interviewed who was a college graduate. He also earned Master's and Ph.D. degrees. For nearly twenty years he was the president of the Jewish Memorial Hospital on Broadway and West 196th Street, where many boxers were treated. Gellman is extremely knowledgeable about brain injury:

"If I knew then what I should have known, I would never have put on a boxing glove in my life. Never. Because, when I got into the medical field, I began to recognize that in your skull, you got a small brain. When you get hit on the chin, that small brain hits the skull and you bleed internally, just like you bleed outside. You get hit on the chin and if you don't 'roll'—that's how they coined that phrase 'roll with the punch'—if you walk in and you get stung with a shot to the nose or the mouth or wherever it might be, and you don't 'roll' with that, that soft brain that rolls around in your skull will hit the skull hard. It's like concrete, that skull of yours. The brain bleeds. And if you bleed internally, you get a concussion.

"Now, you have a lot of fights and you take those shots on the jaw and the chin, by the time you reach the age of forty—like Muhammad Ali—all that bleeding in your skull hardens and when your circulation slows down, you become 'punch-drunk.' You get a 'punch-drunk' syndrome. You can't see the blood, naturally. You see the blood when you get cut on the nose or the face. The reason Ali took those punches was because he knew that if you keep your hands up long enough and tight enough, and you keep hitting so long, you're going to get tired. He waited until the guy punched himself out. In the meantime, he absorbed this punishment, took all his shots, because he was able to take the shots. And winds up, after he reaches the age of forty-five, he's got Parkinson's Syndrome. That's no Parkinson's Syndrome. That's brain damage, plain brain damage. By virtue of the fact that his skull was bleeding that way.

"Today? I think boxing should be outlawed. I'll be the first guy to tell you. I would outlaw it because of the brain damage that I see. Anytime a fighter got really banged up, they would call me. You'd have a fight over in Newark, for example. A guy would take such a terrible beating. The manager knew me. He would say, 'Well, this is a bad business. I'll call Chuck, we'll get our guy over to Jewish Memorial. He'll have his doctors look at him.' I had some pretty good guys in the Sports Medicine Unit. They'd walk in. I'd see the guy with two black eyes, a busted nose, unconscious. And it used to bother me. And the doctor would say to me, 'And you did this?' And I'd say, 'Yeah, I didn't know any better, but I had to make a living.' "

Danny Kapilow was the guiding force behind Ring 8 for many years. He was president of a Teamsters Local and is considered one of the most articulate, effective advocates for benefits to ill and destitute boxers. Kapilow was supposed to fight Fritzie Zivic on August 15, 1942, but that was the day he went into the service.

"About eight or ten years ago, when Ring 8 bought Lou Ambers in from Phoenix to honor him, I reached out for Fritzie Zivic because I wanted to bring him into New York. I found out that he was in the Veterans Administration Hospital in Pittsburgh. So I wrote him a letter inviting him to come in, you know, paying his expenses. And I'll never forget this, because in the letter I reminded him that he and I were supposed to go on August 15, 1942 in the Garden. And that's the very day I went into service and seeing as I got through the war uninjured, that was probably a lucky day for me. He would have probably killed me.

"I wrote that and then a couple of weeks later I got a letter from his wife that said, 'Danny he don't read anything. He don't know anybody. He doesn't remember anything. He's completely gone.' Which is a very sad commentary.

"In my opinion he was gone because of his boxing. But nobody will give you that opinion. But I am a firm believer that the brain damage is horrendous. I grew up with all these kids. I knew them when they started and I see them now. Miltie Kessler, for instance, is one of the few guys who came through it OK. Because he didn't stay around too long, either.

"Maxie Shapiro, though, had a lot of tough fights. And he's not the man he would have been if he hadn't had those fights.

"Allie Stolz is not the person he would have been had he not boxed. Allie was a very bright young fellow, and he was a hell of a boxer. Nobody nailed him more than once every three or four fights with any direct hits. But still, with all of the fights that he had and the talent he fought against, he had problems.

"And I don't know that it hasn't affected me after seventy pro fights. You never know what you could have been. But on the other hand, that's one of the reasons that I quit—I quit early—when I was twenty-seven. And most of that brain damage happens when you start to lose your coordination and you get nailed solid punches. Before that, I can tell you, if I got hit with a solid right hand, every fifth or sixth fight, I was disappointed. But later on, you start to get hit with those things and guys that hung around till they were thirty-five, that's when they began to get the damage. The classic case was Ray Robinson, who was the best of all of them. And he was fine until he stayed around too long.

"When boxers quit at the age of twenty-six, twenty-seven, twenty-eight they were just lucky. With me, I only quit because I was lucky and because I found out they were robbing me and I just wouldn't stand for these guys robbing me and not being able to do anything about it without getting your brains blown out. I said, 'Fuck it, I'll quit. If they're going to keep robbing me, who the hell needs it?' It was lucky, not smart.

"The physical punishment no athlete should have to take, knowing what it does, is the reason boxing should be abolished. I wrote an article that the *New York Times* printed a number of years ago when the AMA came out with a study. And the AMA said what I'm saying. Shortly thereafter, one of boxing's stellar characters, Burt Sugar, who's the worst, well, he writes, 'that's all bullshit, ba ba, ba ba,' you know, and I wrote an article rebutting him which the *Times* printed.

"But nobody pays any attention. The physical and the brain damage that's done is indisputable. It's unable to be remedied. You can't heal it like you do a fractured bone, and it lasts for the entire life. What I found out since is that once the injury is there, not only does it not get better, even after you stop getting hit, it gets progressively worse over the years. And I've seen this because I was with these guys when they started. I was with Sandy Saddler in the gym when he came in from Boston. I was with these guys when I quit, and now I met them thirty years later in the Veteran Boxers, Ring 8, and I can't believe it. Can't believe Ray Robinson. Ray Robinson was a bright, articulate, erudite guy. In the years before he died, it was pitiful. His wife had to lead him around. He couldn't go anyplace without Millie.

"With Muhammad Ali, that bullshit about Parkinson's is fucking bullshit. And I can't believe that somebody doesn't pick it up and say it, all of these so-called reporters. You know where Sandy Saddler is? Did they take you up to see Sandy? We put him in a home in the Bronx, and I can't tell you what he was going through in the years before we were able to get him in there. I mean, horror stories. And he, unable to protect himself in any way. It was horrible.

"But what we do is minimal. And you know what one of the problems is? Most guys won't even come and ask for help. If there's the slightest coherence, they won't come and ask for help because it's like a badge of shame.

"Petey Scalzo. I went to see him. I found out he was in a Veterans Hospital down here in Miami. Two years ago, I went to see him. Petey Scalzo was a very good fighter, had a lot of fights, held a title and after he got finished, he was able to go into show business and make a living successfully, doing the Greek ambassador thing, and he hadn't had a punch for years. When I went to see him in the Veterans Hospital, not only did he not recognize me, he didn't even remember any names we talked about. He didn't even know anything. He was like a walking zombie in a ward there of guys that were shell-shocked and brain-damaged in the war. It was just horrible. And then he died thereafter."

Amazingly enough, in spite of what amounts to an indictment of the brutality of boxing, the boxers, when asked whether such protective devices as headgear should be made mandatory, were unanimous in opposing it, even those who believe the sport should be outlawed or at least severely curtailed.

We're professionals, we're supposed to be able to protect ourselves at all times.

Julie Bort

The public wants to see punishment.

Allie Stolz

Well then, it's like they're sissies. Might as well put on a skirt.

Sammy Farber

The money often was not that great, but the punishment, or specter of it, always was. Why did they do it? Joey Varoff summed it up for many of the boxers.

"Well, there's a thrill. Besides loving boxing, there's a thrill to it. There's something about being in there alone with somebody. I can't explain it to you. I loved it. I loved the sense of challenge. Whether you call it showing off your talent or whatever. Also, it shows you how much guts you really have. You come off the floor, you get knocked down, you get up. You know, I've been knocked down here and there. You get up and it's a matter of self, what you think of yourself, whether you've got courage. I didn't know if I had courage, but I found myself that I had courage. I never quit in a fight. It's something within you."

13

AFTER THE RING

As with all athletes, there came a day in the lives of the boxers when it was time to retire from the arena. The majority of Jewish boxers, however, unlike participants from most other major sports, left the ring while still in their mid-twenties. Either the war provided a natural termination point, or two or more straight defeats convinced them that their career had reached a dead end. "Schoolboy" Bernie Friedkin was twenty-three when he had his last fight in 1940:

"My parents were saying: '*Ven gaist du stop?*'[1] In other words, I had enough, I went up the ladder. Then I lost two fights in a row, which had never happened in my whole career before. So I knew already I'm not gonna go any further. I know I'm startin' to slip! So before I got hurt, I retired. Mom and Pop were after me all the time. But I lost two fights in a row. I lost my desire really. Up 'till now I knew I was going to be champion. And startin' this, when I went as far as I can, so I got out. The money wasn't that great. I was gettin' 500 a fight, of which I wound up with, 250, 300 'leg in bank.'

"When I lost two fights in a row, something clicked in. Had I stayed a little further, I might 've become a little punching bag. Punching bag! I didn't mean "punchy." I say I don't want to be where the other guys could make a reputation at my expense.

"I told my manager, Jay, Frankie Jay Jacobs: 'I'm not goin' any further. I went as far as I could. Now I'm startin' to go down. Before I go down to the bottom, I wanna step out.' My last fight was with Charlie Varre on December 9, 1940. The fight before I lost to Petey Scalzo in a tough fight.

My first fight with him was a draw. I felt I wasn't going any further, that I had lost my youth. I never went to a party or went out. Nothing. In the dressing room before the Varre fight, I says to my manager, Frankie Jay, 'I hope I lose, because I'm getting out and this will clinch it.' 'What kind of talk is that?' he said, 'We'll talk after the fight.'

"Well, it was a pretty good fight, all my fights were, but I had nothing going for me. It was at St. Nick's, main event. Waiting in the corner for the decision, I said to Jay, 'This is it. I'm out, win, lose or draw.' I lost the decision, but I didn't care. It was over for me. Papa was at the fight. When I came out of the dressing room, I said to him, 'That's it, I'm finished. No more fights.' He started to cry, he was so happy.

"Frankie Jay said, 'It's up to you, Bernie.' But I will say a lot of people said to me, 'Hah you'll be back.' 'Cause, other people, you know, they came back.

"But I did not come back because I had gone as far as I could. Always rated one or two, maybe five or six, in my weight class. And I saw, I'm not goin' any further. So why stay in there? Ya know what I mean? And get hurt. My Mama and Papa said, '*Genugga!*' "[2]

Ray Arcel was very influential in Joey Varoff's decision to leave the ring. Varoff began boxing in 1939 when he was seventeen and was in the service until 1946. He then continued fighting until 1950.

"Well, Ray Arcel had a restaurant. Number 1 Fifth Avenue. He knew I wasn't fighting. I couldn't get no fights and I was broke. And I was winning all my fights and getting nowhere. No one would fight me, I was getting discouraged and not making any money and I wasn't fighting often, and he called me and my wife to the restaurant one time and he said, 'Joey, nobody wants to fight you.' I used to take on the toughest and get nowhere. So I got discouraged. I said, 'To hell with it.' I was twenty-seven at the time. I said seventeen to twenty-seven was enough. I got all my marbles. So I got out."

Charlie Gellman was twenty-four when he quit.

"Well, I quit for one reason only. Because, I felt, I got a little bit more common sense, and I decided that this is no career for me and I was advised by Joe Jeannette to get out of there. He says, 'Look. You've reached a point where you're a good club fighter and you can become a journeyman fighter. You'll never be a champ because you're not that good.' He was honest with me. At twenty-four years old, I felt that if I didn't start to think of the future, that if I started taking more punches, I may be walking on my heels. Because no matter how you slice it, the other guy's not standing still and letting you hit him. He's hitting you back."

Marty Pomerantz left training camp to go into business.

"In 1939, I was training for a fight with Pedro Martinez. I was no longer working in the shoe business. I wasn't working because my living at that time was boxing. And I was up at Zeiger's upstate training, and I received a telegram that there was an opportunity for me to go into the shoe business as a partner. We were part of a cooperative, I remember, and somebody died, and there was a chance for me to go in. Kind of have my own business. And I took it. I decided to do it, and I didn't go through with the fight. I left and I think I did the right thing. I wasn't going anywhere as a fighter. You've got to remember there were hundreds and hundreds of fighters in those days. And it was hard to get main events, you had to be connected, much less get a shot at the championship. It was a tough living. Very hard. You had to constantly be in condition because you didn't know. You could be called to fill in. And it was depression times and the money wasn't even that good. So when there was a chance to go into business, I took it."

To Allie Stolz, fighting Bob Montgomery when he was not prepared signaled to him that it was time to stop. It was 1946, and he was twenty-eight years old.

"Well, I decided with the Montgomery fight, when I went on the honeymoon, that was a booboo. That was a goof, and I felt that if I couldn't do what I was supposed to do, this is the end of it. And rightly so, because I got my marbles. If I made another $100,000–$200,000, so what?"

Herbie Kronowitz was a crowd-pleasing fighter and an enthusiastic interviewee. There were not many fights that he thought he lost, and he was never knocked out. From 1946 until 1950 he was ranked in the top ten in the middleweight division. He was twenty-seven when he retired.

"I saw I couldn't get the fights I wanted. And I was fighting guys, why even here in New York, I'd fight a guy, I'd win the fight, I didn't get it. And that used to eat me up.

"I didn't get the decision. I won it. I won the fight but I didn't get it. Because, 'they' have the in. Friends of mine came in to see me before the fight, at least four different fights. They said, 'You better knock 'im out.' I says, 'Believe me I'll kill 'im if I can.' An expression. 'You better knock 'im out or you lose.' 'What do you mean?' They got the referee and one of the judges."

Herbie lost his last six bouts. In his last fight, Joey DeJohn stopped Kronowitz by a technical knockout in the first round.

Very little statistical data has been accumulated on the post–ring occupations of boxers. In 1952, S. Kirson Weinberg and Henry Arond gathered information on ninety-five former boxers, of all ethnic backgrounds, who were either champions or contenders. They discovered the following: eighteen remained in boxing as either trainers or managers; two became writers; twenty-six worked in, owned, or "fronted" for taverns; two were liquor salesmen; eighteen held unskilled jobs (usually in steel mills as the article was Chicago based); six worked in the movies; five were entertainers; three were cab drivers; three had newsstands; two were janitors; three were bookies; three worked at race tracks; and two were in different businesses.[3]

Steven Riess was able to collect information on thirty-six former Jewish boxers and found that only one was a manual worker, four were in the tavern or restaurant business (11.1 percent as compared to 27.4 percent in the Weinberg study), ten remained in boxing (27.4 percent compared to 21.19), and twelve, or 33 percent, owned businesses or had white-collar jobs compared to 2.1 percent in Weinberg's study.[4]

The Jewish boxers whom I interviewed provided their own statistics, which seem to fall somewhere between the Weinberg and the Riess conclusions. But far more interesting were the stories behind the numbers.

As in so many other things, Maxie Shapiro is in a category all his own. In 1948 Maxie stopped boxing for four years and then made a very brief comeback.

"I got into the movie business. I got a Screen Actor's Guild card and I did bits. Small walk-ons. In different movies that came to New York. In fact, I was in Rocky Graziano's movie. *Somebody Up There Likes Me*, with Paul Newman. I got extra parts in movies that paid $25. Today they pay $100 for just a walk-on. I did that. And that's about it.

"Then I fought in '52. I think I won it too. But I couldn't get into the big money. After '52? I didn't do much. I just sort of. . . . I don't know, I can't remember. I can't think what I was. . . . It seems I've been out of work all my life."

Herbie Kronowitz owned taxicabs and then in 1970 became a salesman. Herbie was also a boxing referee and judge for nearly thirty years. Curly Nichols and Joey Baker were in the taxicab business. Sammy Farber owned a bar and grill for thirty-two years and now works for a brokerage company. Julie Bort owned several luncheonettes and tended bar occasionally at Aqueduct Race Track.

Allie Stolz had a number of appearance bookings and entertainment contracts set if he had won the Angott fight. They did not materialize. All he will say is that he was "in business" after his fighting days were over. Al Reid was in the fast-food business for several years with a brother-in-law in California. He then returned to New York. He became a boxing judge. Sigi Ashkenaz became a watchmaker. For fifty years he operated a very successful jewelry business in Norfolk, Virginia.

Bernie Friedkin worked for the Ronzoni Macaroni Company and also as a dispatcher at Kennedy Airport. In an ironic twist, he received the job through the good offices of Harry Davidoff, Al "Bumy" Davis's brother. Friedkin also judged boxing matches. Marty Pomerantz was in the shoe business and then owned taxicabs. Miltie Kessler owned a pool room and a bar with his brother Ruby, who was also a boxer (a brother act was very rare among the Jews). He then sold office equipment for many years and more recently went into business with his son Stephen selling foreign cars in New York. A second son is also in the business.

Miltie believes that athletes generally are not successful in business.

"I don't think it has to do with them being Jewish or anything. I think what happens to boxers is what happens to any person in sports. Or maybe mostly in boxing. Because they really didn't get an education. They boxed probably since they were seventeen or eighteen years till they were twenty-five or twenty-six. They had no education. They didn't know how to do anything. They didn't know how to take care of a business. Most boxers. I mean, what did they know about business? So how could they do good? I'm not speaking for all of them. Actually, I'm not speaking for myself, you know, or a guy like Danny Kapilow, or even Kronowitz. But most of those young guys after they came out of sports, they weren't trained for a business. They didn't have too much education. What could they do?

"They didn't grow up, you know. They didn't mature from eighteen to twenty-five, those seven or eight years. They didn't really know what the world was all about. They were in sports. Somebody was managing their money for them. Their itineraries.

"This is true of Jews, blacks, Irish, Italians. Anyone. Except for the certain individuals that have foresight to be able to take care of themselves.

"You take a guy like Allie Stolz. Had some good paydays. Fought for the championship. And he was an intelligent guy. And he's an intelligent guy to this day. But he just can't make it.

"Because they didn't mature or whatever. They didn't get that experience. I don't know. It was difficult for boxers, after their careers were over, when they were only in their twenties, to come down to earth and to hold down a job from 9 to 5 just like everybody else in society. Very difficult. The more popular they were, the more difficult it became to do something like that.

"I had a problem with it. I wasn't a well-known, popular fighter. I was popular in my area, but if I went out of my neighborhood, nobody knew who I was. But still, when I stopped boxing, when I got knocked out the last time, I felt I needed to be rehabilitated or something. I didn't, but I look back at it now. I was depressed about it, stuff like that. I'm proud now to say that I was a fighter and that I thought I was a good fighter. Some boxers succeeded in business. I can't say that it didn't happen, but very rarely.

"I would do it all over again, but I would do it differently. I would take care of myself. Yeah, I would have trained."

Oscar Goldman began his post-fighting career by taking numbers. He then went into the Army and when he was discharged spent the next thirty-five years working for the Post Office. He has a talent for art and lettering and spent his time making signs, which he liked to do. He also received a pension that he found more than adequate.

Joey Varoff had a career which he loved and of which he is very proud.

"After I quit fighting I said, 'What the hell do I do for a living?' So someone gave me a bartender job. I'm not a drinking man. I hated it. I said, 'I don't want to do this for a living.' So I went to a school to be a policeman for New York City. I knew I was slightly under the height, but they told me, 'Don't worry about it.'

"You had to be 5'8". I was 5'7-7/8". That's why I ended out here. And I studied my ass off and I passed the exam. I got 72. 70 was passing. I just made 72. But the test was tough. I came out high on the list. And what do you think? They failed me for being an eighth of an inch too short. So help me God. I ran into the son of a bitch. I called him an anti-Semite. He wouldn't pass me. I said, 'Look, I've got two children and I'm a prizefighter and I want to be a policeman so bad.' And he says, 'Sorry buddy, you're too short.' If I'd a had a gun, I would have shot him.

"Then someone told me they needed firemen and policemen in Washington, D.C. And the height requirement was a half inch shorter. I took the test and I came out very high. I made a very good mark, and they called me a couple of months later. And so I said to my wife, 'I'll go down myself and I'll try it out.' So I went down there and I loved it. I loved the job.

"It was corny. I always wanted a job with a little prestige and adventure. I wore a beautiful uniform. You fought fires, which was exciting. Even though I got scared many times, it was exciting. Riding fire engines was exciting. Then after a while, you drove fire engines, you know. And it was a thrill. And it was a very well-respected job. I was proud that my kids knew I was a fireman. It was something that I really loved.

"I started out with $2,900 a year, which wasn't bad at that time. And you know what my retirement is? Fifty-five thousand a year. Retirement. I was a chief, don't forget.

"I worked my way up to chief. First a technician, sergeant, lieutenant, captain, acting chief, then chief. All those years.

"Anti-Semitism in the fire department? Definitely. Definitely. Not tremendous, but there always was. And as usual, little Jewish guy, they hear an ex-fighter, everybody wants to try him out. I always made a joke. They tried me out twice a year for thirty years, and I had sixty knockouts.

"I got into a few fights. I can tell you a funny story. I don't look for trouble, but I cannot stand to take shit from anybody. Thank God I could take care of myself. So I went into the fire department, right away I saw a clown sitting there saying, 'Fuck the Jews.' There were no Jews in the fire department, you know, about five out of 1500 men. I remember the first time I heard some officers talking, 'God damn Jew from New York. Too bad Hitler didn't get them all. They killed Jesus.' And all that stuff. I didn't say nothing. You know, I didn't want to get into trouble. I'd get fired. So I let it go over my head and I'd hear other nasty things. I used to tell them in a nice way. 'I don't want to hear this bullshit. I'll knock the shit out of you.' I was in the fire department for two years, and I had a fight with a guy, a big anti-Semite. They transferred me to a different company so it wouldn't make problems. And I was in that new firehouse, and the next thing you know some guy called me a 'Jewboy' and I took him. I thought, Gee, they're going to fire me. I'm taking on everybody. I wasn't taking no crap, you know. But nothing happened and I was there for five years. Then I went to another firehouse and I walked into the door and the first thing some Irish guy said to me, 'Hey Cut-Cock.' I said, 'Oy, Gevalt, another one.' I said to the guy, 'You and I are going to have to go outside.' So I walked to the door and the captain said, 'Hey, that shit don't go around here.'

"The other guy could say what he wants, but I didn't mind. I loved the job. What a job it was. Ah! I loved it.

"My wife used to say to me she never heard me say one time in my career that I didn't want to go to work. Let me tell you some of the goodies about it. When I was a chief, they give you three uniforms. Gold all over the place. Badges, this and that, gold stripes and all that stuff. Beautiful. I had my own office with my name on it. I had my own room with lockers and everything else. I had my own beautiful bathroom. I had my own fire chief's car, red car. And I had a chauffeur. I had an aide who did all my administrative work.

"When I walked into a firehouse, any firehouse in the city, the man at the watch desk, he'd sound two bells and the whole God-damned firehouse got to line up for me at attention and I addressed them. I loved all this crap.

"I was in charge of about five firehouses, about twelve to fifteen pieces of apparatus. About 150 men, I guess. You were a chief no matter where you were in that fire department.

"Oh. What a job that was. And they salute you wherever you go. They gotta salute you. A shmuck like me. You know, I was very happy. I loved it."

Artie Levine had a very successful career financially. After boxing he owned a meat business, set up a local for the teamsters union, and was then a Volkswagen salesman. He is now retired in North Carolina where he lives with his second wife.

Taxicabs seem to have a certain attraction for fighters. This was also Danny Kapilow's entré into his post-boxing world.

"Well, in '47 I packed it in and I made one of the biggest mistakes of my life then, because the first thing I did when I got out I bought a taxicab and the biggest mistake of my life was I sold it back in thirty days rather than stay in that field. I would have been a millionaire by now.

"I would have built a fleet. I remember sitting down with my wife and saying, 'Listen, either I'm going to sell this thing,' and in one month I made a two or three thousand dollar profit, 'or else I'm going to take fifty or sixty thousand and I'm going to buy three or four.' And I decided not to do it and that was probably the biggest financial mistake I made in my life. But I can't complain. Everything worked out OK for me.

"After that, I joined the local of NATSE, the National Alliance of Theatrical and Stage Employees. They did the work in the Coliseum bringing the business shows in and out. I was looking to get a card in the big local, in the theaters, you know; but I started in that local, 829, and from there I got interested in the labor movement, and then later on I was able to get a charter from the Plating Jewelry and Novelty Workers and then I began to organize. And then eventually, I built that local and got a Teamsters charter from Jimmy Hoffa in 1968 and continued in that until I retired in 1986.

"Hoffa said to me when I went to Washington to bring my local into the teamsters and he found out I had been a professional fighter. He said, 'You must have been crazy. How could anybody with any kind of sense do anything as stupid as that?' I'll never forget that. That's the way he felt about it."

Charlie Gellman graduated from Columbia School of Mines (now Engineering) and also earned a Master's and Ph.D. degree. He tells a fascinating story, one that combines his love for boxing with his formal academic training.

"After the war was over, I worked for a company called Para Equipment Company. Para Equipment who did some war work invited me to be the general manager, and they were starting to make bicycles for children. They had a factory and we had metal stamping equipment left over from the war, and I stayed there for a couple of years, from around 1945 to around 1948. Then Israel became a state—and applied for an export-import bank loan from the U.S. government. And they got $200 million as a loan in an effort to develop the country. They set up an office here called the Government of Israel Supply Mission, and they invited me to be the technical advisor for the purchase of steel. The country needed water, and they had to pump the water through steel pipe. They had no facilities for making steel pipe or buying steel pipe. But I was familiar with steel, and they needed somebody to purchase the steel, to get the specifications for them and come over. From that, I went to Israel and then I was asked to help develop the hospitals over there as an engineer. I worked on the Beilinson Hospital, now called the Sheba Hospital, and then, I came back to the states, because my kids were born, I couldn't stay there too long. And I worked through the supply mission to help develop that hospital along with purchasing other material like tractors and all that.

"When Beth David Hospital, at 161 East 90th Street, lost their executive director—this was back in 1952—they were looking for a new director. Louis Glickman, who used to have a big real estate company was a member of the Board of Directors of Beth David. He says, 'I've got just the guy to be the executive director.' And sure enough, I met with Harry Helmsley, Larry Wein, Louis Glickman, and they hired me to be director of Beth David Hospital. Then I went to the United Hospital Fund, took a lot of courses, went to get a degree in public health, and I wind up to run that hospital at Beth David. Then it moved to Grand Central Hospital which is on 42nd Street, which is now the Ford Foundation.

"That became the 42nd Street Beth David Hospital, and I stayed there until about 1962. In 1962, the director of Jewish Memorial Hospital was seventy some years old and he was going to retire. I knew that they were going to shut down Grand Central, so I talked to some of my board members and they knew some of the board members of Jewish Memorial, one of which was Henry Schenk of Trade Bank. And there was Murray Baron who was a lawyer at that bank. And there was Milton Heller and a few other people from plumbing supplies, and I became the executive director of Jewish Memorial Hospital at 196th Street on Broadway, which ultimately led to the presidency of Jewish Memorial. It's not called executive director; they changed the name to president because that became fashionable.

"Jewish Memorial was later torn down. What had happened was Columbia Presbyterian Hospital was at 168th Street and expanding. Funding came through the State Department of Health. They felt that they couldn't have four hospitals up there. They said that the cost was terrific. They had St. Elizabeth, Siddenham Hospital, Jewish Memorial Hospital, and now the Logan Hospital which was formerly the Knickerbocker Hospital, all up in that area. They thought they would close the four hospitals and fund the expanded Columbia Presbyterian. At that time I was almost seventy already, and I had to get out. I didn't mind.

"I'll tell you something. My boxing background had a lot to do with my career. In 1959, the unions started to come into hospitals. What happened is that Leon Davis was the head of Local 199, which was the radical communist union and he wanted to get raises. He had a job to do. The law in 1959 provided that hospitals did not have to be unionized. There was a special law. Because you cannot have a third-party organization get involved in health care. You can't have people quit. You can't have people strike. So he got together with the Central Labor Council which was Harry van Arsdale, and he said 'This is a lucrative market. We're going to organize hospitals and nursing homes and stuff like that.' They get paid dues so it was very lucrative, and they went into a whole big program in 1959, when I was at Grand Central Hospital. They picked on the Jewish hospitals first because they felt we were the most liberal. One was Beth David; the others were Mount Sinai, Beth Israel, Montefiore, Beth Abraham Home. They hit five hospitals. They were going to strike us if we didn't go along with them.

"How did they go about it? With muscle. They put sugar in the gas tanks of our ambulances. They rip the sinks out. They steal your cook. They take him up to the Catskill Mountains, and they lose him so you can't feed the patients. We were horrified by this. I was, at that time, deeply involved in boxing, and I was involved with Ring 8 and Ring 21 and Ring 14; Ring 14 was Hudson County. I brought all the fighters over. And they worked per diem. Mopping the floor, working. Wagner was the mayor. Oh, boy! It was murder! And they started bringing in goons. Well, one guy comes in my office and he wouldn't let me out. And I says, 'If you don't let me out, I'm going to knock the shit out of you.' He wouldn't let me out; I busted his jaw. And they put another guy in, and I busted his jaw. He wouldn't come to my emergency room, so we took him to Bellevue Hospital.

"The doctors, of course, didn't go on strike. So Mayor Wagner calls me down the next day, and he gives me a lecture and sitting alongside of him is Harry van Arsdale and he says, 'We know you were a fighter. We know you're a tough guy. But this is a labor town. You can't do this. You can't do that.'

"Then the television came and all the fighters were around me in my room. I'll never forget. Johnny Colan was there and Mark Hogg was there. Al Reid was there. Phil Reuther was there. Paul Berenbach was there. They were all helping me because I was helping them out.

"Johnny Colan had an insurance agency, but he took time out to come there. He's a sweet guy. He's as fine as silk.

"I became involved in helping the boxers medically. It started at Beth David. I'll tell you one incident. Al Singer got badly beat up. He was involved with the mob and they didn't know what to do with him. And a lot of the cops knew Al was a boxer. He was the lightweight champ. He was beaten by Jimmy McLarnin who I still keep in touch with, by the way.

"Singer was hurt and somehow or other they brought him into St. Claire's Hospital, and along the line, Charlie 'Phil' Rosenberg or Champ Segal or one of those guys said, 'Look, get him over to Charlie Gellman because he got the best over there. Charlie will see that the right doctors get on the case right away.' So they brought him over to my hospital and I tried to talk to Al. And I tell you something, he started to mumble, and I was heartbroken. I remember Al when he was a real clean kid. He was always involved with the mob people, but I saw him and I was shocked. And then I recognized that these guys got nothing. I had to cover myself because I couldn't do things for nothing. I had to find a way to do it. I had a good rapport with the medical board at Beth David, and I said, 'Look fellas, you know, I don't have to tell you that I was a boxer. You know that. There's a lot of very fine boxers out there and you guys are sporting people. Would you be good enough to take whatever insurance they have or any assignment?'

"Most of the boxers were over sixty-five. I think this was before Medicare. But some of them had no money, so there was welfare at that time, and welfare would pay X number of dollars. Would you believe that they all agreed to take whatever they could get? As far as the hospital was concerned, I would arrange with the Social Service Department to apply for welfare for them and whatever they would give me, it would work out. So I got the consent of the Medical Board and then the Board of Trustees.

"When I moved to Jewish Memorial Hospital, I followed the same procedure. But then, when Mickey Walker got into the hospital, I said to my boxing friends, 'Look, some of these expenses I can't take care of because they won't give me allowances for his clothes and pajamas and stuff like that.' So Willie Gilzenberg says, 'Don't worry about it, Charlie. I'll get together with all of the promoters in Pennsylvania and we'll try to get a fund together.'

"Willie Gilzenberg. Late in life he started World Wide Wrestling. I got that money up to about $10,000–$15,000, and I had extra money to use to buy certain things for them. I had trouble with Mickey Walker. Mickey was a rough guy. You couldn't keep him in the hospital. He had eight wives. They used to come and visit him. Once in a while they'd pick him up in a car and go out of there. And I had to go look for him half the time. I had to use the extra money to pay extra guards to watch him.

"Jack Dempsey came into the hospital. He had terrible arthritis. And of course, Jack Dempsey and his wife Deeana, we were very, very close. Jack Dempsey was like my father. He was at my daughter's wedding.

"He was not a rich man, Dempsey. Everyplace he went he never had to pay for a meal. They'd take care of him. I knew his wives. One was Estelle Taylor. One was HannahWilliams. And the last one was Deeana. She was Jewish. Lovely lady. And I knew the children. Dempsey's children used to call me 'Pop.'

"Tommy Loughran came up, Jackie "Kid" Berg came up, he caught his finger in the door of a taxicab. Billy Soose would come over. Johnny Addie died there. When he was critically ill, they rushed him there. Bobby Gleason who ran Gleason's gym died up there. Charlie "Phil" Rosenberg died up there. Babe Orlando. Some of them came too late. Whenever Joe Giardello would come up, he'd come in. Chico Vejar's kid had cerebral palsy. When they needed help, they would call me. There was a relationship that's been going on for twenty some odd years. And I ran clinics for them. When Roberto Duran was training for Sugar Ray Leonard, he hurt his back up in Grossinger's. Ray Arcel called me immediately. He and Freddy Brown. He said, "Look, we got to get him down to you." He came to my hospital. We stabilized him.

"We took care of Gene Tunney. Gene Tunney in my opinion was the greatest heavyweight around. This guy had class. He wasn't too friendly with the Jewish people until he met Bernie Gimbel. It wasn't like he was unfriendly. It was just, he was a little cold. Ultimate gentleman, until he took to drinking later on. Which killed him.

"I used to take him to Jewish Memorial to dry him out. This clean liver. This terrific guy. Later he had a lot of trouble. You know, his daughter killed somebody, I guess her husband or whoever it might be. Another son drowned in an accident. One of his sons was a United States senator. He himself married a rich woman by the name of Polly Lauder. They lived in Greenwich, Connecticut. It was not unusual for her to call me to tell me he fell, he opened his head. The chauffeur would drive him over to Jewish Memorial. He had started to become an alcoholic.

"Oh, I had long days. Calls used to come in 3–4 o'clock in the morning at Jewish Memorial; I ran five ambulances up there and 250 beds. In Beth David there were three hundred beds. I had twenty-six clinics going all the time. And we had a very active emergency room. We had our obstetrics. We delivered almost three thousand babies a year. We had a mental health clinic, affiliation with New York Medical College as a teaching institution. We had quite an organization. No question, the boxing made it all happen."

As in other areas, the values of the Jewish boxers regarding marriage were very traditional. With rare exceptions, they married young Jewish women from their neighborhoods and remained married. Of all the interviewees, only Allie Stolz (twice) and Maxie Shapiro have been divorced. Joey Varoff was the sole boxer to wed out of the Jewish religion. (Ray Arcel, the trainer, married a non-Jew who died, and he later married a Jewish woman.) Every boxer had married.

The script for Joey Varoff's real-life marriage could have been taken from the fictional movie, *His People* (1924).

"My wife and I knew each other since she was nine and I was thirteen. She knew I wanted to be a fighter since I was a youngster. She was not crazy about it, but she accepted it.

"You'll laugh. She came from the lower East Side, right in my neighborhood. An Irish girl, believe it or not. And the only Irish girl in the neighborhood. But there was no problem because she speaks Yiddish, understands Yiddish. Got married in Yiddish. We did everything in Yiddish. So we had no problem.

"My wife knows Yiddish better than Jewish people know it themselves. She was the only Irish girl in the neighborhood. It was very close. We were childhood sweethearts. I was thirteen, she was nine. We were inseparable. And my mother, I loved her, but my mother used to say to me, 'Yossel, Margie is a wonderful, darling girl, but you know, she's an Irish girl and it's not nice.' I was thirteen. I would say, 'Ma. I'm thirteen years old. I'm not getting married.' Ended up getting married when we got old enough.

"My parents weren't happy, but they accepted it. You know, we got married in Jewish and all that stuff. After a while they learned to accept it and love her."

Artie Levine had a problem which was the reverse of Joey Varoff's.

"It was 1946 and I was a comfortable boxer at the time. I could live very comfortably. I had a couple of cars a year. I didn't drink or smoke or anything like that. I met Mimi at a social club in Brooklyn, and we went together for a year. It was a change of life for me. I didn't know there was such a thing you could call love. She was a very intelligent girl. She was a very smart woman and she was a school teacher. She graduated Magna Cum Laude, Phi Beta Kappa, from Pratt Institute and from Queens College. She was an artist, too. And she was very adept. We got along very well. We were married thirty-seven years. We had a very good marriage."

Levine's problem in marrying Mimi was that while his father was Jewish, his mother was not. Technically, he was not a Jew (which in Orthodox and Conservative Judaism is determined by matrilineal descent), and this was important to Mimi's family.

"I didn't even think of religion until Mimi came along. I didn't think of it at all. It wasn't an important factor to me, but it was important to her. That was the stumbling block right from the very beginning. I wasn't Bar Mitzvahed or anything. It was a very difficult thing with her and her father.

"We overcame it together. I went to a *mikvah*, I was immersed in water. I had my pecker, I couldn't use it for a month. I had gotten married a couple days later. I was incapacitated; it was terrible. I had about half an inch cut. It was a very difficult blood letting, in a sense, and I had a Minyan. I think I had twelve men in there. Eight men, I forget exactly what the Minyan was. And I went into a kosher home."

Levine's wife died several years ago, and while visiting a former fighter by the name of Harry Bauman in a nursing home, Levine met a lady who was visiting her mother. The woman is not Jewish, but she and Artie were married in 1987.

"I'm not exactly close with my children, now, because I married out of the faith and I have Jewish children. It makes it very difficult.

"They very definitely resent it. And we're just getting over that together. We're getting through it more or less, and they're calling me, gradually. I'm getting phone calls. For a couple of years, I didn't get phone calls from them. But I'm happy. I have a wonderful home. I'm comfortable. I have a beautiful wife. I married a shikse. And that's all."

So Artie Levine, the non-Jew who married a Jew, became the Jew who married a non-Jew.

Bernie Friedkin was twenty-nine, older than most boxers, when he married Leonore. But Bernie knew what he was waiting for.

"Everything I do, my guiding light is this lady here (pointing to his wife, Leonore Friedkin). Nine years my junior. She watches me like a mother watching their kids. 'Take your pills, take your vitamin pills.' I forget, I don't know, I'm '*fablunget*' [mixed up]. She watches me like a mother watches a baby. So I'm a lucky man.

"We were married in '46. I was twenty-nine, and my mother and father never saw me with a girl. I says, 'When I get married, when you see me with a girl, that's the one I'm gonna marry.' I was very picky. I didn't bring flaunt girls. I come home one day, 'Mom. Pop. I'm gettin' married.' 'Hah? Where? Who?' My brother-in-law was in the jewelry business. He went out and got me a ring which I told him to buy me. Three months later we're married. Now my family loves her more than they love me. 'Cause she earned it.

"I met her in Lake Mohegan. I rented a place there with some friends. And she was there. Her mother had a place there. And I asked her to dance. I took two, three dances with her. I was impressed! I took her to the bar for a drink. She says, 'I'll have a Coca-Cola.' Oh my God, I'm waitin' for this all my life. So people say, 'How do you know she wasn't fooling you?' I said, 'I been around long enough to know the real stuff.' We go to weddings she has a piña colada. A piña colada. You know what that is, a mixed nothing?

Al Reid's wife, Kathryn, was fully an equal partner in his interview:

"When I met Al he was not boxing any longer. I had no regard for boxers at all. And when I did marry him my father said, 'You married a boxer?' My father sang opera. He was a teacher. My mother could read and write, she was a literate woman. Her dad, my 'Zadie' was a very learned man in Europe. I mean, 'You're marrying a boxer?'"

"My parents had a store. My mother-in-law walked by and she cased me. I'll never forget it. I was standing behind the counter, and I was also working in show business. I looked at her and I said, 'Who's that woman?' and then Al introduced me to her. I said to my Mama, '*Du glachst dem?*' She says, 'Yes *A feiner mensch*.' She asked, 'Is he good-natured?' I said, 'Yes.' 'That's good.' And that was it. But my father said, 'A boxer?'

"In those days, people tied in boxers with being rough people, bad people. It's a different life. My father also wasn't so happy that I was a chorus girl. He thought I should've studied more ballet. But I did teach ballet eventually. And the fact that I did a specialty, and that I was innovative, and that I was creative, he only said, 'You should be a ballet dancer, or marry a doctor or a lawyer.' 'Cause everybody in the family is a professional. Well, I married a professional boxer.

"We got married and then we had a Jewish ceremony. First we eloped, and then we had the Jewish ceremony. We had a whole gang of boxers there and showpeople. It was really a glamorous kind of wedding. It was at the Beethoven Hall. Down on the lower East Side. About 14th Street.

"This is funny. Leon Gold was the rabbi. When I worked with Molly Picon, Leon Gold was in the show. And when he saw me, he says, 'What are you doing here?' I says, 'I'm the bride.' And he was the Rabbi!

"Oh God, I have to look at the wedding picture. Patsy Giovanelli, Johnny Colan, Tino Raino—a whole bunch of them. They've been Al's friends since before the service, but especially then."

Every boxer had children. Artie Levine and Sigi Ashkenaz were the only ones who had as many as three; the rest had one or two. As with many other depression-raised families, this may have been a reaction to the relentless battle they and their parents fought to feed larger households during the 1930s.

If the boxers did not pursue educational opportunities or possess degrees, the same can hardly be said for their children, many of whom are college and university trained. The boxers and their wives are extraordinarily proud of the academic and professional achievements of their children.

Sigi Ashkenaz has a son who is an attorney. Al Reid's daughter is a biomedical engineer, and his son is an investment banker. Curly Nichols's son is a college graduate who has elected to own and drive a hansom cab in Central Park. Miltie Kessler's son owns Stephen Kessler Motors. Bernie Friedkin's daughters are teachers.

Among the offspring of the boxers are teachers, businesspeople, civil servants, housewives, accountants, doctors and white-collar employees. Very few are blue-collar workers, and none is remotely connected with boxing or ever has been. Most do not even like the sport, but they are proud of their fathers' achievements.

Among the sons and daughters there are several intermarriages and divorces. The boxers are reticent to speak of them. The fighters are strongly identified with Judaism and the community values with which they grew up (in most instances, largely Jewish). Intermarriage and divorce are not among them. If the boxers do not make a religious judgment about having non-Jewish grandchildren, they certainly make an ethnic and cultural one.

But the thirst for education—the fondest dream of Jewish parents—realizes its full flowering in the boxers' children. Marty Pomerantz's view of education and his wife's role in it was typical of many boxers.

"You know, I told my parents, if I had to do it all over again, and I had a choice—I wasn't sure I had a choice when I was a kid—but if I had a choice between college and boxing, I would have taken college. I regret it. If the world were better educated you wouldn't have this violence, this cocaine, and all this stuff that's going on. But I give my wife a lot of credit. She pushed for education and our kids were educated. And I think it's wonderful."

The boxers are generally close to their children and their remaining siblings. Most of the interviews were conducted during the evenings or on Sunday mornings. I cannot recall a single one that was not interrupted by a telephone call from a child or a sister or a brother.

There is great pride and affection for grandchildren. Of course, Bernie Friedkin carries this to his own benevolent extreme.

Bernie Friedkin: Three geniuses. GENIUSES I tell you. GENIUSES.

Leonore Friedkin: He's going to drive those kids crazy.

Bernie Friedkin: I know! God, I smother them with love. That's my privilege. GENIUSES.

In 1971, 80 percent of American Jews of college age attended an institution of higher education as compared with 50 percent of the remainder of the population. Of the boxers interviewed, nearly 90 percent of their children are college graduates, and many earned advanced degrees.

In their family lives, the boxers adhered to the values and mores of the communities of which they had always remained a part. With regard to education, the boxers have emphasized it for their children with the determination that so many displayed in the ring.

14
THE RISE AND FALL OF JEWISH BOXING

The existence of Jewish boxing, to say nothing of its prominence, appears as an anomaly to most people today. It was largely ignored in the Jewish press of that era and is referred to pejoratively, when at all, in histories of the Jews in this country. The fighters themselves, however, did not make sociological or cultural calculations when they decided to become professionals.

In his Master's thesis, Thomas Jenkins traces the history of boxers over a sixty-year period (1890–1949) and concludes that the second generation of most immigrant nationalities who settled in urban areas produced large numbers of prizefighters. It was a means to earn money and gain social status. Few of the Jewish fighters viewed their careers in terms of social mobility, but virtually all emphasized the economic considerations, especially since most of the boxers grew up in depression years.

To Teddy Brenner, there was nothing unusual about Jewish boys becoming boxers: "When the Irish first landed here, they had to fight for a living. And then the Jewish immigrants arrived. And they had to fight for survival and you had Jewish fighters just like you had Jewish toughguys."

Danny Kapilow comes closest of all the fighters to articulating Jenkins's theme of ethnic succession.

"There was a lot of everything in the minority groups, just as there are today. The Irish and the Italians and the Jews were the minorities then, and they were the ones that needed the money. So they're the ones that turned to professional sports. Just like the blacks and Latins are doing today. There's no place else to go. It was part of ethnic progression. Hell, I always tell everybody that I was too nervous in those years to steal, so boxing was easier than stealing.

"It was an alternative, sure. Lots of guys went in that direction in those years. Jews and non-Jews. A lot of great Irish fighters and a lot of great Irish racketeers. And the same with the Italians, as you well know. Had a lot of great Italian fighters at that time and a lot of great Italian mobsters.

"There might have been a hero or two, but in my opinion it was positively economic. The glory and the adulation were merely secondary. It came, but it wasn't the reason. That was completely secondary. It was just better than a $12 a week job.

"There's no question that the notoriety and the publicity came into it a little bit. But in the beginning, it was just a question of a way to make a dollar. There was a question of, 'Am I going to do this or am I going to stay with this job for $12 a week with a guy that's hollering at me every day and I may not have the job at the end of the month?' And in most cases, you didn't, and had to start to look for another one. And so you wind up in the gym, and if you have any talent it begins to develop and then you start to look that way. I see it that way myself. I might be wrong, you know, some other guys might have had different opinions, but not me."

Artie Levine became a boxer to earn money. He was very successful at it. Still, he thinks it was a mistake.

"Back in those days, you didn't have opportunities to make money. There weren't the opportunities we have today. And I didn't have the desire at the time to stay in school. I should have stayed in school is what I should have done. Stayed in school, gone to college, which I could have done. My family would have sent me to college, I'm sure of that. But I thought I could make my way in boxing and I thought boxing was a bigger thing and you could make more money in boxing and that's what I did. I found it to be so. I made a lot of money, for those years. I would make $18,000, $20,000, $25,000, $35,000, $40,000 a year. On my end of the purse, which was a lot of money over the years. And in those days, you didn't find too many guys who were making more than I was making, I don't believe."

With the passing from the boxing scene of fighters such as Herb Kronowitz, Maxie Shapiro, and Danny Kapilow, the era of Jewish boxing came to an abrupt end. No other group of young Jewish fighters replaced them. In the last forty years, there has been only a scattered handful of Jewish boxers. If the rise of Jewish boxing was consistent with a pattern of ethnic progression, its demise was meteoric, much more rapid than with any other nationality.

The Jewish tradition of learning may have been sublimated to the desperate economic need. But at war's end, it resurfaced, according to Danny Kapilow:

"By 1950, there were no more Jewish boxers. Irish remained, Italians remained, and of course, the blacks started to come up. No more Jewish gangsters either. They started to make their way in our society. The depression was over. You had a prosperity setting in. There were jobs, and the children were able to exist and to better themselves. They ran out of the rackets for the same reason. The racket guy sent his son to college. He became a doctor. He wasn't going to become a soldier in a mob.

"I don't know that it happened more among the Jews than among other ethnic groups. The Irish became very successful in the United States, politically and in the industrial side. The only ones that stayed with it were the Italians through the illegal organizations and they built their money there. Although of course, a lot of Italians, a great many of them, went the other way too, and became judges. And big doctors.

"I didn't take any advantage of the G.I. Bill. But I think that for a lot of guys that had a background of learning, like the Jews had for many centuries, it probably helped.

"You were able to go to college and get some money. And because of the background of learning, in the Jewish history, they might have taken advantage of it more than other people with other backgrounds. I just know that if a guy can make a few bucks outside, he's not going to go into the gym and get his brains knocked out and for three or four years make no money and work your ass off. Roadwork in the morning. Gym in the afternoon. Fights every two weeks. Constant rigorous abstention from girls, from food. So if there's another way, most people are going to do it. The only reason we didn't do in our day, as I said before, is there was really no other way unless you wanted to take a pistol."

Teddy Brenner's son is a neurosurgeon, and his daughter is chairman of the French department at a school in Berkeley, California. The moment opportunities became available, Jewish parents regained the upper hand.

"Well, opportunities became more plentiful for good jobs and going to school became almost an obsession with Jewish families. 'Go to college.' Very few of them ever had college people in their family. And that's the way it gravitated. Also, the G.I. Bill helped a great deal."

To Micky Katz, the precipitous decline of Jewish boxing is unequivocally a matter of culture.

"Definitely. It's for a Jewish boy to be a lawyer or a doctor or, 'my son is an industrial designer.' It's unheard of to be a fighter. So that the Jewish boys, because of the culture, I must say, stay away from it. Money is not an attraction today. The black fellow, the Spanish fellow, the Puerto Rican fellow, he goes in because, for one thing he doesn't want to further his education as much as the Jewish boy, who will learn by the book. And the parents and their disciplinary actions generally have a lot to contribute to a Jewish child furthering their knowledge, knowledge being power. And they emphasize that all the time. So that your question about why they're not here today is emphasized by the fact that if there wasn't the tough times and the depression, they wouldn't have been at all. The one thing I'll never forget. 'Jewish boys are not supposed to be fighters.'

"During the twenties and thirties the boy came home and the parents were happy to take the few dollars if he had a job, to keep their homes going. But when a guy went to the Seward gym and he came back bruised, and, 'oh, what is this all about? This is not for a Jewish boy.' And that was emphasized strongly in the culture. In our culture."

Representing a distinctly minority view, Leo Bodner believes that Jewish boxing could make a comeback, albeit on a smaller scale.

"I don't know of any Jewish boxers whose son became a boxer. But if there was a big Jewish boxer today, a lot of kids would be attracted. Definitely. Not as many, but it could come back.

"It would become popular, if he was a gentleman. You know what I mean? If he wasn't a rough bum, kids would be attracted."

15

RING 8, AGAIN

On a Sunday in December 1992, my wife and I attended the annual Christmas–Chanukah party of Ring 8. It is held in a Queens restaurant in the afternoon, for many of the boxers are reluctant to go out at night. I was especially happy that my wife accompanied me because I wanted her to meet some of the people whom I had interviewed and spoken of at home.

As usual, there was much hugging and backslapping as the boxers greeted each other. This time, a few even embraced me and I wondered if this warm welcome was due to the spirit of the season or whether I was becoming accepted in the fraternity. Many of my interviewees were present. I spent some time with Al Reid who told me that he was not feeling too well, but that complaining would not help. (Six weeks later he was dead.)

I was impressed by the large crowd of nearly three hundred people. Tino Raino, who was undergoing chemotherapy, looked drawn. (He has since died.) He explained that many of the boxers came with their children and grandchildren. It was an event they would not miss. I spoke with the grandson of one of the boxers. He told me that personally he hated boxing, but "I like to see the look on my grandfather's face as he sees his old friends. As long as he is alive and can do it, I'll come with him."

The mood in the banquet room was jovial. The atmosphere was almost genteel. People seemed genuinely pleased to see each other, and there was much table hopping. One of the boxing writers told me, "Did you ever drive with a boxer? He will never speed or break any traffic law. If a car cuts him off, he will let the car have the right of way. He will never fight it. Do you know why? He does not have to prove his manliness. He has done that already. He has been tested under the most grueling fire in sports. Many of these people fought each other in the ring. They bore each other no animosity then, and they have none now. They know they are part of a very unique breed."

Emile Griffith and Sandy Saddler were guests. They were treated with great courtesy. People came over to them, and they were polite and chatty with each visitor. Saddler's life was saved by Ring 8. He was found by Charlie Gellman and Danny Kapilow, placed in a Bronx nursing home, and brought back to health. Tino looked over at Saddler and said, "It's incredible. Sandy was dead. Now look at him. We should be doing much more."

I sat for a time with Herb Kronowitz, who was unusually introspective. "The thing about boxing is that it gave every one of us everything we have. I don't mean just money. It taught us how to live, how to act, how to eat, how to be physically fit. It opened doors to places that we never could have gotten into. Some made more money than others, but every boxer looks at his career as the most important experience in his life."

My notion that the basis of the boxers' being is space rather than time oriented was underscored at the awards ceremony at the conclusion of the party. A number of plaques, which were in the shape of a standing open book, were presented to various individuals who have served Ring 8, or boxing generally, with distinction. As we were leaving, we paused at the awards table to look at them. Not one had a date on it. "Just look at that," I said to Herb Kronowitz, "There's no date. Five years from now no one will remember when these awards were given." Kronowitz examined the plaques thoughtfully for a moment. "What difference does it make?" he wanted to know.

APPENDIXES

APPENDIX A

Jews Who Fought Other Jews for the World Title

CHAMPION	CHALLENGER	TITLE	SITE	DATE	VERDICT
Abe Attell	Kid Goodman	FW	Boston	Feb. 22, 1905	15-round draw; Attell retained crown
Benny Leonard	Charley White	LtW	Benton	July 5, 1920	K.O., 9th round, Leonard
Benny Leonard	Joe Welling	LtW	New York City	Nov. 26, 1920	K.O., 14th round, Leonard
Benny Leonard	Lew Tendler	LtW	New York City	July 24, 1923	Win by 15-round decision, Leonard
Louis "Kid" Kaplan	Danny Kramer	FW	New York City	Jan. 2, 1925	K.O., 9th round, Kaplan
Benny Bass	Red Chapman	FW Elim.	Philadelphia	Sept. 12, 1927	Win by 10-round decision, Bass
Corporal Izzy Schwartz	Newsboy Brown	FW Elim.	New York City	Dec. 16, 1927	Win by 15-round decision, Schwartz
Mushy Callahan	Jackie "Kid" Berg	JWW	London	Feb. 18, 1930	K.O., 10th round, Berg
Maxie Rosenbloom	Abie Bain	LtHW	New York City	Oct. 22, 1930	K.O., 11th round, Rosenbloom
Maxie Rosenbloom	Bob Olin	LtHW	New York City	Nov. 16, 1934	Win by 15-round decision, Olin

APPENDIX B
Jewish World Champions

LIGHT-HEAVYWEIGHTS

"Battling" 1916–1920	
"Slapsie" Maxie Rosenbloom	1930–1934
Bob Olin	1934–1935
Mike Rossman	1978–1979

MIDDLEWEIGHTS

Al McCoy	1914–1917
Ben Jeby	1933
Solly Krieger	1938–1939

WELTERWEIGHTS

Ted "Kid" Lewis	1915–1916, 1917–1919
Jackie Fields	1929–1930, 1932–1933
Barney Ross	1934, 1935–1938

JUNIOR WELTERWEIGHTS

Mushy Callahan	1926–1930
Jackie "Kid" Berg	1930–1931
Barney Ross	1933–1935

LIGHTWEIGHTS

Benny Leonard	1917–1925
Al Singer	1930
Barney Ross	1933, 1935

JUNIOR LIGHTWEIGHTS

Artie O'Leary	1917–1919
Jack Bernstein	1923
Benny Bass	1929–1931

FEATHERWEIGHTS

Abe Attell	1901–1912
Louis "Kid" Kaplan	1925–1927
Benny Bass	1927–1928

BANTAMWEIGHTS

Harry Harris	1901
Abe Goldstein	1924
Charlie "Phil" Rosenberg	1925–1927
Robert Cohen	1954–1956
Alphonse Halimi	1957–1959, 1960–1961

FLYWEIGHTS

"Corporal" Izzy Schwartz	1927–1929
Young Perez	1931–1932

APPENDIX C
The Ten Greatest Jewish Boxers of All Time

1. Benny Leonard
2. Abe Attell
3. Ted "Kid" Lewis
4. Harry Lewis
5. Barney Ross
6. Lew Tendler
7. Charlie White
8. Jackie "Kid" Berg
9. Joe Choyinski
10. Louis "Kid" Kaplan

Source: Appendix C was compiled by Hank Kaplan, Mike Silver, and Vic Zimet.

APPENDIX D
Gallery of Jewish Boxers (1900–Present)

HEAVYWEIGHT

Joe Choyinski	1888–1904
Bob Pastor	1935–1942
Art Lasky	1930–1939
Abe Simon	1935–1942
King Levinsky	1928–1939
Natie Brown	1930s
Bill Weinberg	1940s
Abe Feldman	1930s
Bill Poland	1938–1942
Jack Gross	1926–1932

LIGHT-HEAVYWEIGHT

"Battling" Levinsky***	1926–1927
Maxie Rosenbloom***	1923–1939
Bob Olin***	1929–1939
Yale Okun	1924–1934
Abie Bain	1924–1932
Armand Emanuel	1926–1932
Jack Bloomfield	1920s
Augie Ratner	1916–1925
Mike Rossman***	1973–1983
Herbie Katz	1936–1942

MIDDLEWEIGHT

Ben Jeby***	1928–1936
Al McCoy***	1908–1919
Georgie Abrams	1937–1948
Solly Krieger***	1928–1941

Dave Rosenberg	1919–1925
K.O. Phil Kaplan	1919–1929
Erich Seelig	1930–1940
Artie Levine	1942–1949
Herbie Kronowitz	1939–1950
Harold Green	1942–1953

WELTERWEIGHT

Ted "Kid" Lewis***	1909–1929
Harry Lewis***	1904–1913
Barney Ross***	1929–1938
Matt Wells***	1909–1922
Jackie Fields***	1924–1933
Mushy Callahan*	1924–1930
Phil Bloom	1912–1923
Sammy Luftspring	1936–1941
Al "Bummy" Davis	1937–1946
Mike Kaplan	1935–1942

LIGHTWEIGHT**

Benny Leonard***	1911–1932
Lew Tendler	1913–1928
Charley White	1906–1925
Jackie "Kid" Berg*	1924–1945
Sid Terris	1922–1931
Benny Valgar	1916–1929
Jack Bernstein*	1914–1931
Al Singer***	1927–1935
Solly Seaman	1920–1928
Ray Miller	1924–1933
Ruby Goldstein	1925–1937
Allie Stolz	1937–1946
Maxie Shapiro	1938–1948
Davey Day	1920–1928
Leach Cross	1906–1921
Joe Benjamin	1914–1925

Jack Silver	1922–1929
Sammy Dorfman	1920s
Joe Welling	1911–1924
Eddie "Kid" Wolfe	1928–1935

FEATHERWEIGHT

Abe Attell***	1900–1917
Louis "Kid" Kaplan***	1921–1933
Benny Bass***	1923–1940
Danny Kramer	1919–1928
Harry Blitman	1920s
Danny Frush	1917–1926
Eddie "Kid" Wagner	1920–1927
Lew Feldman	1928–1941
Joey Sangor	1921–1930
Charley Beecher	1920s

BANTAMWEIGHT

Charlie "Phil" Rosenberg***	1921–1929
Harry Harris***	1896–1907
Abe Goldstein***	1916–1927
Monte Attell***	1902–1917
"Newsboy" Brown	1924–1933
Charley Goldman	1904–1915
Young Montreal	1916–1929
Robert Cohen***	1951–1959
Alphonse Halimi***	1955–1964
Joe Burman	1916–1924

FLYWEIGHT

"Corporal" Izzy Schwartz***	1922–1932
Young Perez***	1928–1938
Johnny Rosner	1910–1922
Marty Gold	1930s
Jackie "Kid" Wolf	1910–1915
Sammy Cohen	1920s

Benny Schwartz	1920s
Mannie Wexler	1920s
Phil Tobias	1924–1933
Midget Lou Goldberg (tied for 10th place)	1930s
Alf Mansfield (tied for 10th place)	1900s

Notes:

There are ten outstanding Jewish fighters in each of the traditional weight divisions.

*Berg and Callahan held junior welterweight titles; Jack Bernstein held the junior lightweight title.

**Twenty lightweights were selected because this division had so many outstanding Jewish boxers.

***Indicates World Champion

Source: Appendix D was compiled by Hank Kaplan, Mike Silver, and Vic Zimet.

APPENDIX E
Jews in the Boxing Hall of Fame
(Canastota, New York)

Modern Group	Elected
Benny Leonard	1955
Barney Ross	1956
Lew Tendler	1961
"Slapsie" Maxie Rosenbloom	1972
Jackie "Kid" Berg	1975

Old Timers Group	Elected
Abe Attell	1955
Joe Choyinski	1960
Ted "Kid" Lewis	1964
"Battling" Levinsky	1966
Jackie Fields	1977

Pioneer Group	Elected
Daniel Mendoza	1954

Meritorious Service Group	Elected
Nat Fleischer (Journalist)	1975
Sam Taub (Broadcaster)	1978
Mike Jacobs (Promoter)	1982
Ray Arcel (Trainer)	1982

Wingate Institute, Israel

Benny Leonard	1979
Barney Ross	1979
Jackie Fields	1979
Daniel Mendoza	1981

Abe Attell	1982
"Battling" Levinsky	1982
Ted "Kid" Lewis	1983
"Slapsie" Maxie Rosenbloom	1984

APPENDIX F
Records of World Champions, Interviewees, and Others

	Class	Dates	Total Bouts	W-L	KOs	D	ND
Abrams, Georgie	MW	1937–1948	61	48–10	9	3	0
Ashkenaz, Sigi	WW	1936–1938	25	24–1	9	0	0
Attell, Abe	FW	1900–1917	168	91–10	47	17	50
Attell, Monte	BW	1902–1917	106	28–36	27	14	28
Bain, Abie	LtHW	1924–1932	94	48–11	31	4	31
Bartfield, Soldier	WW	1912–1925	169	32–18	18	8	111
Bass, Benny	LW	1923–1940	197	140–28	59	6	23
Beecher, Willie	LW	1909–1917	65	10–1	10	3	51
Bell, Archie	LW	1924–1932	90	63–18	5	8	1
Benjamin, Joe	LW	1915–1925	64	38–11	13	5	10
Berg, Jackie "Kid"	WW	1924–1945	192	157–26	57	9	0
Berger, Maxie	WW	1935–1946	132	99–24	26	9	0
Bernstein, Jack	LW	1914–1931	107	65–23	17	7	12
Bernstein, Joe	FW	1894–1908	85	32–18	15	35	0
Blitman, Harry	FW	1926–1930	63	52–4	23	2	5
Bloom, Phil	LW	1912–1923	175	43–22	15	11	99
Bort, Julie	LW	1948–1950	70	59–10	12	1	0
Brock, Phil	LW	1904–1914	69	33–9	20	8	19
Brown, Newsboy	FW	1924–1933	64	46–11	8	5	2
Brown, Young Abe	LW	1904–1914	80	21–2	15	2	55
Burman, Joe	BW	1916–1924	120	29–3	20	6	82
Callahan, Frankie	LW	1911–1922	135	21–8	20	2	104
Callahan, Mushy	WW	1924–1932	77	59–13	19	4	1
Choyinski, Joe	HW	1888–1904	78	50–14	25	6	8
Clinton, Johnny	LW	1918–1924	63	45–4	10	7	6
Cohen, Meyer	WW	1920s*	68	46–13	24	2	5
Cohen, Mickey	FW	1930s*	93	60–16	25	6	11

	Class	Dates	Total Bouts	W-L	KOs	D	ND
Cohen, Robert	BW	1951–1958	43	36–4	14	3	0
Davis Al "Bummy"	MW	1937–1948	79	65–10	46	4	0
Day, Davey	LW	1920–1928	73	59–10	29	4	0
Duffy, Oakland Jimmy	WW	1920–1928	79	56–12	6	10	1
Emanuel, Armand	HW	1926–1932	51	40–7	14	2	2
Farber, Sammy	BW	1927–1932	75	55–20	5	0	0
Feldman, Lew	LW	1928–1941	182	115–54	8	13	0
Felix, Harry	LW	1920s*	65	44–7	2	7	7
Fields, Jackie	WW	1924–1933	87	73–9	30	2	3
Foreman, Al	LW	1922–1933	85	67–11	45	7	0
Friedkin, Bernie "Schoolboy"	LW	1935–1943	74	49–10	10	15	0
Friedman, Sailor	LW	1916–1924	82	37–3	22	4	38
Frush, Danny	FW	1917–1926	88	60–10	24	1	17
Gellman, Charlie (Chuck Halper)	MW	1935–1940	65	60–5	22	0	0
Glick, Joey	JLW	1921–1934	206	115–47	27	31	10
Goldman, Charley	BW	1900–1911	137	36–6	20	1	84
Goldman, Oscar	FW	1929–1935	73	58–15	10	0	0
Goldstein, Abe Attell	BW	1916–1927	128	67–16	34	7	38
Goldstein, Ruby	LW	1925–1937	55	50–5	34	0	0
Goodman, Abe Kid	FW	1899–1908	122	55–19	26	43	3
Green, Harold	MW	1942–1953	87	70–14	23	3	0
Green, Johnny	BW	1920s*	62	43–2	8	4	13
Gross, Jack	HW	1926–1932	52	40–8	26	2	2
Halimi, Alphonse	BW	1955–1964	50	41–8	21	1	0
Harmon, Willie	WW	1920s*	96	50–15	24	6	15
Harris, Harry	BW	1895–1904	54	40–2	15	7	5
Herman, Kid	LW	1899–1907	81	48–10	26	21	2
Jackson, Willie	LW	1913–1922	158	25–9	17	8	115
Jacobs, Harry	MW	1930–1937	43	39–2	20	2	0
Jeby, Ben	MW	1928–1936	73	54–14	22	4	1
Kapilow, Danny	WW	1941–1948	68	50–11	16	7	0
Kaplan, K. O. Phil	MW	1919–1929	95	69–14	34	1	11

	Class	Dates	Total Bouts	W-L	KOs	D	ND
Kaplan, Louis Kid	FW	1921–1933	131	101–13	17	10	7
Kessler, Miltie	WW	1940–1945	50	41–9	15	0	0
Kramer, Danny	FW	1919–1928	90	52–22	25	3	13
Krieger, Solly	MW	1928–1942	111	80–24	53	7	0
Kronowitz, Herbie	MW	1941–1950	83	54–24	9	5	0
Lasky, Art	HW	1930–1939	58	42–7	34	4	5
Leach, Cross	LW	1905–1916	154	43–14	25	2	95
Leonard, Benny	LW	1911–1932	210	89–5	71	1	115
Levine, Artie	MW	1941–1949	71	50–15	36	6	0
Levinsky, "Battling"	LHW	1910–1930	172	76–19	34	0	177
Lewis, Harry	WW	1903–1913	171	163–15	47	8	85
Lewis, Ted "Kid"	WW	1909–1929	250	155–24	65	6	65
Lustig, Young	LW	1911–1915	78	11–0	10	3	64
McCoy, Al	MW	1908–1919	157	44–6	26	7	100
Mendelson, Johnny	LW	1916–1927	79	18–5	14	1	55
Miller, Ray	LW	1924–1933	111	75–25	31	4	7
Montreal, Young	FlW	1916–1929	103	56–19	11	6	22
Nichols, Curly	WW	1937–1947	65	50–15	4	0	0
Okun, Yale	HW	1924–1934	92	54–24	11	4	10
O'Leary, Young	BW	1910s*	67	19–2	5	9	46
Olin, Bob	LtHW	1929–1939	85	54–27	25	4	0
Otto, Young	LW	1903–1923	196	93–10	70	4	93
Pomerantz, Marty	LW	1935–1938	30	24–6	6	0	0
Portney, Jack	FW	1927–1938	102	78–13	20	5	6
Ratner, Augie	MW	1916–1925	62	16–16	5	5	25
Reid, Al	FW	1935–1941	100	60–28	2	12	0
Rice, Frankie	FW	1918–1924	101	54–15	41	12	0
Rosenberg, Charlie "Phil"	BW	1921–1929	65	35–16	7	6	8
Rosenberg, Dave	MW	1919–1925	57	39–9	9	4	5
Rosenbloom, "Slapsie" Maxie	LtHW	1923–1939	289	210–35	18	23	21
Rosner, Johnny	FlW	1910–1922	77	11–7	7	1	58
Ross, Barney	WW	1931–1938	82	74–4	24	4	0
Rossman, Mike	LtHW	1973–1983	54	44–74	27	3	0

	Class	Dates	Total Bouts	W-L	KOs	D	ND
Sandwina, Teddy	HW	1926–1932	68	46–16	38	5	1
Sangor, Joey	FW	1920s*	70	16–13	7	3	38
Schlaifer, Morrie	WW	1919–1924	66	28–13	16	2	23
Schwartz, "Corporal" Izzy	FlW	1922–1931	124	69–33	7	10	12
Seaman, Solly	LW	1920–1928	93	60–11	12	14	8
Seelig, Erich	MW	1931–1940	58	0–40	9	7	0
Shapiro, Maxie	LW	1938–1948	123	87–30	26	6	0
Silver, Jack	LW	1922–1929	237	201–7	47	8	21
Simon, Abe	HW	1935–1942	49	38–10	27	1	0
Singer, Al	LW	1927–1931	70	60–8	24	2	0
Stolz, Allie	LW	1937–1946	85	163–10	21	2	0
Tendler, Lew	WW	1913–1928	168	59–11	37	3	95
Terris, Sid	LW	1922–1931	108	85–13	12	4	6
Tiplitz, Joey	LW	1919–1924	73	24–8	16	2	39
Valgar, Benny	LW	1916–1929	191	77–15	19	3	97
Varoff, Joey	LW	1939–1950	65	55–5	5	7	0
Vogel, Sammy	LW	1921–1928	50	39–8	11	1	2
Wagner, Eddie Kid	FW	1920–1927	109	33–18	5	4	55
Welling, Joe	LW	1911–1924	129	26–19	14	4	80
Wells, Matt	WW	1909–1922	77	28–18	6	2	29
White, Charley	LW	1906–1923	145	80–15	51	0	50
Wolfe, Eddie Kid	FW	1928–1935	103	66–24	12	11	2
Yanger, Benny	LW	1899–1909	84	51–10	25	20	3

Notes:
   *Exact dates have not been established or could not be found.
   Names in parentheses indicate other names that the boxers fought under.

FIW	= Flyweight (112 pounds)		HW	=	Heavyweight (Above 175 pounds)
BW	= Bantamweight (118 pounds)				
FW	= Featherweight (126 pounds)		W	=	Wins
LW	= Lightweight (135 pounds)		KO	=	Knockout
WW	= Welterweight (147 pounds)		D	=	Draw
MW	= Middleweight (160 pounds)		ND	=	No decision or newspaper decision
LtHW	= Light-Heavyweight (175 pounds)				

NOTES

Chapter 1: Introduction

1. *American Hebrew*, December 27, 1907.

2. Steven A. Riess, "A Fighting Chance: The Jewish American Boxing Experience." *American Jewish History* 74 (March 1985): 229.

3. See Barney Ross, and Martin Abrahamson, *No Man Stands Alone: The Story of Barney Ross* (Lippincott, 1957) in which he states: "The news from Germany made me feel. . . . I was fighting for all my people" (pp. 150–153).

4. S. Kirson Weinberg and Henry Arond, "The Occupational Culture of the Boxer," *American Journal of Sociology* 57 (March 1952).

5. Celia Heller, *On the Edge of Destruction: Jews of Poland Between the Two World Wars* (Schocken Books, 1980), p. 100.

6. Thomas Jenkins, "Changes in Ethnic and Racial Representation Among Professional Boxers: A Study in Ethnic Succession," M.A. thesis, University of Chicago, 1955.

Chapter 2: A Brief History

1. Todd M. Endelman, *The Jews of Georgian England 1714–1830* (Philadelphia: Jewish Publication Society, 1979), pp. 219–223.

Chapter 4: *Es Haypt Zuch Nisht Un* (It Doesn't Exist)

1. *New York Daily Forward*, March 9, 1928.

2. Abraham Cahan, "The New Writers and the Ghetto," *Bookman* 39 (August 1914): 633.

Chapter 5: In the Beginning

1. In this manner, Jewish youth often learned to fight on the streets. Benny Leonard's tale of fighting Irish and Italian kids falls into this pattern.

2. The film *Hester Street* graphically describes this phenomenon.

3. In "Introduction," David Berger, ed., *The Legacy of Jewish Migration: 1881 and Its Impact* (Holt, Rinehart and Winston, 1983).

4. Ritual slaughterer.

5. Jewish Study Room.

6. Armand Emanuel, in an earlier era, was a lawyer.

7. Most boxing people put Maxie's date of birth at 1914.

8. Sabbath observance.

9. *New York Times*, June 26, 1926.

10. Shame and disgrace.

11. The New York Coliseum, located in the Bronx, is often referred to as the Bronx Coliseum.

12. Deriving pride.

13. "May he rest in peace."

Chapter 6: Benny, Barney, and the Fans

1. Cited in Peter Levine, *Ellis Island to Ebbets Field: Sport and the American Jewish Experience* (Oxford University Press, 1992), p. 139.

2. Ibid., p. 178.

3. *Ring Magazine*, November 1929, p. 24.

Chapter 7: Anti-Semitism

1. Henry Feingold, *A Time for Searching: Entering the Mainstream: 1920–1945* (Johns Hopkins University Press, 1992), p. 11.

2. Ibid., p. 17.

3. Ibid., p. 251.

4. Leonard Dinnerstein, *Anti-Semitism in America* (New York: Jewish Publication Society, 1994).

5. Feingold, *A Time for Searching*, p. 11.

Chapter 8: The War

1. Deborah Dash Moore, "When Jews Were G.I.'s" (David W. Belin Lecture in American Jewish Affairs, March 7, 1994).

2. Bort had been knocked out by Charlie Fusari, a welterweight contender.

Chapter 9: The Main Event

1. *New York Times*, May 16, 1942.
2. Ibid., December 1, 1939.
3. "Did you get killed?"
4. *New York Times*, November 16, 1934.

Chapter 10: The Money

1. "Put it in the bank."

Chapter 11: The Wise Guys

1. Albert Fried, *The Rise and Fall of the Jewish Gangster in America* (Holt, Rinehart and Winston, 1980).
2. Peter Levine, *Ellis Island to Ebbets Field: Sport and the American Jewish Experience* (Oxford University Press, 1992), p. 153.
3. Howard Sachar, *A History of the Jews in America* (Alfred A. Knopf, 1992).

Chapter 12: A Dangerous Sport

1. *Journal of the American Medical Association* (JAMA), January 14, 1983, p. 254.
2. Goldstein refereed only once after the Griffith–Paret fight.

Chapter 13: After the Ring

1. "When are you going to stop?"
2. "Enough!"
3. S. Kirson Weinberg and Henry Arond, "The Occupational Culture of the Boxer," *American Journal of Sociology* 57 (March 1952), p. 469.
4. Steven Riess, "A Fighting Chance: The Jewish American Boxing Experience," *American Jewish History* 74 (March 1985): 252–253.

BIBLIOGRAPHY

Books

Abrahams, Israel. *Jewish Life in the Middle Ages*. Athenaeum Press, 1896.

Adelman, Melvin. *A Sporting Time: New York City and the Rise of Modern Athletics*. University of Illinois Press, 1986.

Andre, Sam, and Nat Fleischer. *A Pictorial History of Boxing*. Citadel Press, 1991.

Baron, Salo W. *The Russian Jews Under Tsars and Soviets*. Schocken Books, 1987.

Berger, David, ed. *The Legacy of Jewish Migration: 1881 and Its Impact*. Holt, Rinehart and Winston, 1983.

Blady, Ken. *The Jewish Boxers' Hall of Fame*. Shapolsky Publishers, 1988.

Cahan, Abraham. *The Imported Bridegroom and Other Stories of the New York Ghetto*. Houghton Mifflin and Co., 1898.

Collins, Nigel. *Boxing Babylon: Behind the Shadowy World of the Prize Ring*. Citadel Press, 1990.

Daniel, Daniel M. *The Mike Jacobs Story*. Magazine Publishing, 1950.

Dinnerstein, Leonard. *Anti-Semitism in America*. Jewish Publication Society, 1994.

Early, Gerald. *Tuxedo Junction*. Ecco Press, 1989.

Endelman, Todd M. *The Jews of Georgian England 1714–1830*. Jewish Publication Society, 1979.

Feingold, Henry. *A Time for Searching: Entering the Mainstream: 1920–1945*. The Jewish People in America, vol. 4. Johns Hopkins University Press, 1992.

Fleischer, Nat. *Fifty Years at Ringside*. Ring Magazine Books, 1958.

——— . *Leonard the Magnificent*. Ring Magazine Books, 1947.

Frank, Stanley. *The Jew in Sports*. Miles Publishing, 1936.

Fried, Albert. *The Rise and Fall of the Jewish Gangster in America*. Holt, Rinehart and Winston, 1980.

Gilfoyle, Timothy J. *City of Eros: New York City Prostitution and the Commercialization of Sex, 1790–1920*. W. W. Norton, 1992.

Goldstein, Ruby, and Frank Graham. *Third Man in the Ring*. Funk and Wagnall, 1959.

Goodman, Cary. *Choosing Sides: Playground and Street Life on the Lower East Side*. Schocken Books, 1979.

Guttman, Allen. *From Ritual to Record: The Nature of Modern Sports*. Columbia University Press, 1978.

Hauser, Thomas. *Black Lights: Inside the World of Professional Boxing*. Simon and Schuster, 1986.

Heller, Celia. *On the Edge of Destruction: Jews of Poland Between the Two World Wars*. Schocken Books, 1980.

Heller, Peter. *In This Corner*. Dell Publishing, 1973.

Hemingway, Ernest. *The Sun Also Rises*. Charles Scribner's Sons, 1926.

Hindus, Milton, ed. *The Old East Side*. Jewish Publication Society, 1971.

Howe, Irving. *World of Our Fathers*. Harcourt Brace Jovanovich, 1976.

Johnson, Jack. *Autobiography: In the Ring and Out*. Citadel Press, 1992.

Joselit, Jenna Weisman. *New York's Jewish Jews: The Orthodox Community in the Inter-War Years*. Indiana University Press, 1990.

―――― . *Our Gang: Jewish Crime and the New York Jewish Community*. Indiana University Press, 1983.

Landesman, Alter. *Brownsville: The Birth, Development and Passing of a Community in New York*. New York: Bloch Publishing, 1969.

Levine, Peter. *Ellis Island to Ebbets Field: Sport and the American Jewish Experience*. Oxford University Press, 1992.

Liebling, A. J. *A Neutral Corner*. Simon and Schuster, 1990.

―――― . *The Sweet Science*. Penguin Books, 1956.

Luftspring, Sammy. *Call Me Sammy*. Prentice-Hall of Canada, 1975.

Moore, Deborah Dash. *At Home in America: Second Generation New York Jews*. Columbia University Press, 1981.

1981 Ring Record Book and Boxing Encyclopedia. Athenaeum Press, 1982.

Oates, Joyce Carol. *On Boxing*. Zebra Books, 1988.

Oates, Joyce Carol, and Daniel Halpern, eds. *Reading the Fights*. Prentice-Hall Press, 1988.

Odd, Gilbert E. *Ring Battles of the Century*. Nicholson and Winston, 1980.

Postal, Bernard, Jesse Silver, and Ray Silver. *Encyclopedia of Jews in Sports*. Bloch Publishing, 1965.

Ribalow, Harold U. *The Jew in American Sports*. Bloch Publishing, 1966.

Riess, Steven A. *City Games: The Evolution of American Urban Society and the Rise of Sports*. University of Illinois Press, 1989.

Rischin, Moses. *The Promised City: New York's Jews, 1870–1914.* Harvard University Press, 1962.

Ross, Barney, and Martin Abrahamson. *No Man Stands Alone: The True Story of Barney Ross.* Lippincott, 1957.

Roth, Philip. *Patrimony.* Simon and Schuster, 1991.

Sachar, Howard. *A History of the Jews in America.* Alfred A. Knopf, 1992.

Sammons, Jeffrey T. *Beyond the Ring: The Role of Boxing in American Society.* University of Illinois Press, 1990.

Segal, Hyman. *They Called Him Champ.* Citadel Press, 1959.

Shutte, William. *Fighting Dentist: The Boxing Career of Dr. Leach Cross.* Self-published, 1977.

Sorin, Gerald. *The Nurturing Neighborhood: The Brownsville Boys' Club and Jewish Community in Urban America, 1940–1990.* New York University Press, 1990.

Articles

Cahan, Abraham. "The New Writers and the Ghetto," *Bookman* 39 (August 1914): 633. A short story by Aaron Weitzman.

Gehring, Frederick P. "The Gentle Champion: Barney Ross." *Jewish Digest* (March 1968).

Guttman, Allen. "Out of the Ghetto and into the Field: Jewish Writers and the Theme of Sport." *American Jewish History* 74 (March 1985): 274–286.

Hoberman, John M. "Sport and the Myth of the Jewish Body," paper presented at the annual meeting of the North American Society for Sports History, Clemson University, Clemson, South Carolina (May 27, 1989).

Jenkins, Thomas. "Changes in Ethnic and Racial Representation Among Professional Boxers: A Study in Ethnic Succession," Master's Thesis, University of Chicago, 1955.

Lardner, John. "That Was Pugilism; The White Hopes—I," *New Yorker* (June 25, 1949): 56–67; "The White Hopes—II," *New Yorker* (July 2, 1949): 36–46.

Raskus, Bernard. "A Jewish View of Boxing," *Jewish Digest* (September 1965): 57–60.

"Report by Council on Scientific Affairs." *Journal of the American Medical Association* (January 14, 1983): 254–257.

Riess, Steven A. "A Fighting Chance: The Jewish American Boxing Experience," *American Jewish History* 74 (March 1985): 222–253.

Ross, Dr. Ronald J.; Dr. Monroe Cole; Dr. Jay S. Thompson; and Dr. Kyung H. Lim. "Boxers—Computed Tomography, EEG and Neurological Evaluation," *Journal of the American Medical Association* (January 14, 1983): 211–213.

Steiner, Desiree. "My Father, the Boxer," *Jewish Digest* (July 1973): 63–66.

Weinberg, S. Kirson, and Henry Arond. "The Occupational Culture of the Boxer," *American Journal of Sociology* 57 (March 1952): 460–469.

York, John D. "Professional Boxing: A Social Constructionist Perspective" (Master's Thesis, University of Houston, 1982).

Articles (from *Ring Magazine*)

Albertanti, Albert. "Mike Jacobs, Successor to Tex Rickard" (July 1936): 7, 8, 43.

———. "When the Swells Put Glamour into Boxing" (November 1928): 22, 35.

Albertanti, Francis. "Maxie Rosenbloom" (September 1926):16–17.

Berg, Marty. "New York Boxing Gossip" (November 1929): 24.

Carroll, Ted. "Army Gets East Side Jewel" (August 1942): 22, 23, 42.

———. "A Champion to Remember" (July 1947): 9–10.

Cross Counter. "The Pride of the Ghetto" (May 1945): 18–19.

Editor, *Ring Magazine*. "Stolz Is the Fighter of the Month" (January 1946): 35.

Fleischer, Nat. "Alias Leach Cross" (September 1948): 22.

———. "Leach Cross Reminisces" (June 1928): 9–11.

Leseman, Charles. "Fought Seven Champions But Never Held a Crown" (October 1947): 22–23.

MacAdam, Jack. "England's Mike Jacobs Is Fishmonger Jack Solomons" (January 1946): 7, 11.

Miller, Bill. "The Jew in Boxing" (December 1932): 8–9.

Ring Interviewer. "Waxman Key Figure in Dempsey Success" (April 1961): 22, 47.

Rose, Charley. "The Fighting Dentist" (January 1952): 34, 43.

Schulberg, Budd. "The Great Benny Leonard" (May 1980): 32–37.

The Sportsman. "Shadows of the Past" (March 1944): 17, 44.

Newspapers

Boxing News

The Day (Der Tag)

The Freiheit

Jewish Daily Forward

The Morning Journal

National Police Gazette

New York Post

New York Times

Interviews

*Ray Arcel (conducted by Eli Wohlgelernter on behalf of The American Jewish Committee) — October 11, 1983 and November 8, 1983

Sigi Ashkenaz (Sidney Ashe) — August 30, 1992

Marty Baker — January 30, 1992

Leo Bodner — January 19, 1992

*Julie Bort — February 23, 1992

Teddy Brenner — March 3, 1992

Sammy Farber — February 10, 1992

Bernie Friedkin — February 11, 1992

*Rivi Garbowitz — February 16, 1993

Charlie Gellman — February 12, 1992

Herbert Goldman — July 7, 1992

*Oscar Goldman — January 23, 1992

Randy Gordon — June 18, 1992

Danny Kapilow — June 30, 1992

Hank Kaplan — February 16, 1993

*Micky Katz — January 27, 1992

Miltie Kessler — June 29, 1992

Herbie Kronowitz — January 29, 1992

Artie Levine — February 16, 1992

Rose Lewis — February 9, 1992

Harry Markson — February 18, 1992

*Curly Nichols — July 2, 1992

Marty Pomerantz — March 9, 1992

*Al Reid — February 4, 1992

Martha Rosenfeld — March 24, 1992

Eva and Frank Shain — June 24, 1992

Anne Shapiro — March 17, 1992

Maxie Shapiro — February 2, 1992

Allie Stolz — February 6, 1992

*Joey Varoff — June 28, 1992

Vic Zimet — February 5, 1992

*Deceased

INDEX

About the Author

ALLEN BODNER is an attorney with a remarkable entry into the world of
boxing, as his father was an amateur boxer during the 1920s and a professional manager during the 1930s and 1940s.